50% OFF PSAT Test Prep Course

Dear Customer,

We consider it an honor and a privilege that you chose our PSAT Study Guide. As a way of showing our appreciation and to help us better serve you, we have partnered with Mometrix Test Preparation to offer you **50% off their online PSAT Prep Course.** Many PSAT courses are needlessly expensive and don't deliver enough value. With their course, you get access to the best PSAT prep material, and you only pay half price.

Mometrix has structured their online course to perfectly complement your printed study guide. The PSAT Test Prep Course contains **in-depth lessons** that cover all the most important topics, over **1,100 practice questions** to ensure you feel prepared, more than **500 flashcards** for studying on the go, and over **230 instructional videos**.

Online PSAT Prep Course

Topics Covered:	**Course Features:**
Reading	PSAT Study Guide
○ Information and Ideas ○ Making and Evaluating Predictions ○ Drawing Conclusions and Summarizing	○ Get access to content from the best reviewed study guide available.
Writing	Track Your Progress
○ Writing Essays ○ Parts of Speech ○ Common Sentence Errors	○ Their customized course allows you to check off content you have studied or feel confident with.
Mathematics	8 Full-Length Practice Tests
○ Foundational Math Concepts ○ Problem Solving and Data Analysis ○ Algebra and Advanced Math	○ With 1,100+ practice questions and lesson reviews, you can test yourself again and again to build confidence.
And More!	PSAT Flashcards
	○ Their course includes a flashcard mode consisting of over 500 content cards to help you study.

To receive this discount, visit them at www.mometrix.com/university/psat or simply scan this QR code with your smartphone. At the checkout page, enter the discount code: **TPBPSAT50**

If you have any questions or concerns, please contact them at universityhelp@mometrix.com.

SCAN HERE

FREE Test Taking Tips Video/DVD Offer

To better serve you, we created videos covering test taking tips that we want to give you for FREE.
These videos cover world-class tips that will help you succeed on your test.

We just ask that you send us feedback about this product. Please let us know what you thought about it—whether good, bad, or indifferent.

To get your **FREE videos**, you can use the QR code below or email freevideos@studyguideteam.com with "Free Videos" in the subject line and the following information in the body of the email:

> a. The title of your product
>
> b. Your product rating on a scale of 1-5, with 5 being the highest
>
> c. Your feedback about the product

If you have any questions or concerns, please don't hesitate to contact us at info@studyguideteam.com.

Thank you!

PSAT Prep 2023-2024 with 6 Practice Tests

PSAT NMSQT Study Guide and Review Book for Reading, Writing, and Math on the College Board Exam [7th Edition]

Joshua Rueda

Written and edited by TPB Publishing.

Interested in buying more than 10 copies of our product? Contact us about bulk discounts:
bulkorders@studyguideteam.com

ISBN 13: 9781637753811
ISBN 10: 1637753810

Table of Contents

Welcome

Dear Reader,

Welcome to your new Test Prep Books study guide! We are pleased that you chose us to help you prepare for your exam. There are many study options to choose from, and we appreciate you choosing us. Studying can be a daunting task, but we have designed a smart, effective study guide to help prepare you for what lies ahead.

Whether you're a parent helping your child learn and grow, a high school student working hard to get into your dream college, or a nursing student studying for a complex exam, we want to help give you the tools you need to succeed. We hope this study guide gives you the skills and the confidence to thrive, and we can't thank you enough for allowing us to be part of your journey.

In an effort to continue to improve our products, we welcome feedback from our customers. We look forward to hearing from you. Suggestions, success stories, and criticisms can all be communicated by emailing us at info@studyguideteam.com.

Sincerely,
Test Prep Books Team

FREE Videos/DVD OFFER

Doing well on your exam requires both knowing the test content and understanding how to use that knowledge to do well on the test. We offer completely FREE test taking tip videos. **These videos cover world-class tips that you can use to succeed on your test.**

To get your **FREE videos**, you can use the QR code below or email freevideos@studyguideteam.com with "Free Videos" in the subject line and the following information in the body of the email:

    a. The title of your product
    b. Your product rating on a scale of 1-5, with 5 being the highest
    c. Your feedback about the product

If you have any questions or concerns, please don't hesitate to contact us at info@studyguideteam.com.

Quick Overview

As you draw closer to taking your exam, effective preparation becomes more and more important. Thankfully, you have this study guide to help you get ready. Use this guide to help keep your studying on track and refer to it often.

This study guide contains several key sections that will help you be successful on your exam. The guide contains tips for what you should do the night before and the day of the test. Also included are test-taking tips. Knowing the right information is not always enough. Many well-prepared test takers struggle with exams. These tips will help equip you to accurately read, assess, and answer test questions.

A large part of the guide is devoted to showing you what content to expect on the exam and to helping you better understand that content. In this guide are practice test questions so that you can see how well you have grasped the content. Then, answer explanations are provided so that you can understand why you missed certain questions.

Don't try to cram the night before you take your exam. This is not a wise strategy for a few reasons. First, your retention of the information will be low. Your time would be better used by reviewing information you already know rather than trying to learn a lot of new information. Second, you will likely become stressed as you try to gain a large amount of knowledge in a short amount of time. Third, you will be depriving yourself of sleep. So be sure to go to bed at a reasonable time the night before. Being well-rested helps you focus and remain calm.

Be sure to eat a substantial breakfast the morning of the exam. If you are taking the exam in the afternoon, be sure to have a good lunch as well. Being hungry is distracting and can make it difficult to focus. You have hopefully spent lots of time preparing for the exam. Don't let an empty stomach get in the way of success!

When travelling to the testing center, leave earlier than needed. That way, you have a buffer in case you experience any delays. This will help you remain calm and will keep you from missing your appointment time at the testing center.

Be sure to pace yourself during the exam. Don't try to rush through the exam. There is no need to risk performing poorly on the exam just so you can leave the testing center early. Allow yourself to use all of the allotted time if needed.

Remain positive while taking the exam even if you feel like you are performing poorly. Thinking about the content you should have mastered will not help you perform better on the exam.

Once the exam is complete, take some time to relax. Even if you feel that you need to take the exam again, you will be well served by some down time before you begin studying again. It's often easier to convince yourself to study if you know that it will come with a reward!

Test-Taking Strategies

1. Predicting the Answer

When you feel confident in your preparation for a multiple-choice test, try predicting the answer before reading the answer choices. This is especially useful on questions that test objective factual knowledge. By predicting the answer before reading the available choices, you eliminate the possibility that you will be distracted or led astray by an incorrect answer choice. You will feel more confident in your selection if you read the question, predict the answer, and then find your prediction among the answer choices. After using this strategy, be sure to still read all of the answer choices carefully and completely. If you feel unprepared, you should not attempt to predict the answers. This would be a waste of time and an opportunity for your mind to wander in the wrong direction.

2. Reading the Whole Question

Too often, test takers scan a multiple-choice question, recognize a few familiar words, and immediately jump to the answer choices. Test authors are aware of this common impatience, and they will sometimes prey upon it. For instance, a test author might subtly turn the question into a negative, or he or she might redirect the focus of the question right at the end. The only way to avoid falling into these traps is to read the entirety of the question carefully before reading the answer choices.

3. Looking for Wrong Answers

Long and complicated multiple-choice questions can be intimidating. One way to simplify a difficult multiple-choice question is to eliminate all of the answer choices that are clearly wrong. In most sets of answers, there will be at least one selection that can be dismissed right away. If the test is administered on paper, the test taker could draw a line through it to indicate that it may be ignored; otherwise, the test taker will have to perform this operation mentally or on scratch paper. In either case, once the obviously incorrect answers have been eliminated, the remaining choices may be considered. Sometimes identifying the clearly wrong answers will give the test taker some information about the correct answer. For instance, if one of the remaining answer choices is a direct opposite of one of the eliminated answer choices, it may well be the correct answer. The opposite of obviously wrong is obviously right! Of course, this is not always the case. Some answers are obviously incorrect simply because they are irrelevant to the question being asked. Still, identifying and eliminating some incorrect answer choices is a good way to simplify a multiple-choice question.

4. Don't Overanalyze

Anxious test takers often overanalyze questions. When you are nervous, your brain will often run wild, causing you to make associations and discover clues that don't actually exist. If you feel that this may be a problem for you, do whatever you can to slow down during the test. Try taking a deep breath or counting to ten. As you read and consider the question, restrict yourself to the particular words used by the author. Avoid thought tangents about what the author *really* meant, or what he or she was *trying* to say. The only things that matter on a multiple-choice test are the words that are actually in the question. You must avoid reading too much into a multiple-choice question, or supposing that the writer meant something other than what he or she wrote.

5. No Need for Panic

It is wise to learn as many strategies as possible before taking a multiple-choice test, but it is likely that you will come across a few questions for which you simply don't know the answer. In this situation, avoid panicking. Because most multiple-choice tests include dozens of questions, the relative value of a single wrong answer is small. As much as possible, you should compartmentalize each question on a multiple-choice test. In other words, you should not allow your feelings about one question to affect your success on the others. When you find a question that you either don't understand or don't know how to answer, just take a deep breath and do your best. Read the entire question slowly and carefully. Try rephrasing the question a couple of different ways. Then, read all of the answer choices carefully. After eliminating obviously wrong answers, make a selection and move on to the next question.

6. Confusing Answer Choices

When working on a difficult multiple-choice question, there may be a tendency to focus on the answer choices that are the easiest to understand. Many people, whether consciously or not, gravitate to the answer choices that require the least concentration, knowledge, and memory. This is a mistake. When you come across an answer choice that is confusing, you should give it extra attention. A question might be confusing because you do not know the subject matter to which it refers. If this is the case, don't

 eliminate the answer before you have affirmatively settled on another. When you come across an answer choice of this type, set it aside as you look at the remaining choices. If you can confidently assert that one of the other choices is correct, you can leave the confusing answer aside. Otherwise, you will need to take a moment to try to better understand the confusing answer choice. Rephrasing is one way to tease out the sense of a confusing answer choice.

7. Your First Instinct

Many people struggle with multiple-choice tests because they overthink the questions. If you have studied sufficiently for the test, you should be prepared to trust your first instinct once you have carefully and completely read the question and all of the answer choices. There is a great deal of research suggesting that the mind can come to the correct conclusion very quickly once it has obtained all of the relevant information. At times, it may seem to you as if your intuition is working faster even than your reasoning mind. This may in fact be true. The knowledge you obtain while studying may be retrieved from your subconscious before you have a chance to work out the associations that support it. Verify your instinct by working out the reasons that it should be trusted.

8. Key Words

Many test takers struggle with multiple-choice questions because they have poor reading comprehension skills. Quickly reading and understanding a multiple-choice question requires a mixture of skill and experience. To help with this, try jotting down a few key words and phrases on a piece of scrap paper. Doing this concentrates the process of reading and forces the mind to weigh the relative importance of the question's parts. In selecting words and phrases to write down, the test taker thinks

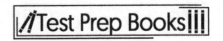

about the question more deeply and carefully. This is especially true for multiple-choice questions that are preceded by a long prompt.

9. Subtle Negatives

One of the oldest tricks in the multiple-choice test writer's book is to subtly reverse the meaning of a question with a word like *not* or *except*. If you are not paying attention to each word in the question, you can easily be led astray by this trick. For instance, a common question format is, "Which of the following is...?" Obviously, if the question instead is, "Which of the following is not...?," then the answer will be quite different. Even worse, the test makers are aware of the potential for this mistake and will include one answer choice that would be correct if the question were not negated or reversed. A test taker who misses the reversal will find what he or she believes to be a correct answer and will be so confident that he or she will fail to reread the question and discover the original error. The only way to avoid this is to practice a wide variety of multiple-choice questions and to pay close attention to each and every word.

10. Reading Every Answer Choice

It may seem obvious, but you should always read every one of the answer choices! Too many test takers fall into the habit of scanning the question and assuming that they understand the question because they recognize a few key words. From there, they pick the first answer choice that answers the question they believe they have read. Test takers who read all of the answer choices might discover that one of the latter answer choices is actually *more* correct. Moreover, reading all of the answer choices can remind you of facts related to the question that can help you arrive at the correct answer. Sometimes, a misstatement or incorrect detail in one of the latter answer choices will trigger your memory of the subject and will enable you to find the right answer. Failing to read all of the answer choices is like not reading all of the items on a restaurant menu: you might miss out on the perfect choice.

11. Spot the Hedges

One of the keys to success on multiple-choice tests is paying close attention to every word. This is never truer than with words like *almost*, *most*, *some*, and *sometimes*. These words are called "hedges" because they indicate that a statement is not totally true or not true in every place and time. An absolute statement will contain no hedges, but in many subjects, the answers are not always straightforward or absolute. There are always exceptions to the rules in these subjects. For this reason,

you should favor those multiple-choice questions that contain hedging language. The presence of qualifying words indicates that the author is taking special care with his or her words, which is certainly important when composing the right answer. After all, there are many ways to be wrong, but there is only one way to be right! For this reason, it is wise to avoid answers that are absolute when taking a multiple-choice test. An absolute answer is one that says things are either all one way or all another. They often include words like *every*, *always*, *best*, and *never*. If you are taking a multiple-choice test in a subject that doesn't lend itself to absolute answers, be on your guard if you see any of these words.

12. Long Answers

In many subject areas, the answers are not simple. As already mentioned, the right answer often requires hedges. Another common feature of the answers to a complex or subjective question are qualifying clauses, which are groups of words that subtly modify the meaning of the sentence. If the question or answer choice describes a rule to which there are exceptions or the subject matter is complicated, ambiguous, or confusing, the correct answer will require many words in order to be expressed clearly and accurately. In essence, you should not be deterred by answer choices that seem excessively long. Oftentimes, the author of the text will not be able to write the correct answer without offering some qualifications and modifications. Your job is to read the answer choices thoroughly and completely and to select the one that most accurately and precisely answers the question.

13. Restating to Understand

Sometimes, a question on a multiple-choice test is difficult not because of what it asks but because of how it is written. If this is the case, restate the question or answer choice in different words. This process serves a couple of important purposes. First, it forces you to concentrate on the core of the question. In order to rephrase the question accurately, you have to understand it well. Rephrasing the question will concentrate your mind on the key words and ideas. Second, it will present the information to your mind in a fresh way. This process may trigger your memory and render some useful scrap of information picked up while studying.

14. True Statements

Sometimes an answer choice will be true in itself, but it does not answer the question. This is one of the main reasons why it is essential to read the question carefully and completely before proceeding to the answer choices. Too often, test takers skip ahead to the answer choices and look for true statements. Having found one of these, they are content to select it without reference to the question above. The savvy test taker will always read the entire question before turning to the answer choices. Then, having settled on a correct answer choice, he or she will refer to the original question and ensure that the selected answer is relevant. The mistake of choosing a correct-but-irrelevant answer choice is especially common on questions related to specific pieces of objective knowledge.

15. No Patterns

One of the more dangerous ideas that circulates about multiple-choice tests is that the correct answers tend to fall into patterns. These erroneous ideas range from a belief that B and C are the most common right answers, to the idea that an unprepared test-taker should answer "A-B-A-C-A-D-A-B-A." It cannot be emphasized enough that pattern-seeking of this type is exactly the WRONG way to approach a multiple-choice test. To begin with, it is highly unlikely that the test maker will plot the correct answers according to some predetermined pattern. The questions are scrambled and delivered in a random order. Furthermore, even if the test maker was following a pattern in the assignation of correct answers, there is no reason why the test taker would know which pattern he or she was using. Any attempt to discern a pattern in the answer choices is a waste of time and a distraction from the real work of taking the test. A test taker would be much better served by extra preparation before the test than by reliance on a pattern in the answers.

Bonus Content

We host multiple bonus items online, including all six practice tests in digital format. Scan the QR code or go to this link to access this content:

testprepbooks.com/bonus/psat

The first time you access the page, you will need to register as a "new user" and verify your email address.

If you have any issues, please email support@testprepbooks.com

Introduction to the PSAT

Function of the Test

The Preliminary SAT/National Merit Scholarship Qualifying Test (PSAT/NMSQT) is an introductory version of the SAT exam. Given by the College Board with support from the National Merit Scholarship Corporation (NMSC), the PSAT is designed to help U.S. students get ready for the SAT or ACT. It also serves as a qualifying measure to identify students for college scholarships, including the National Merit Scholarship Program. Students taking the PSAT/NMSQT are automatically considered for the National Merit Scholarship Program, a contest that recognizes and awards scholars based on academic performance. About 50,000 pupils are acknowledged for extraordinary PSAT scores every year. Approximately 16,000 of these students become National Merit Semifinalists, and about half of this group is awarded scholarships.

Over 3.5 million high school students take the PSAT every year. Most are sophomore or junior high school students residing in the U.S. However, younger students may also register to take the PSAT. Students who are not U.S. citizens or residents can take the PSAT as well, by locating and contacting a local school that offers it.

Test Administration

The PSAT/NMSQT is offered on various dates in the fall at schools throughout the United States. Some schools will pay all or part of the exam registration fee for their pupils. Since the financial responsibility of the student for the exam is different for each school, it is best to consult the school's guidance department for specifics.

Tenth grade students who would like another chance to take the PSAT can take the PSAT 10 in the spring at various schools throughout the U.S. In addition to serving as a practice test for the SAT, scholarship programs use the PSAT 10 to screen for prospective students, but unlike the PSAT/NMSQT, it is not part of the National Merit Scholarship Program.

Students with documented disabilities can contact the College Board to make alternative arrangements to take the PSAT. All reasonable applications are reviewed.

Test Format

The PSAT gauges a student's proficiency in three areas: Reading, Mathematics, and Writing and Language. All the tests that fall under the SAT umbrella (including the PSAT) were redesigned in 2015. The revised PSAT is very similar to the new SAT in substance, structure, and scoring methodology, except that the PSAT does not include an essay. 1520 is the highest possible score for the PSAT.

The reading portion of the PSAT measures comprehension, requiring candidates to read multi-paragraph fiction and non-fiction segments including informational visuals, such as charts, tables and graphs, and answer questions based on this content. Three critical sectors are tested for the math section: Solving problems and analyzing data, Algebra, and complex equations and operations. The writing and language portion requires students to evaluate and edit writing and graphics to obtain an answer that correctly conveys the information given in the passage.

The PSAT contains 139 multiple-choice questions, with each section comprising over 40 questions. A different length of time is given for each section, for a total of two hours, 45 minutes.

Section	Time (In Minutes)	Number of Questions
Reading	60	47
Writing and Language	35	44
Mathematics	70	48
Total	**165**	**139**

Scoring

Scores for the newly revised PSAT are based on a scale of 320 to 1520. Scores range from 160-760 for the Math section and 160-760 for the Reading and Writing and Language combined. The PSAT also no longer penalizes for incorrect answers, as it did in the previous version. Therefore, a student's raw score is the number of correctly answered questions. Score reports also list sub-scores for math, reading and writing on a scale from 8 to 38, in order to give candidates an idea of strengths and weaknesses. Mean, or average, scores received by characteristic U.S. test-takers, are broken down by grade level.

The report ranks scores based on a percentile between 1 and 99 so students can see how they measured up to other test takers. Average (50th percentile), scores range from about 470 to 480 in each section, for a total of 940 to 960. Good scores are typically defined as higher than 50 percent. Scores of 95 percent or higher are in contention for National Merit Semifinalist and Finalist slots, but scholarships usually only go to the top one percent of 10th graders taking the PSAT.

Recent/Future Developments

A redesigned version of the PSAT was launched in October 2015. Changes include a longer total length (2 hours, 45 minutes, versus the previous time of 2 hours, 10 minutes), a total of four multiple-choice answers per question instead of five as in the past, and no guessing penalty, so students earn points based only on questions answered correctly. The revised PSAT also has more of a well-rounded emphasis on life skills and the thinking needed at a college level, incorporating concepts learned in science, history and social studies into the reading, math and writing sections. It is important to note that since the redesigned PSAT is different than in the past, scores on previous tests should not be compared to those taken in the current year.

When the PSAT was revamped, a number of new Services for Students with Disabilities (SSD) regulations occurred as well. For example, the PSAT/NMSQT printed test manual for nonstandard testers (often referred to as the "pink book") is no longer used. Instead, every candidate will use the standard exam booklet unless an alternative design (such as large print, Braille, MP3 Audio, and Assistive Technology Compatible) is requested.

There is also a new option allowing students to save time by completing classifying data prior to the exam by choosing the pre-administration option on the PSAT registration website. And starting in January 2015, the College Board forged new collaborations with five scholarship providers to expand scholarship opportunities earlier in students' high school careers.

Study Prep Plan for the PSAT

1 **Schedule** - Use one of our study schedules below or come up with one of your own.

2 **Relax** - Test anxiety can hurt even the best students. There are many ways to reduce stress. Find the one that works best for you.

3 **Execute** - Once you have a good plan in place, be sure to stick to it.

One Week Study Schedule		
Day 1	Reading Test
Day 2	Math Test
Day 3	Passport to Advanced Math
Day 4	Practice Tests #1 & #2
Day 5	Practice Tests #3 & #4
Day 6	Practice Tests #5 & #6
Day 7	Take Your Exam!

Two Week Study Schedule			
Day 1	Reading Test	Day 8	Practice Test #1
Day 2	Analysis of History/ Social Studies Excerpts	Day 9	Practice Test #2
Day 3	Standard English Conventions	Day 10	Practice Test #3
Day 4	Math Test	Day 11	Practice Test #4
Day 5	Problem-Solving and Data Analysis	Day 12	Practice Test #5
Day 6	Passport to Advanced Math	Day 13	Practice Test #6
Day 7	Additional Topics	Day 14	Take Your Exam!

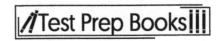

One Month Study Schedule							
Day 1	Reading Test	Day 11	Math Test	Day 21	Additional Topics
Day 2	Words in Context	Day 12	Creating, Solving, and Interpreting Systems...	Day 22	Degrees and Radians
Day 3	Rhetoric and Synthesis	Day 13	Algebraically Solving Systems of Two Linear...	Day 23	Complementary Angle Theorem
Day 4	Analysis of History/ Social Studies Excerpts	Day 14	Problem-Solving and Data Analysis	Day 24	Practice Test #1
Day 5	Analysis of Science Excerpts	Day 15	Given a Scatterplot, Using Linear...	Day 25	Practice Test #2
Day 6	Writing and Language Test	Day 16	Comparing Linear Growth with...	Day 26	Practice Test #3
Day 7	Effective Language Use	Day 17	Passport to Advanced Math	Day 27	Practice Test #4
Day 8	Standard English Conventions	Day 18	Adding, Subtracting, and Multiplying...	Day 28	Practice Test #5
Day 9	Pronouns	Day 19	Rewriting Simple Rational Expressions	Day 29	Practice Test #6
Day 10	Punctuation	Day 20	Understanding a Nonlinear...	Day 30	Take Your Exam!

Build your own prep plan by visiting:

testprepbooks.com/prep

As you study for your test, we'd like to take the opportunity to remind you that you are capable of great things! With the right tools and dedication, you truly can do anything you set your mind to. The fact that you are holding this book right now shows how committed you are. In case no one has told you lately, you've got this! Our intention behind including this coloring page is to give you the chance to take some time to engage your creative side when you need a little brain-break from studying. As a company, we want to encourage people like you to achieve their dreams by providing good quality study materials for the tests and certifications that improve careers and change lives. As individuals, many of us have taken such tests in our careers, and we know how challenging this process can be. While we can't come alongside you and cheer you on personally, we can offer you the space to recall your purpose, reconnect with your passion, and refresh your brain through an artistic practice. We wish you every success, and happy studying!

Reading Test

The purpose of this guide is to help test takers understand the basic principles of reading comprehension questions contained in the Preliminary SAT/National Merit Qualifying Test (PSAT/NMSQT). Studying this guide will help determine the types of questions that the test contains and how best to address them, provided the test's parameters. This guide is not all-inclusive, and does not contain actual test material. This guide is, and should be used, only as preparation to improve student's reading skills for the PSAT Reading Comprehension section.

Each section addresses key skills test takers need to master in order to successfully complete the Reading portion of the PSAT. Each section is further broken down into sub-skills. All of the topics and related subtopics address testable material. Careful use of this guide should fully prepare test takers for a successful test experience.

Command of Evidence

Command of evidence, or the ability to use contextual clues, factual statements, and corroborative phrases to support an author's message or intent, is an important part of the PSAT/NMSQT. A test taker's ability to parse out factual information and draw conclusions based on evidence is important to critical reading comprehension. The test will ask students to read text passages, and then answer questions based on information contained in them. These types of questions may ask test takers to identify stated facts. They may also require test takers to draw logical conclusions, identify data based on graphs, make inferences, and to generally display analytical thinking skills.

Finding Evidence in a Passage

The basic tenet of reading comprehension is the ability to read and understand a text. One way to understand a text is to look for information that supports the author's main idea, topic, or position statement. This information may be factual, or it may be based on the author's opinion. This section will focus on the test taker's ability to identify factual information, as opposed to opinionated bias. The PSAT/NMSQT will ask test takers to read passages containing factual information, and then logically relate those passages by drawing conclusions based on evidence.

In order to identify factual information within one or more text passages, begin by looking for statements of fact. Factual statements can be either true or false. Identifying factual statements as opposed to opinion statements is important in demonstrating full command of evidence in reading. For example, the statement *The temperature outside was unbearably hot* may seem like a fact; however, it's not. While anyone can point to a temperature gauge as factual evidence, the statement itself reflects only an opinion. Some people may find the temperature unbearably hot. Others may find it comfortably warm. Thus, the sentence, *The temperature outside was unbearably hot,* reflects the opinion of the author who found it unbearable. If the text passage followed up the sentence with atmospheric conditions indicating heat indices above 140 degrees Fahrenheit, then the reader knows there is factual information that supports the author's assertion of *unbearably hot.*

In looking for information that can be proven or disproven, it's helpful to scan for dates, numbers, timelines, equations, statistics, and other similar data within any given text passage. These types of indicators will point to proven particulars. For example, the statement, *The temperature outside was unbearably hot on that summer day, July 10, 1913,* most likely indicates factual information, even if the

13

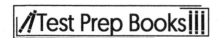

reader is unaware that this is the hottest day on record in the United States. Be careful when reading biased words from an author. Biased words indicate opinion, as opposed to fact. The following list contains a sampling of common biased words:

- Good/bad
- Great/greatest
- Better/best/worst
- Amazing
- Terrible/bad/awful
- Beautiful/handsome/ugly
- More/most
- Exciting/dull/boring
- Favorite
- Very
- Probably/should/seem/possibly

Remember, most of what is written is actually opinion or carefully worded information that seems like fact when it isn't. To say, *duplicating DNA results is not cost-effective* sounds like it could be a scientific fact, but it isn't. Factual information can be verified through independent sources.

The simplest type of test question may provide a text passage, then ask the test taker to distinguish the correct factual supporting statement that best answers the corresponding question on the test. However, be aware that most questions may ask the test taker to read more than one text passage and identify which answer best supports an author's topic. While the ability to identify factual information is critical, these types of questions require the test taker to identify chunks of details, and then relate them to one another.

Displaying Analytical Thinking Skills

Analytical thinking involves being able to break down visual information into manageable portions in order to solve complex problems or process difficult concepts. This skill encompasses all aspects of command of evidence in reading comprehension.

A reader can approach analytical thinking in a series of steps. First, when approaching visual material, a reader should identify an author's thought process. Is the line of reasoning clear from the presented passage, or does it require inference and coming to a conclusion independent of the author? Next, a reader should evaluate the author's line of reasoning to determine if the logic is sound. Look for evidentiary clues and cited sources. Do these hold up under the author's argument? Third, look for bias. Bias includes generalized, emotional statements that will not hold up under scrutiny, as they are not based on fact. From there, a reader should ask if the presented evidence is trustworthy. Are the facts cited from reliable sources? Are they current? Is there any new factual information that has come to light since the passage was written that renders the argument useless? Next, a reader should carefully think about information that opposes the author's view. Do the author's arguments guide the reader to identical thoughts, or is there room for sound arguments? Finally, a reader should always be able to identify an author's conclusion and be able to weigh its effectiveness.

The ability to display analytical thinking skills while reading is key in any standardized testing situation. Test takers should be able to critically evaluate the information provided, and then answer questions related to content by using the steps above.

14

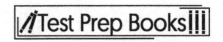

Making Inferences

Simply put, an inference is an educated guess drawn from evidence, logic, and reasoning. The key to making inferences is identifying clues within a passage, and then using common sense to arrive at a reasonable conclusion. Consider it "reading between the lines."

One way to make an inference is to look for main topics. When doing so, pay particular attention to any titles, headlines, or opening statements made by the author. Topic sentences or repetitive ideas can be clues in gleaning inferred ideas. For example, if a passage contains the phrase *While some consider DNA testing to be infallible, it is an inherently flawed technique,* the test taker can infer the rest of the passage will contain information that points to problems with DNA testing.

The test taker may be asked to make an inference based on prior knowledge but may also be asked to make predictions based on new ideas. For example, the test taker may have no prior knowledge of DNA other than its genetic property to replicate. However, if the reader is given passages on the flaws of DNA testing with enough factual evidence, the test taker may arrive at the inferred conclusion that the author does not support the infallibility of DNA testing in all identification cases.

When making inferences, it is important to remember that the critical thinking process involved must be fluid and open to change. While a reader may infer an idea from a main topic, general statement, or other clues, they must be open to receiving new information within a particular passage. New ideas presented by an author may require the test taker to alter an inference. Similarly, when asked questions that require making an inference, it's important to read the entire test passage and all of the answer options. Often, a test taker will need to refine a general inference based on new ideas that may be presented within the test itself.

Author's Use of Evidence to Support Claims

Authors utilize a wide range of techniques to tell a story or communicate information. Readers should be familiar with the most common of these techniques. Techniques of writing are also commonly known as rhetorical devices, and they are some of the evidence that authors use to support claims.

In nonfiction writing, authors employ argumentative techniques to present their opinion to readers in the most convincing way. Persuasive writing usually includes at least one type of appeal: an appeal to logic (logos), emotion (pathos), or credibility and trustworthiness (ethos). When a writer appeals to logic, they are asking readers to agree with them based on research, evidence, and an established line of reasoning. An author's argument might also appeal to readers' emotions, perhaps by including personal stories and anecdotes (a short narrative of a specific event). A final type of appeal, appeal to authority, asks the reader to agree with the author's argument on the basis of their expertise or credentials. Consider three different approaches to arguing the same opinion:

Logic (Logos)

Below is an example of an appeal to logic. The author uses evidence to disprove the logic of the school's rule (the rule was supposed to reduce discipline problems, but the number of problems has not been reduced; therefore, the rule is not working) and call for its repeal.

> Our school should abolish its current ban on campus cell phone use. The ban was adopted last year as an attempt to reduce class disruptions and help students focus more on their lessons.

15

However, since the rule was enacted, there has been no change in the number of disciplinary problems in class. Therefore, the rule is ineffective and should be done away with.

Emotion (Pathos)

An author's argument might also appeal to readers' emotions, perhaps by including personal stories and anecdotes.

The next example presents an appeal to emotion. By sharing the personal anecdote of one student and speaking about emotional topics like family relationships, the author invokes the reader's empathy in asking them to reconsider the school rule.

> Our school should abolish its current ban on campus cell phone use. If students aren't able to use their phones during the school day, many of them feel isolated from their loved ones. For example, last semester, one student's grandmother had a heart attack in the morning. However, because he couldn't use his cell phone, the student didn't know about his grandmother's accident until the end of the day—when she had already passed away, and it was too late to say goodbye. By preventing students from contacting their friends and family, our school is placing undue stress and anxiety on students.

Credibility (Ethos)

Finally, an appeal to authority includes a statement from a relevant expert. In this case, the author uses a doctor in the field of education to support the argument. All three examples begin from the same opinion—the school's phone ban needs to change—but rely on different argumentative styles to persuade the reader.

> Our school should abolish its current ban on campus cell phone use. According to Dr. Bartholomew Everett, a leading educational expert, "Research studies show that cell phone usage has no real impact on student attentiveness. Rather, phones provide a valuable technological resource for learning. Schools need to learn how to integrate this new technology into their curriculum." Rather than banning phones altogether, our school should follow the advice of experts and allow students to use phones as part of their learning.

Informational Graphics

A test taker's ability to draw conclusions from an informational graphic is a sub-skill in displaying one's command of reading evidence. Drawing conclusions requires the reader to consider all information provided in the passage, then to use logic to piece it together to form a reasonably correct resolution. In this case, a test taker must look for facts as well as opinionated statements. Both should be considered in order to arrive at a conclusion. These types of questions test one's ability to conduct logical and analytical thinking.

Identifying data-driven evidence in informational graphics is very similar to analyzing factual information. However, it often involves the use of graphics in order to do so. In these types of questions, the test taker will be presented with a graph, or organizational tool, and asked questions regarding the information it contains. On the following page, review the pie chart organizing percentages of primary occupations of public transportation passengers in US cities.

This figure depicts the jobs of passengers taking public transportation in U.S. cities. A corresponding PSAT question may have the test taker study the chart, then answer a question regarding the values. For

example, is the number of students relying on public transportation greater or less than the number of the unemployed? Similarly, the test may ask if people employed outside the home are less likely to use public transportation than homemakers. Note that the phrase *less likely* may weigh into the reader's choice of optional answers and that the test taker should look for additional passage data to arrive at a conclusion one way or another.

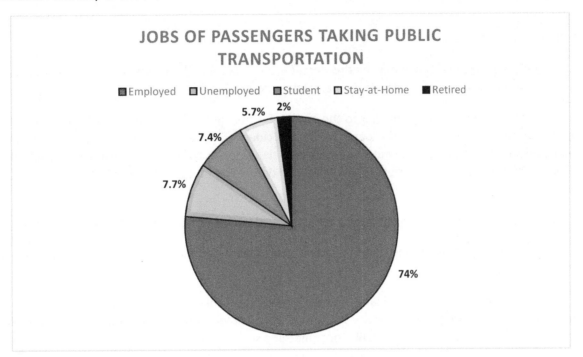

The PSAT/NMSQT will also test the ability to draw a conclusion by presenting the test taker with more than one passage, and then ask questions that require the reader to compare the passages in order to arrive at a logical conclusion. For example, a text passage may describe the flaws in DNA testing, and then describe the near infallibility of it in the next. The test taker then may be required to glean the evidence in both passages, then answer a question such as *the central idea in the first paragraph is ...* followed by *which choice regarding the infallibility of DNA testing best refutes the previous question?* In this example, the test taker must carefully find a central concept of the flaws of DNA testing based on the two passages, and then rely on that choice to best answer the subsequent question regarding its infallibility.

Words in Context

In order to successfully complete the reading comprehension section of the PSAT/NMSQT, the test taker should be able to identify words in context. This involves a set of skills that requires the test taker to answer questions about unfamiliar words within a particular text passage. Additionally, the test taker may be asked to answer critical thinking questions based on unfamiliar word meanings. Identifying the meaning of different words in context is very much like solving a puzzle. By using a variety of techniques, a test taker should be able to correctly identify the meaning of unfamiliar words and concepts with ease.

17

Using Context Clues

A context clue is a hint that an author provides to the reader in order to help define difficult or unique words. When reading a passage, a test taker should take note of any unfamiliar words, and then examine the sentence around them to look for clues to the word meanings.

Let's look at an example:

> He faced a *conundrum* in making this decision. He felt as if he had come to a crossroads. This was truly a puzzle, and what he did next would determine the course of his future.

The word *conundrum* may be unfamiliar to the reader. By looking at context clues, the reader should be able to determine its meaning. In this passage, context clues include the idea of making a decision and of being unsure. Furthermore, the author restates the definition of conundrum in using the word *puzzle* as a synonym. Therefore, the reader should be able to determine that the definition of the word *conundrum* is a difficult puzzle.

Similarly, a reader can determine difficult vocabulary by identifying antonyms. Let's look at an example:

> Her *gregarious* nature was completely opposite of her twin's, who was shy, retiring, and socially nervous.

The word *gregarious* may be unfamiliar. However, by looking at the surrounding context clues, the reader can determine that *gregarious* does not mean shy. The twins' personalities are being contrasted. Therefore, *gregarious* must mean sociable, or something similar to it.

At times, an author will provide contextual clues through a cause and effect relationship. Look at the next sentence as an example:

> The athletes were excited with *elation* when they won the tournament; unfortunately, their off-court antics caused them to forfeit the win.

The word elated may be unfamiliar to the reader. However, the author defines the word by presenting a cause and effect relationship. The athletes were so elated at the win that their behavior went overboard, and they had to forfeit. In this instance, *elated* must mean something akin to overjoyed, happy, and overexcited.

Cause and effect is one technique authors use to demonstrate relationships. A cause is why something happens. The effect is what happens as a result. For example, a reader may encounter text such as *Because he was unable to sleep, he was often restless and irritable during the day.* The cause is insomnia due to lack of sleep. The effect is being restless and irritable. When reading for a cause and effect relationship, look for words such as "if", "then", "such", and "because." By using cause and effect, an author can describe direct relationships, and convey an overall theme, particularly when taking a stance on their topic.

An author can also provide contextual clues through comparison and contrast. Let's look at an example:

> Her torpid state caused her parents, and her physician, to worry about her seemingly sluggish well-being.

18

The word *torpid* is probably unfamiliar to the reader. However, the author has compared *torpid* to a state of being and, moreover, one that's worrisome. Therefore, the reader should be able to determine that *torpid* is not a positive, healthy state of being. In fact, through the use of comparison, it means sluggish. Similarly, an author may contrast an unfamiliar word with an idea. In the sentence *Her torpid state was completely opposite of her usual, bubbly self,* the meaning of *torpid*, or sluggish, is contrasted with the words *bubbly self*.

A test taker should be able to critically assess and determine unfamiliar word meanings through the use of an author's context clues in order to fully comprehend difficult text passages.

Relating Unfamiliar Words to Familiar Words

The PSAT/NMSQT will test a reader's ability to use context clues, and then relate unfamiliar words to more familiar ones. Using the word *torpid* as an example, the test may ask the test taker to relate the meaning of the word to a list of vocabulary options and choose the more familiar word as closest in meaning. In this case, the test may say something like the following:

Which of the following words means the same as the word *torpid* in the above passage?

Then they will provide the test taker with a list of familiar options such as happy, disgruntled, sluggish, and animated. By using context clues, the reader has already determined the meaning of *torpid* as slow or sluggish, so the reader should be able to correctly identify the word *sluggish* as the correct answer.

One effective way to relate unfamiliar word meanings to more familiar ones is to substitute the provided word in each answer option for the unfamiliar word in question. Although this will not always lead to a correct answer every time, this strategy will help the test taker narrow answer options. Be careful when utilizing this strategy. Pay close attention to the meaning of sentences and answer choices because it's easy to mistake answer choices as correct when they are easily substituted, especially when they are the same part of speech. Does the sentence mean the same thing with the substituted word option in place or does it change entirely? Does the substituted word make sense? Does it possibly mean the same as the unfamiliar word in question?

How an Author's Word Choice Shapes Meaning, Style, and Tone

Authors choose their words carefully in order to artfully depict meaning, style, and tone, which is most commonly inferred through the use of adjectives and verbs. The *tone* is the predominant emotion present in the text, and represents the attitude or feelings that an author has towards a character or event.

To review, an adjective is a word used to describe something, and usually precedes the noun, a person, place, or object. A verb is a word describing an action. For example, the sentence "The scary woodpecker ate the spider" includes the adjective "scary," the noun "woodpecker," and the verb "ate." Reading this sentence may rouse some negative feelings, as the word "scary" carries a negative charge. The *charge* is the emotional connotation that can be derived from the adjectives and verbs and is either positive or negative. Recognizing the charge of a particular sentence or passage is an effective way to understand the meaning and tone the author is trying to convey.

Many authors have conflicting charges within the same text, but a definitive tone can be inferred by understanding the meaning of the charges relative to each other. It's important to recognize key

19

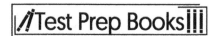

conjunctions, or words that link sentences or clauses together. There are several types and subtypes of conjunctions. Three are most important for reading comprehension:

- *Cumulative conjunctions* add one statement to another.
- Examples: and, both, also, as well as, not only
- e.g. The juice is sweet *and* sour.
- *Adversative conjunctions* are used to contrast two clauses.
- Examples: but, while, still, yet, nevertheless
- e.g. She was tired, *but* she was happy.
- *Alternative conjunctions* express two alternatives.
- Examples: or, either, neither, nor, else, otherwise
- e.g. He must eat, *or* he will die.

Identifying the meaning and tone of a text can be accomplished with the following steps:

- Identify the adjectives and verbs.
- Recognize any important conjunctions.
- Label the adjectives and verbs as positive or negative.
- Understand what the charge means about the text.

To demonstrate these steps, examine the following passage from the classic children's poem, "The Sheep":

>Lazy sheep, pray tell me why
>
>In the pleasant fields you lie,
>
>Eating grass, and daisies white,
>
>From the morning till the night?
>
>Everything can something do,
>
>But what kind of use are you?

–Taylor, Jane and Ann. "The Sheep."

This selection is a good example of conflicting charges that work together to express an overall tone. Following the first two steps, identify the adjectives, verbs, and conjunctions within the passage. For this example, the adjectives are <u>underlined</u>, the verbs are in **bold**, and the conjunctions *italicized*:

>_Lazy_ sheep, pray **tell** me why
>
>In the <u>pleasant</u> fields you **lie**,
>
>**Eating** grass, and daisies <u>white,</u>
>
>From the morning till the night?
>
>Everything can something do,
>
>*But* what kind of use are you?

20

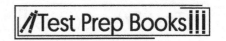

For step three, read the passage and judge whether feelings of positivity or negativity arose. Then assign a charge to each of the words that were outlined. This can be done in a table format, or simply by writing a + or − next to the word.

The word <u>lazy</u> carries a negative connotation; it usually denotes somebody unwilling to work. To **tell** someone something has an exclusively neutral connotation, as it depends on what's being told, which has not yet been revealed at this point, so a charge can be assigned later. The word <u>pleasant</u> is an inherently positive word. To **lie** could be positive or negative depending on the context, but as the subject (the sheep) is lying in a pleasant field, then this is a positive experience. **Eating** is also generally positive.

After labeling the charges for each word, it might be inferred that the tone of this poem is happy and maybe even admiring or innocuously envious. However, notice the adversative conjunction, "but" and what follows. The author has listed all the pleasant things this sheep gets to do all day, but the tone changes when the author asks, "What kind of use are you?" Asking someone to prove their value is a rather hurtful thing to do, as it implies that the person asking the question doesn't believe the subject has any value, so this could be listed under negative charges. Referring back to the verb **tell**, after reading the whole passage, it can be deduced that the author is asking the sheep to tell what use the sheep is, so this has a negative charge.

+	−
<ul><li>Pleasant</li><li>Lie in fields</li><li>From morning to night</li></ul>	<ul><li>Lazy</li><li>Tell me</li><li>What kind of use are you</li></ul>

Upon examining the charges, it might seem like there's an even amount of positive and negative emotion in this selection, and that's where the conjunction "but" becomes crucial to identifying the tone. The conjunction "but" indicates there's a contrasting view to the pleasantness of the sheep's daily life, and this view is that the sheep is lazy and useless, which is also indicated by the first line, "lazy sheep, pray tell me why."

It might be helpful to look at questions pertaining to tone. For this selection, consider the following question:

The author of the poem regards the sheep with a feeling of what?
    a. Respect
    b. Disgust
    c. Apprehension
    d. Intrigue

Considering the author views the sheep as lazy with nothing to offer, Choice *A* appears to reflect the opposite of what the author is feeling.

Choice *B* seems to mirror the author's feelings towards the sheep, as laziness is considered a disreputable trait, and people (or personified animals, in this case) with unfavorable traits might be viewed with disgust.

Choice *C* doesn't make sense within context, as laziness isn't usually feared.

Choice *D* is tricky, as it may be tempting to argue that the author is intrigued with the sheep because they ask, "pray tell me why." This is another out-of-scope answer choice as it doesn't *quite* describe the feelings the author experiences and there's also a much better fit in Choice *B*.

Rhetoric and Synthesis

Rhetoric

The PSAT/NMSQT will test a reader's ability to identify an author's use of rhetoric within text passages. Rhetoric is the use of positional or persuasive language to convey one or more central ideas. The idea behind the use of rhetoric is to convince the reader of something. Its use is meant to persuade or motivate the reader. An author may choose to appeal to their audience through logic, emotion, the use of ideology, or by conveying that the central idea is timely, and thus, important to the reader. There are a variety of rhetorical techniques an author can use to achieve this goal.

An author may choose to use traditional elements of style to persuade the reader. They may also use a story's setting, mood, characters, or a central conflict to build emotion in the reader. Similarly, an author may choose to use specific techniques such as alliteration, irony, metaphor, simile, hyperbole, allegory, imagery, onomatopoeia, and personification to persuasively illustrate one or more central ideas they wish the reader to adopt. In order to be successful in a standardized reading comprehension test situation, a reader needs to be well acquainted in recognizing rhetoric and rhetorical devices.

Identifying Elements of Style

A writer's style is unique. The combinations of elements are carefully designed to create an effect on the reader. For example, the novels of J.K. Rowling are very different in style than the novels of Stephen King, yet both are designed to tell a compelling tale and to entertain readers. Furthermore, the articles found in *National Geographic* are vastly different from those a reader may encounter in *People* magazine, yet both have the same objective: to inform the reader. The difference is in the elements of style.

While there are many elements of style an author can employ, it's important to look at three things: the words they choose to use, the voice an author selects, and the fluency of sentence structure. Word choice is critical in persuasive or pictorial writing. While effective authors will choose words that are succinct, different authors will choose various words based on what they are trying to accomplish. For example, a reader would not expect to encounter the same words in a gothic novel that they would read in a scholastic article on gene therapy. An author whose intent is to paint a picture of a foreboding scene, will choose different words than an author who wants to persuade the reader that a particular political party has the most sound, ideological platform. A romance novelist will sound very different than a true crime writer.

The voice an author selects is also important to note. An author's voice is that element of style that indicates their personality. It's important that authors move us as readers; therefore, they will choose a voice that helps them do that. An author's voice may be satirical or authoritative. It may be light-hearted

or serious in tone. It may be silly or humorous as well. Voice, as an element of style, can be vague in nature and difficult to identify, since it's also referred to as an author's tone, but it is that element unique to the author. It is the author's "self." A reader can expect an author's voice to vary across literary genres. A non-fiction author will generally employ a more neutral voice than an author of fiction, but use caution when trying to identify voice. Do not confuse an author's voice with a particular character's voice.

Another critical element of style involves how an author structures their sentences. An effective writer—one who wants to paint a vivid picture or strongly illustrate a central idea—will use a variety of sentence structures and sentence lengths. A reader is more likely to be confused if an author uses choppy, unrelated sentences. Similarly, a reader will become bored and lose interest if an author repeatedly uses the same sentence structure. Good writing is fluent. It flows. Varying sentence structure keeps a reader engaged and helps reading comprehension. Consider the following example:

> The morning started off early. It was bright out. It was just daylight. The Moon was still in the sky. He was tired from his sleepless night.

Then consider this text:

> Morning hit hard. He didn't remember the last time light hurt this bad. Sleep had been absent, and the very thought of moving towards the new day seemed like a hurdle he couldn't overcome.

Note the variety in sentence structure. The second passage is more interesting to read because the sentence fluency is more effective. Both passages paint the picture of a central character's reaction to dawn, but the second passage is more effective because it uses a variety of sentences and is more fluent than the first.

Elements of style can also include more recognizable components such as a story's setting, the type of narrative an author chooses, the mood they set, and the character conflicts employed. The ability to effectively understand the use of rhetoric demands the reader take note of an author's word choices, writing voice, and the ease of fluency employed to persuade, entertain, illustrate, or otherwise captivate a reader.

Identifying Rhetorical Devices

If a writer feels strongly about a subject, or has a passion for it, strong words and phrases can be chosen. Think of the types of rhetoric (or language) our politicians use. Each word, phrase, and idea is carefully crafted to elicit a response. Hopefully, that response is one of agreement to a certain point of view, especially among voters. Authors use the same types of language to achieve the same results. For example, the word "bad" has a certain connotation, but the words "horrid," "repugnant," and "abhorrent" paint a far better picture for the reader. They're more precise. They're interesting to read, and they should all illicit stronger feelings in the reader than the word "bad." An author generally uses other devices beyond mere word choice to persuade, convince, entertain, or otherwise engage a reader.

Rhetorical devices are those elements an author utilizes in painting sensory, and hopefully persuasive ideas to which a reader can relate. They are numerable. Test takers will likely encounter one or more standardized test questions addressing various rhetorical devices. This study guide will address the more common types: alliteration, irony, metaphor, simile, hyperbole, allegory, imagery, onomatopoeia, and personification, providing examples of each.

23

Alliteration is a device that uses repetitive beginning sounds in words to appeal to the reader. Classic tongue twisters are a great example of alliteration. *She sells sea shells down by the sea shore* is an extreme example of alliteration. Authors will use alliterative devices to capture a reader's attention. It's interesting to note that marketing also utilizes alliteration in the same way. A reader will likely remember products that have the brand name and item starting with the same letter. Similarly, many songs, poems, and catchy phrases use this device. It's memorable. Use of alliteration draws a reader's attention to ideas that an author wants to highlight.

Irony is a device that authors use when pitting two contrasting items or ideas against each other in order to create an effect. It's frequently used when an author wants to employ humor or convey a sarcastic tone. Additionally, it's often used in fictional works to build tension between characters, or between a particular character and the reader. An author may use *verbal irony* (sarcasm), *situational irony* (where actions or events have the opposite effect than what's expected), and *dramatic irony* (where the reader knows something a character does not). Examples of irony include:

- Dramatic Irony: An author describing the presence of a hidden killer in a murder mystery, unbeknownst to the characters but known to the reader.

- Situational Irony: An author relating the tale of a fire captain who loses her home in a five-alarm conflagration.

- Verbal Irony: This is where an author or character says one thing but means another. For example, telling a police officer "Thanks a lot" after receiving a ticket.

Metaphor is a device that uses a figure of speech to paint a visual picture of something that is not literally applicable. Authors relate strong images to readers, and evoke similar strong feelings using metaphors. Most often, authors will mention one thing in comparison to another more familiar to the reader. It's important to note that metaphors do not use the comparative words "like" or "as." At times, metaphors encompass common phrases such as clichés. At other times, authors may use mixed metaphors in making identification between two dissimilar things. Examples of metaphors include:

- An author describing a character's anger as *a flaming sheet of fire.*
- An author relating a politician as having been a folding chair under close questioning.
- A novel's character telling another character to *take a flying hike.*
- Shakespeare's assertion that *all the world's a stage.*

Simile is a device that compares two dissimilar things using the words "like" and "as." When using similes, an author tries to catch a reader's attention and use comparison of unlike items to make a point. Similes are commonly used and often develop into figures of speech and catch phrases.

Examples of similes include:

- An author describing a character as having a complexion like a faded lily.

- An investigative journalist describing his interview subject as being like cold steel and with a demeanor hard as ice.

- An author asserting the current political arena is just like a three-ring circus and as dry as day old bread.

Similes and metaphors can be confusing. When utilizing simile, an author will state one thing is like another. A metaphor states one thing is another. An example of the difference would be if an author states a character is *just like a fierce tiger and twice as angry,* as opposed to stating the character *is a fierce tiger and twice as angry.*

Hyperbole is simply an exaggeration that is not taken literally. A potential test taker will have heard or employed hyperbole in daily speech, as it is a common device we all use. Authors will use hyperbole to draw a reader's eye toward important points and to illicit strong emotional and relatable responses. Examples of hyperbole include:

- An author describing a character as being as big as a house and twice the circumference of a city block.

- An author stating the city's water problem as being old as the hills and more expensive than a king's ransom in spent tax dollars.

- A journalist stating the mayoral candidate died of embarrassment when her tax records were made public.

Allegories are stories or poems with hidden meanings, usually a political or moral one. Authors will frequently use allegory when leading the reader to a conclusion. Allegories are similar to parables, symbols, and analogies. Often, an author will employ the use of allegory to make political, historical, moral, or social observations. As an example, Jonathan Swift's work *Gulliver's Travels into Several Remote Nations of the World* is an allegory in and of itself. The work is a political allegory of England during Jonathan Swift's lifetime. Set in the travel journal style plot of a giant amongst smaller people, and a smaller Gulliver amongst the larger, it is a commentary on Swift's political stance of existing issues of his age. Many fictional works are entire allegories in and of themselves. George Orwell's *Animal Farm* is a story of animals that conquer man and form their own farm society with swine at the top; however, it is not a literal story in any sense. It's Orwell's political allegory of Russian society during and after the Communist revolution of 1917. Other examples of allegory in popular culture include:

- Aesop's fable "The Tortoise and the Hare," which teaches readers that being steady is more important than being fast and impulsive.

- The popular *Hunger Games* by Suzanne Collins that teaches readers that media can numb society to what is truly real and important.

- Dr. Seuss's *Yertle the Turtle* which is a warning against totalitarianism and, at the time it was written, against the despotic rule of Adolf Hitler.

Imagery is a rhetorical device that an author employs when they use visual or descriptive language to evoke a reader's emotion. Use of imagery as a rhetorical device is broader in scope than this study guide addresses, but in general, the function of imagery is to create a vibrant scene in the reader's imagination and, in turn, tease the reader's ability to identify through strong emotion and sensory experience. In the simplest of terms, imagery, as a rhetoric device, beautifies literature.

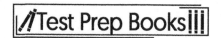
An example of poetic imagery is below:

> Pain has an element of blank
> It cannot recollect
> When it began, or if there were
> A day when it was not.
> It has no future but itself,
> Its infinite realms contain
> Its past, enlightened to perceive
> New periods of pain.

In the above poem, Emily Dickenson uses strong imagery. Pain is equivalent to an "element of blank" or of nothingness. Pain cannot recollect a beginning or end, as if it was a person (see *personification* below). Dickenson appeals to the reader's sense of a painful experience by discussing the unlikelihood that discomfort sees a future, but does visualize a past and present. She simply indicates that pain, through the use of imagery, is cyclical and never ending. Dickenson's theme is one of painful depression, and it is through the use of imagery that she conveys this to her readers.

Onomatopoeia is the author's use of words that create sound. Words like *pop* and *sizzle* are examples of onomatopoeia. When an author wants to draw a reader's attention in an auditory sense, they will use onomatopoeia. An author may also use onomatopoeia to create sounds as interjection or commentary. Examples include:

- An author describing a cat's vocalization as the kitten's chirrup echoed throughout the empty cabin.
- A description of a campfire as crackling and whining against its burning green wood.
- An author relating the sound of a car accident as *metallic screeching against crunching asphalt*.
- A description of an animal roadblock as being *a symphonic melody of groans, baas, and moans*.

Personification is a rhetorical device that an author uses to attribute human qualities to inanimate objects or animals. Once again, this device is useful when an author wants the reader to strongly relate to an idea. As in the example of George Orwell's *Animal Farm*, many of the animals are given the human abilities to speak, reason, apply logic, and otherwise interact as humans do. This helps the reader see how easily it is for any society to segregate into the haves and the have-nots through the manipulation of power. Personification is a device that enables the reader to empathize through human experience.

Examples of personification include:

- An author describing the wind as *whispering through the trees*.

- A description of a stone wall as being a hardened, unmovable creature made of cement and brick.

- An author attributing a city building as having slit eyes and an unapproachable, foreboding façade.

- An author describing spring as a beautiful bride, blooming in white, ready for summer's matrimony.

When identifying rhetorical devices, look for words and phrases that capture one's attention. Make note of the author's use of comparison between the inanimate and the animate. Consider words that make the reader feel sounds and envision imagery. Pay attention to the rhythm of fluid sentences and to the use of words that evoke emotion. The ability to identify rhetorical devices is another step in achieving successful reading comprehension and in being able to correctly answer standardized questions related to those devices.

Synthesis

Synthesis in reading involves the ability to fully comprehend text passages, and then going further by making new connections to see things in a new or different way. It involves a full thought process and requires readers to change the way they think about what they read. The PSAT/NMSQT will require a test taker to integrate new information that he or she already knows, and demonstrate an ability to express new thoughts.

Synthesis goes further than summary. When summarizing, a reader collects all of the information an author presents in a text passage, and restates it in an effective manner. Synthesis requires that the test taker not only summarize reading material, but be able to express new ideas based on the author's message. It is a full culmination of all reading comprehension strategies. It will require the test taker to order, recount, summarize, and recreate information into a whole new idea.

In utilizing synthesis, a reader must be able to form mental images about what they read, recall any background information they have about the topic, ask critical questions about the material, determine the importance of points an author makes, make inferences based on the reading, and finally be able to form new ideas based on all of the above skills. Synthesis requires the reader to make connections, visualize concepts, determine their importance, ask questions, make inferences, then fully synthesize all of this information into new thought.

Making Connections in Reading

There are three helpful thinking strategies to keep in mind when attempting to synthesize text passages:

- Think about how the content of a passage relates to life experience.
- Think about how the content of a passage relates to other text.
- Think about how the content of a passage relates to the world in general.

When reading a given passage, the test taker should actively think about how the content relates to their life experience. While the author's message may express an opinion different from what the reader believes, or express ideas with which the reader is unfamiliar, a good reader will try to relate any of the author's details to their own familiar ground. A reader should use context clues to understand unfamiliar terminology, and recognize familiar information they have encountered in prior experience. Bringing prior life experience and knowledge to the test-taking situation is helpful in making connections. The ability to relate an unfamiliar idea to something the reader already knows is critical in understanding unique and new ideas.

When trying to make connections while reading, keep the following questions in mind:

- How does this feel familiar in personal experience?
- How is this similar to or different from other reading?
- How is this familiar in the real world?
- How does this relate to the world in general?

A reader should ask themselves these questions during the act of reading in order to actively make connections to past and present experiences. Utilizing the ability to make connections is an important step in achieving synthesis.

Determining Importance in Reading

Being able to determine what is most important while reading is critical to synthesis. It is the difference between being able to tell what is necessary to full comprehension and that which is interesting but not necessary.

When determining the importance of an author's ideas, consider the following:

- Ask how critical an author's particular idea, assertion, or concept is to the overall message.

- Ask "is this an interesting fact or is this information essential to understanding the author's main idea?"

- Make a simple chart. On one side, list all of the important, essential points an author makes and on the other, list all of the interesting yet non-critical ideas.

- Highlight, circle, or underline any dates or data in non-fiction passages. Pay attention to headings, captions, and any graphs or diagrams.

- When reading a fictional passage, delineate important information such as theme, character, setting, conflict (what the problem is), and resolution (how the problem is fixed). Most often, these are the most important aspects contained in fictional text.

- If a non-fiction passage is instructional in nature, take physical note of any steps in the order of their importance as presented by the author. Look for words such as *first*, *next*, *then*, and *last*.

Determining the importance of an author's ideas is critical to synthesis in that it requires the test taker to parse out any unnecessary information and demonstrate they have the ability to make sound determination on what is important to the author, and what is merely a supporting or less critical detail.

Asking Questions While Reading

A reader must ask questions while reading. This demonstrates their ability to critically approach information and apply higher thinking skills to an author's content. Some of these questions have been addressed earlier in this section. A reader must ask what is or isn't important, what relates to their experience, and what relates to the world in general. However, it's important to ask other questions as

well in order to make connections and synthesize reading material. Consider the following partial list of possibilities:

- What type of passage is this? Is it fiction? Non-fiction? Does it include data?

- Based on the type of passage, what information should be noted in order to make connections, visualize details, and determine importance?

- What is the author's message or theme? What is it they want the reader to understand?

- Is this passage trying to convince readers of something? What is it? If so, is the argument logical, convincing, and effective? How so? If not, how not?

- What do readers already know about this topic? Are there other viewpoints that support or contradict it?

- Is the information in this passage current and up to date?

- Is the author trying to teach readers a lesson? If so, what is it? Is there a moral to this story?

- How does this passage relate to experience?

- What is not as understandable in this passage? What context clues can help with understanding?

- What conclusions can be drawn? What predictions can be made?

Again, the above should be considered only a small example of the possibilities. Any question the reader asks while reading will help achieve synthesis and full reading comprehension.

Analysis of History/Social Studies Excerpts

The PSAT/NMSQT will test for the ability to read substantial, historically based excerpts, and then answer comprehension questions based on content. The test taker will encounter at least two U.S. history, or social science, passages within the test. One is likely to be from a U.S. founding document or work that has had great impact on history. The test may also include one or more passages from social sciences such as economics, psychology, or sociology.

For these types of questions, the test taker will need to utilize all the reading comprehension skills discussed above, but mastery of further skills will help. This section addresses those skills.

Comprehending Test Questions Prior to Reading

While preparing for a historical passage on a standardized test, first read the test questions, and then quickly scan the test answers prior to reading the passage itself. Notice there is a difference between the terms *read* and *scans*. Reading involves full concentration while addressing every word. Scanning involves quickly glancing at text in chunks, noting important dates, words, and ideas along the way. Reading the test questions will help the test taker know what information to focus on in the historical passage. Scanning answers will help the test taker focus on possible answer options while reading the passage.

When reading standardized test questions that address historical passages, be sure to clearly understand what each question is asking. Is a question asking about vocabulary? Is another asking for the test taker to find a specific historical fact? Do any of the questions require the test taker to draw conclusions, identify an author's topic, tone, or position? Knowing what content to address will help the test taker focus on the information they will be asked about later. However, the test taker should approach this reading comprehension technique with some caution. It is tempting to only look for the right answers within any given passage. However, do not put on "reading blinders" and ignore all other information presented in a passage. It is important to fully read every passage and not just scan it. Strictly looking for what may be the right answers to test questions can cause the test taker to ignore important contextual clues that actually require critical thinking in order to identify correct answers. Scanning a passage for what appears to be wrong answers can have a similar result.

When reading the test questions prior to tackling a historical passage, be sure to understand what skills the test is assessing, and then fully read the related passage with those skills in mind. Focus on every word in both the test questions and the passage itself. Read with a critical eye and a logical mind.

Reading for Factual Information

Standardized test questions that ask for factual information are usually straightforward. These types of questions will either ask the test taker to confirm a fact by choosing a correct answer, or to select a correct answer based on a negative fact question.

For example, the test taker may encounter a passage from Lincoln's Gettysburg Address. A corresponding test question may ask the following:

> Which war is Abraham Lincoln referring to in the following sentence? Now we are engaged in a great civil war, testing whether that nation, or any nation so conceived and so dedicated, can long endure.

This type of question is asking the test taker to confirm a simple fact. Given options such as World War I, the War of Spanish Succession, World War II, and the American Civil War, the test taker should be able to correctly identify the American Civil War based on the words "civil war" within the passage itself, and, hopefully, through general knowledge. In this case, reading the test question and scanning answer options ahead of reading the Gettysburg Address would help quickly identify the correct answer. Similarly, a test taker may be asked to confirm a historical fact based on a negative fact question. For example, a passage's corresponding test question may ask the following:

> Which option is incorrect based on the above passage?

Given a variety of choices speaking about which war Abraham Lincoln was addressing, the test taker would need to eliminate all correct answers pertaining to the American Civil War and choose the answer choice referencing a different war. In other words, the correct answer is the one that contradicts the information in the passage.

It is important to remember that reading for factual information is straightforward. The test taker must distinguish fact from bias. Factual statements can be proven or disproven independent of the author and from a variety of other sources. Remember, successfully answering questions regarding factual information may require the test taker to re-read the passage, as these types of questions test for attention to detail.

30

Reading for Tone, Message, and Effect

The PSAT/NMSQT does not just address a test taker's ability to find facts within a historical reading passage; it also evaluates a reader's ability to determine an author's viewpoint through the use of tone, message, and overall effect. This type of reading comprehension requires inference skills, deductive reasoning skills, the ability to draw logical conclusions, and overall critical thinking skills. Reading for factual information is straightforward. Reading for an author's tone, message, and overall effect is not. It's key to read carefully when asked test questions that address a test taker's ability to identify these writing devices. These are not questions that can be easily answered by quickly scanning for the right information.

Tone

An author's *tone* is the use of particular words, phrases, and writing style to convey an overall meaning. Tone expresses the author's attitude towards a particular topic. For example, a historical reading passage may begin like the following:

> The presidential election of 1960 ushered in a new era, a new Camelot, a new phase of forward thinking in U.S. politics that embraced brash action and unrest and responded with admirable leadership.

From this opening statement, a reader can draw some conclusions about the author's attitude towards President John F. Kennedy. Furthermore, the reader can make additional, educated guesses about the state of the Union during the 1960 presidential election. By close reading, the test taker can determine that the repeated use of the word *new* and words such as *admirable leadership* indicate the author's tone of admiration regarding President Kennedy's boldness. In addition, the author assesses that the era during President Kennedy's administration was problematic through the use of the words *brash action* and *unrest*. Therefore, if a test taker encountered a test question asking about the author's use of tone and their assessment of the Kennedy administration, the test taker should be able to identify an answer indicating admiration. Similarly, if asked about the state of the Union during the 1960s, a test taker should be able to correctly identify an answer indicating political unrest.

When identifying an author's tone, the following list of words may be helpful. This is not an inclusive list. Generally, parts of speech that indicate attitude will also indicate tone:

- Comical
- Angry
- Ambivalent
- Scary
- Lyrical
- Matter-of-fact
- Judgmental
- Sarcastic
- Malicious
- Objective
- Pessimistic
- Patronizing
- Gloomy

31

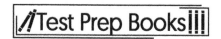

- Instructional
- Satirical
- Formal
- Casual

Message

An author's *message* is the same as the overall meaning of a passage. It is the main idea, or the main concept the author wishes to convey. An author's message may be stated outright, or it may be implied. Regardless, the test taker will need to use careful reading skills to identify an author's message or purpose.

Often, the message of a particular passage can be determined by thinking about why the author wrote the information. Many historical passages are written to inform and to teach readers established, factual information. However, many historical works are also written to convey biased ideas to readers. Gleaning bias from an author's message in a historical passage can be difficult, especially if the reader is presented with a variety of established facts as well. Readers tend to accept historical writing as factual. This is not always the case. Any discerning reader who has tackled historical information on topics such as United States political party agendas can attest that two or more works on the same topic may have completely different messages supporting or refuting the value of the identical policies.

Therefore, it is important to critically assess an author's message separate from factual information. One author, for example, may point to the rise of unorthodox political candidates in an election year based on the failures of the political party in office while another may point to the rise of the same candidates in the same election year based on the current party's successes. The historical facts of what has occurred leading up to an election year are not in refute. Labeling those facts as a failure or a success is a bias within an author's overall *message*, as is excluding factual information in order to further a particular point. In a standardized testing situation, a reader must be able to critically assess what the author is trying to say separate from the historical facts that surround their message.

Using the example of Lincoln's Gettysburg Address, a test question may ask the following:

What message is the speaker trying to convey through this address?

Then they will ask the test taker to select an answer that best expresses Lincoln's *message* to his audience. Based on the options given, a test taker should be able to select the answer expressing the idea that Lincoln's audience should recognize the efforts of those who died in the war as a sacrifice to preserving human equality and self-government.

Effect

An author may want to challenge a reader's intellect, inspire imagination, or spur emotion. An author may present information to appeal to a physical, aesthetic, or transformational sense. Take the following text as an example:

In 1963, Martin Luther King stated "I have a dream." The gathering at the Lincoln Memorial was the beginning of the Civil Rights movement and, with its reference to the Emancipation Proclamation, Dr. King's words electrified those who wanted freedom and equality while rising from hatred and slavery. It was the beginning of radical change.

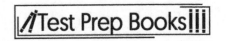

The test taker may be asked about the effect this statement might have on King's audience. Through careful reading of the passage, the test taker should be able to choose an answer that best identifies an effect of grabbing the audience's attention. The historical facts are in place: King made the speech in 1963 at the Lincoln Memorial, kicked off the civil rights movement, and referenced the Emancipation Proclamation. The words *electrified* and *radical change* indicate the effect the author wants the reader to understand as a result of King's speech. In this historical passage, facts are facts. However, the author's message goes beyond the facts to indicate the effect the message had on the audience and, in addition, the effect the event should have on the reader.

When reading historical passages, the test taker should perform due diligence in their awareness of the test questions and answers up front. From there, the test taker should carefully, and critically, read all historical excerpts with an eye for detail, tone, message (biased or unbiased), and effect. Being able to synthesize these skills will result in success in a standardized testing situation.

Analysis of Science Excerpts

The PSAT/NMSQT includes at least two science passages that address the fundamental concepts of Earth science, biology, chemistry, and/or physics. While prior general knowledge of these subjects is helpful in determining correct test answers, the test taker's ability to comprehend the passages is key to success. When reading scientific excerpts, the test taker must be able to examine quantitative information, identify hypotheses, interpret data, and consider implications of the material they are presented with. It is helpful, at this point, to reference the above section on comprehending test questions prior to reading. The same rules apply: read questions and scan questions, along with their answers, prior to fully reading a passage. Be informed prior to approaching a scientific text. A test taker should know what they will be asked and how to apply their reading skills. In this section of the test, it is also likely that a test taker will encounter graphs and charts to assess their ability to interpret scientific data with an appropriate conclusion. This section may use the identification of hypotheses, the reading and examination of data, and the interpretation of data representation passages to determine the skill levels of test takers in the comprehension of scientific data.

Examine Hypotheses

When presented with fundamental, scientific concepts, it is important to read for understanding. The most basic skill in achieving this literacy is to understand the concept of hypothesis and, moreover, to be able to identify it in a particular passage. A hypothesis is a proposed idea that needs further investigation in order to be proven true or false. While it can be considered an educated guess, a hypothesis goes more in depth in its attempt to explain something that is not currently accepted within scientific theory. It requires further experimentation and data gathering to test its validity and is subject to change, based on scientifically conducted test results. Being able to read a science passage and understand its main purpose, including any hypotheses, helps the test taker understand data-driven evidence. It helps the test taker to be able to correctly answer questions about the science excerpt they are asked to read.

When reading to identify a hypothesis, a test taker should ask, "What is the passage trying to establish? What is the passage's main idea? What evidence does the passage contain that either supports or refutes this idea?" Asking oneself these questions will help identify a hypothesis. Additionally, hypotheses are logical statements that are testable and use very precise language.

Review the following hypothesis example:

> Consuming excess sugar in the form of beverages has a greater impact on childhood obesity and subsequent weight gain than excessive sugar from food.

While this is likely a true statement, it is still only a conceptual idea in a text passage regarding how sugar consumption affects childhood obesity, unless the passage also contains tested data that either proves or disproves the statement. A test taker could expect the rest of the passage to cite data proving that children who drink empty calories gain more weight and are more likely to be obese than children who eat sugary snacks.

A hypothesis goes further in that, given its ability to be proven or disproven, it may result in further hypotheses that require extended research. For example, the hypothesis regarding sugar consumption in drinks, after undergoing rigorous testing, may lead scientists to state another hypothesis such as the following:

> Consuming excess sugar in the form of beverages as opposed to food items is a habit found in mostly sedentary children.

This new, working hypothesis further focuses not just on the source of an excess of calories, but tries an "educated guess" that empty caloric intake has a direct, subsequent impact on physical behavior.

The data-driven chart below is similar to an illustration a test taker might see in relation to the hypothesis on sugar consumption in children:

The Effect of Excess Sugar on Activity

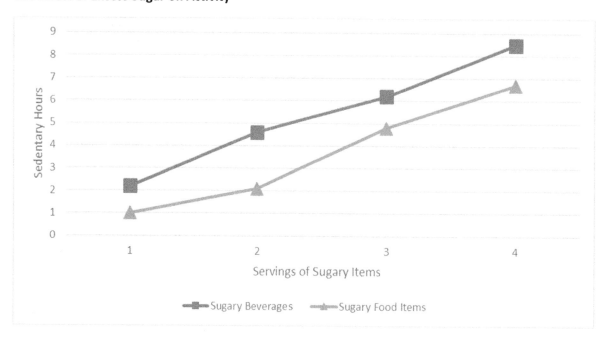

While this guide will address other data-driven passages a test taker could expect to see within a given science excerpt, note that the hypothesis regarding childhood sugar intake and rate of exercise has undergone scientific examination and yielded results that support its truth.

When reading a science passage to determine its hypothesis, a test taker should look for a concept that attempts to explain a phenomenon, is testable, is logical, is precisely worded, and yields data-driven results. The test taker should scan the presented passage for any word or data-driven clues that will help identify the hypothesis, and then be able to correctly answer test questions regarding the hypothesis by using their critical thinking skills.

Interpreting Data and Considering Implications

The PSAT/NMSQT is likely to contain one or more data-driven science passages that require the test taker to examine evidence within a particular type of graphic. The test taker will then be required to interpret the data and answer questions demonstrating their ability to draw logical conclusions.

In general, there are two types of data: qualitative and quantitative. Science passages may contain both, but simply put, quantitative data is reflected numerically and qualitative is not. Qualitative data is based on its qualities. In other words, qualitative data tends to present information more in subjective generalities (for example, relating to size or appearance). Quantitative data is based on numerical findings such as percentages. Quantitative data will be described in numerical terms. While both types of data are valid, the test taker will more likely be faced with having to interpret quantitative data through one or more graphic(s), and then be required to answer questions regarding the numerical data. The section of this study guide briefly addresses how data may be displayed in line graphs, bar charts, circle graphs, and scatter plots. A test taker should take the time to learn the skills it takes to interpret quantitative data. An example of a line graph is as follows:

Cell Phone Use in Kiteville, 2000-2006

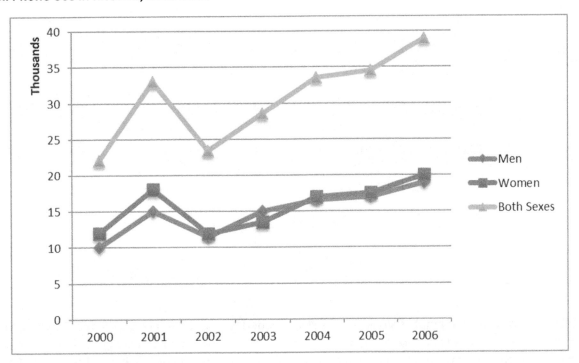

A line graph presents quantitative data on both horizontal (side to side) and vertical (up and down) axes. It requires the test taker to examine information across varying data points. When reading a line graph, a test taker should pay attention to any headings, as these indicate a title for the data it contains. In the

35

above example, the test taker can anticipate the line graph contains numerical data regarding the use of cellphones during a certain time period. From there, a test taker should carefully read any outlying words or phrases that will help determine the meaning of data within the horizontal and vertical axes. In this example, the vertical axis displays the total number of people in increments of 5,000. Horizontally, the graph displays yearly markers, and the reader can assume the data presented accounts for a full calendar year. In addition, the line graph also uses different shapes to mark its data points. Some data points represent the number of men. Some data points represent the number of women, and a third type of data point represents the number of both sexes combined.

A test taker may be asked to read and interpret the graph's data, then answer questions about it. For example, the test may ask, *In which year did men seem to decrease cellphone use?* then require the test taker to select the correct answer. Similarly, the test taker may encounter a question such as *Which year yielded the highest number of cellphone users overall?* The test taker should be able to identify the correct answer as 2006.

A bar graph presents quantitative data through the use of lines or rectangles. The height and length of these lines or rectangles corresponds to numerical data. The data presented may represent information over time, showing shaded data over time or over other defined parameters. A bar graph will also utilize horizontal and vertical axes. An example of a bar graph is as follows:

Population Growth in Major U.S. Cities

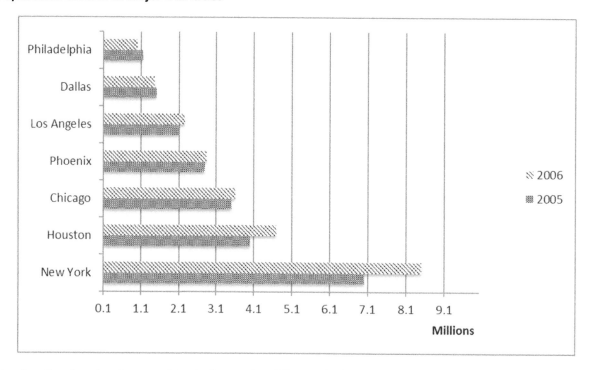

Reading the data in a bar graph is similar to the skills needed to read a line graph. The test taker should read and comprehend all heading information, as well as information provided along the horizontal and vertical axes. Note that the graph pertains to the population of some major U.S. cities. The "values" of these cities can be found along the left side of the graph, along the vertical axis. The population values can be found along the horizontal axes. Notice how the graph uses shaded bars to depict the change in population over time, as the heading indicates. Therefore, when the test taker is asked a question such as, *Which major U.S. city experienced the greatest amount of population growth during the depicted two*

year cycle, the reader should be able to determine a correct answer of New York. It is important to pay particular attention to color, length, data points, and both axes, as well as any outlying header information in order to be able to answer graph-like test questions.

A circle graph (also sometimes referred to as a pie chart) presents quantitative data in the form of a circle. The same principles apply: the test taker should look for numerical data within the confines of the circle itself but also note any outlying information that may be included in a header, footer, or to the side of the circle. A circle graph will not depict horizontal or vertical axis information, but will instead rely on the reader's ability to visually take note of segmented circle pieces and apply information accordingly. An example of a circle graph is as follows:

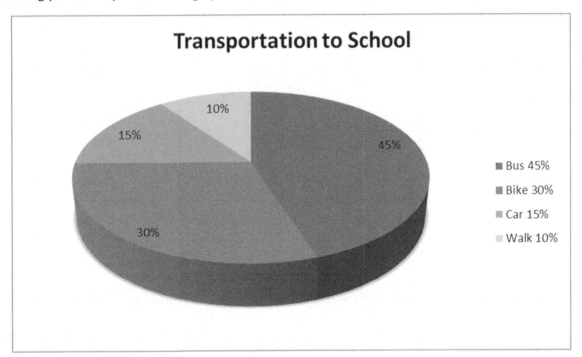

Transportation to School

- Bus 45%
- Bike 30%
- Car 15%
- Walk 10%

Notice the heading "Transportation to School." This should indicate to the test taker that the topic of the circle graph is how people traditionally get to school. To the right of the graph, the reader should comprehend that the data percentages contained within it directly correspond to the method of transportation. In this graph, the data is represented through the use shades and pattern. Each transportation method has its own shade. For example, if the test taker was then asked, *Which method of school transportation is most widely utilized,* the reader should be able to identify school bus as the correct answer.

Be wary of test questions that ask test takers to draw conclusions based on information that is not present. For example, it is not possible to determine, given the parameters of this circle graph, whether the population presented is of a particular gender or ethnic group. This graph does not represent data from a particular city or school district. It does not distinguish between student grade levels and, although the reader could infer that the typical student must be of driving age if cars are included, this is not necessarily the case. Elementary school students may rely on parents or others to drive them by personal methods. Therefore, do not read too much into data that is not presented. Only rely on the quantitative data that is presented in order to answer questions.

A scatter plot or scatter diagram is a graph that depicts quantitative data across plotted points. It will involve at least two sets of data. It will also involve horizontal and vertical axes.

An example of a scatter plot is as follows:

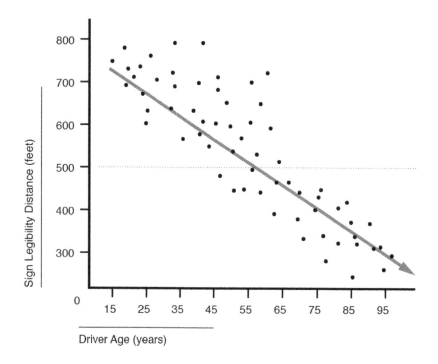

The skills needed to address a scatter plot are essentially the same as in other graph examples. Note any topic headings, as well as horizontal or vertical axis information. In the sample above, the reader can determine the data addresses a driver's ability to correctly and legibly read road signs as related to their age. Again, note the information that is absent. The test taker is not given the data to assess a time period, location, or driver gender. It simply requires the reader to note an approximate age to the ability to correctly identify road signs from a distance measured in feet. Notice that the overall graph also displays a trend. In this case, the data indicates a negative one and possibly supports the hypothesis that as a driver ages, their ability to correctly read a road sign at over 500 feet tends to decline over time. If the test taker were to be asked, *At what approximation in feet does a fifty-six-year-old driver correctly see and read a street sign,* the answer would be the option closest to 700 feet.

Reading and examining scientific data in excerpts involves all of a reader's contextual reading, data interpretation, drawing logical conclusions based only on the information presented, and their application of critical thinking skills across a set of interpretive questions. Thorough comprehension and attention to detail is necessary to achieve test success.

Writing and Language Test

The PSAT Writing and Language Test contains a series of passages that must be read along with questions pertaining to each passage. The task is not to recall or restate a passage's content, but to analyze *how* the content is presented and answer questions about how to improve it.

Expression of Ideas

This test is about *how* the information is communicated rather than the subject matter itself. The good news is there isn't any writing! Instead, it's like being an editor helping the writer find the best ways to express their ideas. Things to consider include: how well a topic is developed, how accurately facts are presented, whether the writing flows logically and cohesively, and how effectively the writer uses language. This can seem like a lot to remember, but these concepts are the same ones taught way back in elementary school.

One last thing to remember while going through this guide is not to be intimidated by the terminology. Phrases like "pronoun-antecedent agreement" and "possessive determiners" can sound confusing and complicated, but the ideas are often quite simple and easy to understand. Though proper terminology is used to explain the rules and guidelines, the PSAT Writing and Language Test is not a technical grammar test.

Organization

Good writing is not merely a random collection of sentences. No matter how well written, sentences must relate and coordinate appropriately to one another. If not, the writing seems random, haphazard, and disorganized. Therefore, good writing must be *organized* (where each sentence fits a larger context and relates to the sentences around it).

Transition Words
The writer should act as a guide, showing the reader how all the sentences fit together. Consider this example:

> Seat belts save more lives than any other automobile safety feature. Many studies show that airbags save lives as well. Not all cars have airbags. Many older cars don't. Air bags aren't entirely reliable. Studies show that in 15% of accidents, airbags don't deploy as designed. Seat belt malfunctions are extremely rare.

There's nothing wrong with any of these sentences individually, but together they're disjointed and difficult to follow. The best way for the writer to communicate information is through the use of *transition words*. Here are examples of transition words and phrases that tie sentences together, enabling a more natural flow:

- To show causality: *as a result*, *therefore*, and *consequently*
- To compare and contrast: *however, but*, and *on the other hand*
- To introduce examples: *for instance, namely*, and *including*
- To show order of importance: *foremost, primarily, secondly*, and *lastly*

The above is not a complete list of transitions. There are many more that can be used; however, most fit into these or similar categories. The important point is that the words should clearly show the relationship between sentences, supporting information, and the main idea.

Here is an update to the previous example using transition words. These changes make it easier to read and bring clarity to the writer's points:

> Seat belts save more lives than any other automobile safety feature. Many studies show that airbags save lives as well. However, not all cars have airbags. For instance, some older cars don't. Furthermore, air bags aren't entirely reliable. For example, studies show that in 15% of accidents, airbags don't deploy as designed. But, on the other hand, seat belt malfunctions are extremely rare.

Also be prepared to analyze whether the writer is using the best transition word or phrase for the situation. Take this sentence for example: "As a result, seat belt malfunctions are extremely rare." This sentence doesn't make sense in the context above because the writer is trying to show the *contrast* between seat belts and airbags, not the causality.

Logical Sequence

Even if the writer includes plenty of information to support their point, the writing is only effective when the information is in a logical order. *Logical sequencing* is really just common sense, but it's also an important writing technique. First, the writer should introduce the main idea, whether for a paragraph, a section, or the entire piece. Second, they should present evidence to support the main idea by using transitional language. This shows the reader how the information relates to the main idea and to the sentences around it. The writer should then take time to interpret the information, making sure necessary connections are obvious to the reader. Finally, the writer can summarize the information in a closing section.

Although most writing follows this pattern, it isn't a set rule. Sometimes writers change the order for effect. For example, the writer can begin with a surprising piece of supporting information to grab the reader's attention, and then transition to the main idea. Thus, if a passage doesn't follow the logical order, don't immediately assume it's wrong. However, most writing usually settles into a logical sequence after a nontraditional beginning.

Focus

Good writing stays *focused* and on topic. During the test, determine the main idea for each passage and then look for times when the writer strays from the point they're trying to make. Let's go back to the seat belt example. If the writer suddenly begins talking about how well airbags, crumple zones, or other safety features work to save lives, they might be losing focus from the topic of "safety belts."

Focus can also refer to individual sentences. Sometimes the writer does address the main topic, but in a confusing way. For example:

> Thanks to seat belt usage, survival in serious car accidents has shown a consistently steady increase since the development of the retractable seat belt in the 1950s.

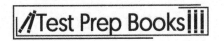

This statement is definitely on topic, but it's not easy to follow. A simpler, more focused version of this sentence might look like this:

Seat belts have consistently prevented car fatalities since the 1950s.

Providing *adequate information* is another aspect of focused writing. Statements like "seat belts are important" and "many people drive cars" are true, but they're so general that they don't contribute much to the writer's case. When reading a passage, watch for these kinds of unfocused statements.

Introductions and Conclusions

Examining the writer's strategies for introductions and conclusions puts the reader in the right mindset to interpret the rest of the passage. Look for methods the writer might use for introductions such as:

- Stating the main point immediately, followed by outlining how the rest of the piece supports this claim.

- Establishing important, smaller pieces of the main idea first, and then grouping these points into a case for the main idea.

- Opening with a quotation, anecdote, question, seeming paradox, or other piece of interesting information, and then using it to lead to the main point.

Whatever method the writer chooses, the introduction should make their intention clear, establish their voice as a credible one, and encourage a person to continue reading.

Conclusions tend to follow a similar pattern. In them, the writer restates their main idea a final time, often after summarizing the smaller pieces of that idea. If the introduction uses a quote or anecdote to grab the reader's attention, the conclusion often makes reference to it again. Whatever way the writer chooses to arrange the conclusion, the final restatement of the main idea should be clear and simple for the reader to interpret.

Finally, conclusions shouldn't introduce any new information.

Precision

People often think of *precision* in terms of math, but precise word choice is another key to successful writing. Since language itself is imprecise, it's important for the writer to find the exact word or words to convey the full, intended meaning of a given situation. For example:

The number of deaths has gone down since seat belt laws started.

There are several problems with this sentence. First, the word *deaths* is too general. From the context, it's assumed that the writer is referring only to *deaths* caused by car accidents. However, without clarification, the sentence lacks impact and is probably untrue. The phrase "gone down" might be accurate, but a more precise word could provide more information and greater accuracy. Did the numbers show a slow and steady decrease of highway fatalities or a sudden drop? If the latter is true, the writer is missing a chance to make their point more dramatically. Instead of "gone down" they could substitute *plummeted*, *fallen drastically*, or *rapidly diminished* to bring the information to life. Also, the phrase "seat belt laws" is unclear. Does it refer to laws requiring cars to include seat belts or to laws

41

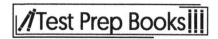

requiring drivers and passengers to use them? Finally, *started* is not a strong verb. Words like *enacted* or *adopted* are more direct and make the content more real. When put together, these changes create a far more powerful sentence:

> The number of highway fatalities has plummeted since laws requiring seat belt usage were enacted.

However, it's important to note that precise word choice can sometimes be taken too far. If the writer of the sentence above takes precision to an extreme, it might result in the following:

> The incidence of high-speed, automobile accident related fatalities has decreased 75% and continued to remain at historical lows since the initial set of federal legislations requiring seat belt use were enacted in 1992.

This sentence is extremely precise, but it takes so long to achieve that precision that it suffers from a lack of clarity. Precise writing is about finding the right balance between information and flow. This is also an issue of *conciseness* (discussed in the next section).

The last thing to consider with precision is a word choice that's not only unclear or uninteresting, but also confusing or misleading. For example:

> The number of highway fatalities has become hugely lower since laws requiring seat belt use were enacted.

In this case, the reader might be confused by the word *hugely*. Huge means large, but here the writer uses *hugely* to describe something small. Though most readers can decipher this, doing so disconnects them from the flow of the writing and makes the writer's point less effective.

On the test, there can be questions asking for alternatives to the writer's word choice. In answering these questions, always consider the context and look for a balance between precision and flow.

Conciseness

"Less is more" is a good rule to follow when writing a sentence. Unfortunately, writers often include extra words and phrases that seem necessary at the time, but add nothing to the main idea. This confuses the reader and creates unnecessary repetition. Writing that lacks *conciseness* is usually guilty of excessive wordiness and redundant phrases. Here's an example containing both of these issues:

> When legislators decided to begin creating legislation making it mandatory for automobile drivers and passengers to make use of seat belts while in cars, a large number of them made those laws for reasons that were political reasons.

There are several empty or "fluff" words here that take up too much space. These can be eliminated while still maintaining the writer's meaning. For example:

- "decided to begin" could be shortened to "began"
- "making it mandatory for" could be shortened to "requiring"
- "make use of" could be shortened to "use"
- "a large number" could be shortened to "many"

42

In addition, there are several examples of redundancy that can be eliminated:

- "legislators decided to begin creating legislation" and "made those laws"
- "automobile drivers and passengers" and "while in cars"
- "reasons that were political reasons"

These changes are incorporated as follows:

> When legislators began requiring drivers and passengers to use seat belts, many of them did so for political reasons.

If asked to identify a redundant phrase on the test, look for words that are close together with the same (or similar) meanings.

Proposition

The *proposition* (also called the *claim* since it can be true or false) is a clear statement of the point or idea the writer is trying to make. The length or format of a proposition can vary, but it often takes the form of a *topic sentence*. A good topic sentence is:

- Clear: does not weave a complicated web of words for the reader to decode or unwrap

- Concise: presents only the information needed to make the claim and doesn't clutter up the statement with unnecessary details

- Precise: clarifies the exact point the writer wants to make and doesn't use broad, overreaching statements

Look at the following example:

> The civil rights movement, from its genesis in the Emancipation Proclamation to its current struggles with de facto discrimination, has changed the face of the United States more than any other factor in its history.

Is the statement clear? Yes, the statement is fairly clear, although other words can be substituted for "genesis" and "de facto" to make it easier to understand.

Is the statement concise? No, the statement is not concise. Details about the Emancipation Proclamation and the current state of the movement are unnecessary for a topic sentence. Those details should be saved for the body of the text.

Is the statement precise? No, the statement is not precise. What exactly does the writer mean by "changed the face of the United States"? The writer should be more specific about the effects of the movement. Also, suggesting that something has a greater impact than anything else in U.S. history is far too ambitious a statement to make.

A better version might look like this:

> The civil rights movement has greatly increased the career opportunities available for Black Americans.

43

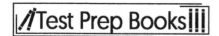
The unnecessary language and details are removed, and the claim can now be measured and supported.

Support

Once the main idea or proposition is stated, the writer attempts to prove or *support* the claim with text evidence and supporting details.

Take for example the sentence, "Seat belts save lives." Though most people can't argue with this statement, its impact on the reader is much greater when supported by additional content. The writer can support this idea by:

- Providing statistics on the rate of highway fatalities alongside statistics for estimated seat belt usage.

- Explaining the science behind a car accident and what happens to a passenger who doesn't use a seat belt.

- Offering anecdotal evidence or true stories from reliable sources on how seat belts prevent fatal injuries in car crashes.

However, using only one form of supporting evidence is not nearly as effective as using a variety to support a claim. Presenting only a list of statistics can be boring to the reader, but providing a true story that's both interesting and humanizing helps. In addition, one example isn't always enough to prove the writer's larger point, so combining it with other examples is extremely effective for the writing. Thus, when reading a passage, don't just look for a single form of supporting evidence.

Another key aspect of supporting evidence is a *reliable source*. Does the writer include the source of the information? If so, is the source well known and trustworthy? Is there a potential for bias? For example, a seat belt study done by a seat belt manufacturer may have its own agenda to promote.

Effective Language Use

Language can be analyzed in a variety of ways. But one of the primary ways is its effectiveness in communicating and especially convincing others.

Rhetoric is a literary technique used to make the writing (or speaking) more effective or persuasive. Rhetoric makes use of other effective language devices such as irony, metaphors, allusion, and repetition. An example of the rhetorical use of repetition would be: "Let go, I say, let go!!!".

Figures of Speech

A *figure of speech* (sometimes called an *idiom*) is a rhetorical device. It's a phrase that's not intended to be taken literally.

When the writer uses a figure of speech, their intention must be clear if it's to be used effectively. Some phrases can be interpreted in a number of ways, causing confusion for the reader. In the PSAT Writing and Language Test, questions may ask for an alternative to a problematic word or phrase. Look for clues to the writer's true intention to determine the best replacement. Likewise, some figures of speech may seem out of place in a more formal piece of writing. To show this, here is the previous seat belt example but with one slight change:

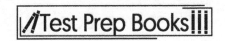

Seat belts save more lives than any other automobile safety feature. Many studies show that airbags save lives as well. However, not all cars have airbags. For instance, some older cars don't. In addition, air bags aren't entirely reliable. For example, studies show that in 15% of accidents, airbags don't deploy as designed. But, on the other hand, seat belt malfunctions happen once in a blue moon.

Most people know that "once in a blue moon" refers to something that rarely happens. However, because the rest of the paragraph is straightforward and direct, using this figurative phrase distracts the reader. In this example, the earlier version is much more effective.

Now it's important to take a moment and review the meaning of the word *literally*. This is because it's one of the most misunderstood and misused words in the English language. *Literally* means that something is exactly what it says it is, and there can be no interpretation or exaggeration. Unfortunately, *literally* is often used for emphasis as in the following example:

> This morning, I literally couldn't get out of bed.

This sentence meant to say that the person was extremely tired and wasn't able to get up. However, the sentence can't *literally* be true unless that person was tied down to the bed, paralyzed, or affected by a strange situation that the writer (most likely) didn't intend. Here's another example:

> I literally died laughing.

The writer tried to say that something was very funny. However, unless they're writing this from beyond the grave, it can't *literally* be true.

Rhetorical Fallacies

A *rhetorical fallacy* is an argument that doesn't make sense. It usually involves distracting the reader from the issue at hand in some way. There are many kinds of rhetorical fallacies. Here are just a few, along with examples of each:

- *Ad Hominem*: Makes an irrelevant attack against the person making the claim, rather than addressing the claim itself.

    - Senator Wilson opposed the new seat belt legislation, but should we really listen to someone who's been divorced four times?

- *Exaggeration*: Represents an idea or person in an obviously excessive manner.

    - Senator Wilson opposed the new seat belt legislation. Maybe she thinks if more people die in car accidents, it will help with overpopulation.

- *Stereotyping (or Categorical Claim)*: Claims that all people of a certain group are the same in some way.

    - Senator Wilson still opposes the new seat belt legislation. You know women can never admit when they're wrong.

When examining a possible rhetorical fallacy, carefully consider the point the writer is trying to make and if the argument directly relates to that point. If something feels wrong, there's a good chance that a

45

fallacy is at play. The PSAT Writing and Language Test doesn't expect the fallacy to be named using specific terms like those above. However, questions can include identifying why something is a fallacy or suggesting a sounder argument.

Style, Tone, and Mood

Style, *tone*, and *mood* are often thought to be the same thing. Though they're closely related, there are important differences to keep in mind. The easiest way to do this is to remember that style "creates and affects" tone and mood. More specifically, style is *how the writer uses words* to create the desired tone and mood for their writing.

Style

Style can include any number of technical writing choices, and some may have to be analyzed on the test. A few examples of style choices include:

- Sentence Construction: When presenting facts, does the writer use shorter sentences to create a quicker sense of the supporting evidence, or do they use longer sentences to elaborate and explain the information?

- Technical Language: Does the writer use jargon to demonstrate their expertise in the subject, or do they use ordinary language to help the reader understand things in simple terms?

- Formal Language: Does the writer refrain from using contractions such as *won't* or *can't* to create a more formal tone, or do they use a colloquial, conversational style to connect to the reader?

- Formatting: Does the writer use a series of shorter paragraphs to help the reader follow a line of argument, or do they use longer paragraphs to examine an issue in great detail and demonstrate their knowledge of the topic?

On the test, examine the writer's style and how their writing choices affect the way the passage comes across.

Tone

Tone refers to the writer's attitude toward the subject matter. Tone conveys how the writer feels about characters, situations, events, ideas, etc. Nonfiction writing is sometimes thought to have no tone at all, but this is incorrect.

A lot of nonfiction writing has a neutral tone, which is an extremely important tone for the writer to take. A neutral tone demonstrates that the writer is presenting a topic impartially and letting the information speak for itself. On the other hand, nonfiction writing can be just as effective and appropriate if the tone isn't neutral. For instance, take the previous examples involving seat belt use. In them, the writer mostly chooses to retain a neutral tone when presenting information. If the writer would instead include their own personal experience of losing a friend or family member in a car accident, the tone would change dramatically. The tone would no longer be neutral. Now it would show that the writer has a personal stake in the content, allowing them to interpret the information in a different way. When analyzing tone, consider what the writer is trying to achieve in the passage, and how they *create* the tone using style.

46

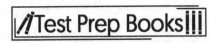

Mood

Mood refers to the feelings and atmosphere that the writer's words create for the reader. Like tone, many nonfiction pieces can have a neutral mood. To return to the previous example, if the writer would choose to include information about a person they know being killed in a car accident, the passage would suddenly carry an emotional component that is absent in the previous examples. Depending on how they present the information, the writer can create a sad, angry, or even hopeful mood. When analyzing the mood, consider what the writer wants to accomplish and whether the best choice was made to achieve that end.

Consistency

Whatever style, tone, and mood the writer uses, good writing should remain *consistent* throughout. If the writer chooses to include the tragic, personal experience above, it would affect the style, tone, and mood of the entire piece. It would seem out of place for such an example to be used in the middle of a neutral, measured, and analytical piece. To adjust the rest of the piece, the writer needs to make additional choices to remain consistent. For example, the writer might decide to use the word *tragedy* in place of the more neutral *fatality*, or they could describe a series of car-related deaths as an *epidemic*. Adverbs and adjectives such as *devastating* or *horribly* could be included to maintain this consistent attitude toward the content. When analyzing writing, look for sudden shifts in style, tone, and mood, and consider whether the writer would be wiser to maintain the prevailing strategy.

Syntax

Syntax is the order of words in a sentence. While most of the writing on the test has proper syntax, there may be questions on ways to vary the syntax for effectiveness. One of the easiest writing mistakes to spot is *repetitive sentence structure*. For example:

> Seat belts are important. They save lives. People don't like to use them. We have to pass seat belt laws. Then more people will wear seat belts. More lives will be saved.

What's the first thing that comes to mind when reading this example? The short, choppy, and repetitive sentences! In fact, most people notice this syntax issue more than the content itself. By combining some sentences and changing the syntax of others, the writer can create a more effective writing passage:

> Seat belts are important because they save lives. Since people don't like to use seat belts, though, more laws requiring their usage need to be passed. Only then will more people wear them and only then will more lives be saved.

Many rhetorical devices can be used to vary syntax (more than can possibly be named here). These often have intimidating names like *anadiplosis*, *metastasis*, and *paremptosis*. The test questions don't ask for definitions of these tricky techniques, but they can ask how the writer plays with the words and what effect that has on the writing. For example, *anadiplosis* is when the last word (or phrase) from a sentence is used to begin the next sentence:

> Cars are driven by people. People cause accidents. Accidents cost taxpayers money.

The test doesn't ask for this technique by name, but be prepared to recognize what the writer is doing and why they're using the technique in this situation. In this example, the writer is probably using *anadiplosis* to demonstrate causation.

47

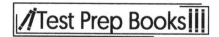

Quantitative Information

Some writing in the test contains *infographics* such as charts, tables, or graphs. In these cases, interpret the information presented and determine how well it supports the claims made in the text. For example, if the writer makes a case that seat belts save more lives than other automobile safety measures, they might want to include a graph (like the one below) showing the number of lives saved by seat belts versus those saved by air bags.

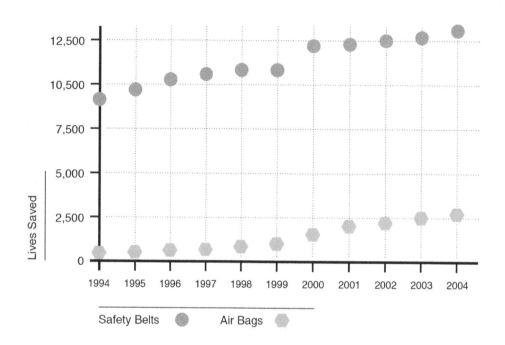

Based on data from the National Highway Traffic Safety Administration

If the graph clearly shows a higher number of lives are saved by seat belts, then it's effective. However, if the graph shows air bags save more lives than seat belts, then it doesn't support the writer's case.

Finally, graphs should be easy to understand. Their information should immediately be clear to the reader at a glance. Here are some basic things to keep in mind when interpreting infographics:

- In a *bar graph*, higher bars represent larger numbers. Lower bars represent smaller numbers.

- *Line graphs* often show trends over time. Points that are higher represent larger numbers than points that are lower. A line that consistently ascends from left to right shows a steady increase over time. A line that consistently descends from left to right shows a steady decrease over time. A line that bounces up and down represents instability or inconsistency in the trend. When interpreting a line graph, determine the point the writer is trying to make, and then see if the graph supports that point.

- *Pie charts* are used to show proportions or percentages of a whole but are less effective in showing change over time.

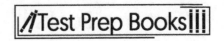

- *Tables* present information in numerical form, not as graphics. When interpreting a table, make sure to look for patterns in the numbers.

There can also be timelines, illustrations, or maps on the test. When interpreting these, keep in mind the writer's intentions and determine whether or not the graphic supports the case.

Standard English Conventions

Most of the topics discussed so far deal with the writer's choices and their effectiveness in a particular writing piece. In many cases, even ineffective writing can be grammatically correct. The following sections examine writing problems that actually break the rules of Standard English. These aren't questions of intent or judgment calls by the writer. These are mistakes that *must* be corrected.

Sentence Structure

Fragments and Run-Ons

A *sentence fragment* is a failed attempt to create a complete sentence because it's missing a required noun or verb. Fragments don't function properly because there isn't enough information to understand the writer's intended meaning. For example:

> Seat belt use corresponds to a lower rate of hospital visits, reducing strain on an already overburdened healthcare system. Insurance claims as well.

Look at the last sentence: *Insurance claims as well.* What does this mean? This is a fragment because it has a noun but no verb, and it leaves the reader guessing what the writer means about insurance claims. Many readers can probably infer what the writer means, but this distracts them from the flow of the writer's argument. Choosing a suitable replacement for a sentence fragment may be one of the questions on the test. The fragment is probably related to the surrounding content, so look at the overall point the writer is trying to make and choose the answer that best fits that idea.

Remember that sometimes a fragment can *look* like a complete sentence or have all the nouns and verbs it needs to make sense. Consider the following two examples:

> Seat belt use corresponds to a lower rate of hospital visits.

> Although seat belt use corresponds to a lower rate of hospital visits.

Both examples above have nouns and verbs, but only the first sentence is correct. The second sentence is a fragment, even though it's actually longer. The key is the writer's use of the word *although*. Starting a sentence with *although* turns that part into a *subordinate clause* (more on that next). Keep in mind that one doesn't have to remember that it's called a subordinate clause on the test. Just be able to recognize that the words form an incomplete thought and identify the problem as a sentence fragment.

A *run-on sentence* is, in some ways, the opposite of a fragment. It contains two or more sentences that have been improperly forced together into one. An example of a run-on sentence looks something like this:

> Seat belt use corresponds to a lower rate of hospital visits it also leads to fewer insurance claims.

Here, there are two separate ideas in one sentence. It's difficult for the reader to follow the writer's thinking because there is no transition from one idea to the next. On the test, choose the best way to correct the run-on sentence.

Here are two possibilities for the sentence above:

> Seat belt use corresponds to a lower rate of hospital visits. It also leads to fewer insurance claims.

> Seat belt use corresponds to a lower rate of hospital visits, but it also leads to fewer insurance claims.

Both solutions are grammatically correct, so which one is the best choice? That depends on the point that the writer is trying to make. Always read the surrounding text to determine what the writer wants to demonstrate, and choose the option that best supports that thought.

Subordination and Coordination

With terms like "coordinate clause" and "subordinating conjunction," grammar terminology can scare people! So, just for a minute, forget about the terms and look at how the sentences work.

Sometimes a sentence has two ideas that work together. For example, say the writer wants to make the following points:

> Seat belt laws have saved an estimated 50,000 lives.

> More lives are saved by seat belts every year.

These two ideas are directly related and appear to be of equal importance. Therefore, they can be joined with a simple "and" as follows:

> Seat belt laws have saved an estimated 50,000 lives, and more lives are saved by seat belts every year.

The word *and* in the sentence helps the two ideas work together or, in other words, it "coordinates" them. It also serves as a junction where the two ideas come together, better known as a *conjunction*. Therefore, the word *and* is known as a *coordinating conjunction* (a word that helps bring two equal ideas together). Now that the ideas are joined together by a conjunction, they are known as *clauses*. Other coordinating conjunctions include *or*, *but*, and *so*.

Sometimes, however, two ideas in a sentence are *not* of equal importance:

> Seat belt laws have saved an estimated 50,000 lives.

> Many more lives could be saved with stronger federal seat belt laws.

In this case, combining the two with a coordinating conjunction (*and*) creates an awkward sentence:

> Seat belt laws have saved an estimated 50,000 lives, and many more lives could be saved with stronger federal seat belt laws.

Now the writer uses a word to show the reader which clause is the most important (or the "boss") of the sentence:

50

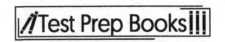
Although seat belt laws have saved an estimated 50,000 lives, many more lives could be saved with stronger federal seat belt laws.

In this example, the second clause is the key point that the writer wants to make, and the first clause works to set up that point. Since the first clause "works for" the second, it's called the *subordinate clause*. The word *although* tells the reader that this idea isn't as important as the clause that follows. This word is called the *subordinating conjunction*. Other subordinating conjunctions include *after*, *because*, *if*, *since*, *unless*, and many more. As mentioned before, it's easy to spot subordinate clauses because they don't stand on their own (as shown in this previous example):

Although seat belt laws have saved an estimated 50,000 lives

This is not a complete thought. It needs the other clause (called the *independent clause*) to make sense. On the test, when asked to choose the best subordinating conjunction for a sentence, look at the surrounding text. Choose the word that best allows the sentence to support the writer's argument.

Parallel Structure

Parallel structure usually has to do with lists. Look at the following sentence and spot the mistake:

Increased seat belt legislation has been supported by the automotive industry, the insurance industry, and doctors.

Many people don't see anything wrong, but the word *doctors* breaks the sentence's parallel structure. The previous items in the list refer to an industry as a singular noun, so every item in the list must follow that same format:

Increased seat belt legislation has been supported by the automotive industry, the insurance industry, and the healthcare industry.

Another common mistake in parallel structure might look like this:

Before the accident, Maria enjoyed swimming, running, and played soccer.

Here, the words "played soccer" break the parallel structure. To correct it, the writer must change the final item in the list to match the format of the previous two:

Before the accident, Maria enjoyed swimming, running, and playing soccer.

Usage

Modifier Placement

Modifiers are words or phrases (often adjectives or nouns) that add detail to, explain, or limit the meaning of other parts of a sentence. Look at the following example:

A big pine tree is in the yard.

In the sentence, the words *big* (an adjective) and *pine* (a noun) modify *tree* (the head noun).

All related parts of a sentence must be placed together correctly. *Misplaced* and *dangling modifiers* are common writing mistakes. In fact, they're so common that many people are accustomed to seeing them

51

and can decipher an incorrect sentence without much difficulty. On the test, expect to be asked to identify and correct this kind of error.

Misplaced Modifiers

Since *modifiers* refer to something else in the sentence (*big* and *pine* refer to *tree* in the example above), they need to be placed close to what they modify. If a modifier is so far away that the reader isn't sure what it's describing, it becomes a *misplaced modifier*. For example:

> Seat belts almost saved 5,000 lives in 2009.

It's likely that the writer means that the total number of lives saved by seat belts in 2009 is close to 5,000. However, due to the misplaced modifier (*almost*), the sentence actually says there are 5,000 instances when seat belts *almost saved lives*. In this case, the position of the modifier is actually the difference between life and death (at least in the meaning of the sentence). A clearer way to write the sentence is:

> Seat belts saved almost 5,000 lives in 2009.

Now that the modifier is close to the 5,000 lives it references, the sentence's meaning is clearer.

Another common example of a misplaced modifier occurs when the writer uses the modifier to begin a sentence. For example:

> Having saved 5,000 lives in 2009, Senator Wilson praised the seat belt legislation.

It seems unlikely that Senator Wilson saved 5,000 lives on her own, but that's what the writer is saying in this sentence. To correct this error, the writer should move the modifier closer to the intended object it modifies. Here are two possible solutions:

> Having saved 5,000 lives in 2009, the seat belt legislation was praised by Senator Wilson.

> Senator Wilson praised the seat belt legislation, which saved 5,000 lives in 2009.

When choosing a solution for a misplaced modifier, look for an option that places the modifier close to the object or idea it describes.

Dangling Modifiers

A modifier must have a target word or phrase that it's modifying. Without this, it's a *dangling modifier*. Dangling modifiers are usually found at the beginning of sentences:

> After passing the new law, there is sure to be an improvement in highway safety.

This sentence doesn't say anything about who is passing the law. Therefore, "After passing the new law" is a dangling modifier because it doesn't modify anything in the sentence. To correct this type of error, determine what the writer intended the modifier to point to:

> After passing the new law, legislators are sure to see an improvement in highway safety.

"After passing the new law" now points to *legislators*, which makes the sentence clearer and eliminates the dangling modifier.

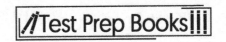

Shifts in Construction

It's been said several times already that *good writing must be consistent*. Another common writing mistake occurs when the writer unintentionally shifts verb tense, voice, or noun-pronoun agreement. This shift can take place within a sentence, within a paragraph, or over the course of an entire piece of writing. On the test, questions may ask that this kind of error be identified. Here are some examples.

Shift in Verb Tense

Even though test questions don't ask for verb tenses to be identified, they may cover recognizing when these tenses change unexpectedly:

> During the accident, the airbags malfunction, and the passengers were injured.

In this sentence, the writer unintentionally shifts from present tense ("airbags malfunction" is happening *now)* to past tense ("passengers were injured" has *already happened*.) This is very confusing. To correct this error, the writer must stay in the same tense throughout. Two possible solutions are:

> During the accident, the airbags malfunctioned, and the passengers were injured.

> During the accident, the airbags malfunction, and the passengers are injured.

Shift in Voice

Sometimes the writer accidentally slips from active voice to passive voice in the middle of a sentence. This is a difficult mistake to catch because it's something people often do when speaking to one another. First, it's important to understand the difference between active and passive voice. Most sentences are written in *active voice*, which means that the noun is doing what the verb in the sentence says. For example:

> Seat belts save lives.

Here, the noun (*seat belt*) is doing the saving. However, in *passive voice*, the verb is doing something to the noun:

> Lives are saved.

In this case, the noun (*lives*) is the thing *being saved*. Passive voice is difficult for many people to identify and understand, but there's a simple (and memorable) way to check: simply add "by zombies" to the end of the verb and, if it makes sense, then the verb is written in passive voice. For example: "My car was wrecked...by zombies." Also, in the above example, "Lives are saved...by zombies." If the zombie trick doesn't work, then the sentence is in active voice.

Here's what a shift in voice looks like in a sentence:

> When Amy buckled her seat belt, a satisfying click was heard.

The writer shifts from active voice in the beginning of the sentence to passive voice after the comma (remember, "a satisfying click was heard...by zombies"). To fix this mistake, the writer must remain in active voice throughout:

> When Amy buckled her seat belt, she heard a satisfying click.

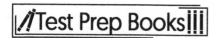

This sentence is now grammatically correct, easier to read...and zombie free!

Shift in Noun-Pronoun Agreement

Pronouns are used to replace nouns so sentences don't have a lot of unnecessary repetition. This repetition can make a sentence seem awkward as in the following example:

> Seat belts are important because seat belts save lives, but seat belts can't do so unless seat belts are used.

Replacing some of the nouns (*seat belts*) with a pronoun (*they*) improves the flow of the sentence:

> Seat belts are important because they save lives, but they can't do so unless they are used.

A pronoun should agree in number (singular or plural) with the noun that precedes it. Another common writing error is the shift in *noun-pronoun agreement*. Here's an example:

> When people are getting in a car, he should always remember to buckle his seatbelt.

The first half of the sentence talks about a plural (*people*), while the second half refers to a singular person (*he* and *his*). These don't agree, so the sentence should be rewritten as:

> When people are getting in a car, they should always remember to buckle their seatbelt.

Pronouns

Pronoun Person

Pronoun person refers to the narrative voice the writer uses in a piece of writing. A great deal of nonfiction is written in third person, which uses pronouns like *he, she, it,* and *they* to convey meaning. Occasionally a writer uses first person (*I, me, we,* etc.) or second person (*you*). Any choice of pronoun person can be appropriate for a particular situation, but the writer must remain consistent and logical.

Test questions may cover examining samples that should stay in a single pronoun person, be it first, second, or third. Look out for shifts between words like *you* and *I* or *he* and *they*.

Pronoun Clarity

Pronouns always refer back to a noun. However, as the writer composes longer, more complicated sentences, the reader may be unsure which noun the pronoun should replace. For example:

> An amendment was made to the bill, but now it has been voted down.

Was the amendment voted down or the entire bill? It's impossible to tell from this sentence. To correct this error, the writer needs to restate the appropriate noun rather than using a pronoun:

> An amendment was made to the bill, but now the bill has been voted down.

Pronouns in Combination

Writers often make mistakes when choosing pronouns to use in combination with other nouns. The most common mistakes are found in sentences like this:

> Please join Senator Wilson and I at the event tomorrow.

Notice anything wrong? Though many people think the sentence sounds perfectly fine, the use of the pronoun *I* is actually incorrect. To double-check this, take the other person out of the sentence:

> Please join I at the event tomorrow.

Now the sentence is obviously incorrect, as it should read, "Please join *me* at the event tomorrow." Thus, the first sentence should replace *I* with *me*:

> Please join Senator Wilson and me at the event tomorrow.

For many people, this sounds wrong because they're used to hearing and saying it incorrectly. Take extra care when answering this kind of question and follow the double-checking procedure.

Agreement

In English writing, certain words connect to other words. People often learn these connections (or *agreements*) as young children and use the correct combinations without a second thought. However, the questions on the test dealing with agreement probably aren't simple ones.

Subject-Verb Agreement

Which of the following sentences is correct?

> A large crowd of protesters was on hand.

> A large crowd of protesters were on hand.

Many people would say the second sentence is correct, but they'd be wrong. However, they probably wouldn't be alone. Most people just look at two words: *protesters were*. Together they make sense. They sound right. The problem is that the verb *were* doesn't refer to the word *protesters*. Here, the word *protesters* is part of a prepositional phrase that clarifies the actual subject of the sentence (*crowd*). Take the phrase "of protesters" away and re-examine the sentences:

> A large crowd was on hand.

> A large crowd were on hand.

Without the prepositional phrase to separate the subject and verb, the answer is obvious. The first sentence is correct. On the test, look for confusing prepositional phrases when answering questions about subject-verb agreement. Take the phrase away, and then recheck the sentence.

Noun Agreement

Nouns that refer to other nouns must also match in number. Take the following example:

> John and Emily both served as an intern for Senator Wilson.

Two people are involved in this sentence: John and Emily. Therefore, the word *intern* should be plural to match. Here is how the sentence should read:

> John and Emily both served as interns for Senator Wilson.

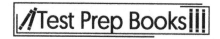
Frequently Confused Words

The English language is interesting because many of its words sound so similar or identical that they confuse readers and writers alike. Errors involving these words are hard to spot because they *sound* right even when they're wrong. Also, because these mistakes are so pervasive, many people think they're correct. Here are a few examples that may be encountered on the test:

They're vs. Their vs. There

This set of words is probably the all-time winner of misuse. The word *they're* is a contraction of "they are." Remember that contractions combine two words, using an apostrophe to replace any eliminated letters. If a question asks whether the writer is using the word *they're* correctly, change the word to "they are" and reread the sentence. Look at the following example:

> Legislators can be proud of they're work on this issue.

This sentence *sounds* correct, but replace the contraction *they're* with "they are" to see what happens:

> Legislators can be proud of they are work on this issue.

The result doesn't make sense, which shows that it's an incorrect use of the word *they're*. Did the writer mean to use the word *their* instead? The word *their* indicates possession because it shows that something *belongs* to something else. Now put the word *their* into the sentence:

> Legislators can be proud of their work on this issue.

To check the answer, find the word that comes right after the word *their* (which in this case is *work*). Pose this question: whose *work* is it? If the question can be answered in the sentence, then the word signifies possession. In the sentence above, it's the legislators' work. Therefore, the writer is using the word *their* correctly.

If the words *they're* and *their* don't make sense in the sentence, then the correct word is almost always *there*. The word *there* can be used in many different ways, so it's easy to remember to use it when *they're* and *their* don't work. Now test these methods with the following sentences:

> Their going to have a hard time passing these laws.

> Enforcement officials will have there hands full.

> They're are many issues to consider when discussing car safety.

In the first sentence, asking the question "Whose going is it?" doesn't make sense. Thus the word *their* is wrong. However, when replaced with the conjunction *they're* (or *they are*), the sentence works. Thus the correct word for the first sentence should be *they're*.

In the second sentence, ask this question: "Whose hands are full?" The answer (*enforcement officials*) is correct in the sentence. Therefore, the word *their* should replace *there* in this sentence.

In the third sentence, changing the word *they're* to "they are" ("They are are many issues") doesn't make sense. Ask this question: "Whose are is it?" This makes even less sense, since neither of the words *they're* or *their* makes sense. Therefore, the correct word must be *there*.

Who's vs. Whose

Who's is a contraction of "who is" while the word *whose* indicates possession. Look at the following sentence:

> Who's job is it to protect America's drivers?

The easiest way to check for correct usage is to replace the word *who's* with "who is" and see if the sentence makes sense:

> Who is job is it to protect America's drivers?

By changing the contraction to "Who is" the sentence no longer makes sense. Therefore, the correct word must be *whose*.

Your vs. You're

The word *your* indicates possession, while *you're* is a contraction for "you are." Look at the following example:

> Your going to have to write your congressman if you want to see action.

Again, the easiest way to check correct usage is to replace the word *Your* with "You are" and see if the sentence still makes sense.

> You are going to have to write your congressman if you want to see action.

By replacing Your with "You are," the sentence still makes sense. Thus, in this case, the writer should have used "You're."

Its vs. It's

Its is a word that indicates possession, while the word *it's* is a contraction of "it is." Once again, the easiest way to check for correct usage is to replace the word with "it is" and see if the sentence makes sense. Look at the following sentence:

> It's going to take a lot of work to pass this law.

Replacing *it's* with "it is" results in this: "It is going to take a lot of work to pass this law." This makes sense, so the contraction (*it's*) is correct. Now look at another example:

> The car company will have to redesign it's vehicles.

Replacing *it's* with "it is" results in this: "The car company will have to redesign it is vehicles." This sentence doesn't make sense, so the contraction (*it's*) is incorrect.

Than vs. Then

Than is used in sentences that involve comparisons, while *then* is used to indicate an order of events. Consider the following sentence:

> Japan has more traffic fatalities than the U.S.

The use of the word *than* is correct because it compares Japan to the U.S. Now look at another example:

Laws must be passed, and then we'll see a change in behavior.

Here the use of the word *then* is correct because one thing happens after the other.

Affect vs. Effect

Affect is a verb that means to change something, while *effect* is a noun that indicates such a change. Look at the following sentence:

There are thousands of people affected by the new law.

This sentence is correct because *affected* is a verb that tells what's happening. Now look at this sentence:

The law will have a dramatic effect.

This sentence is also correct because *effect* is a noun and the thing that happens.

Note that a noun version of *affect* is occasionally used. It means "emotion" or "desire," usually in a psychological sense.

Two vs. Too vs. To

Two is the number (2). *Too* refers to an amount of something, or it can mean *also*. *To* is used for everything else. Look at the following sentence:

Two senators still haven't signed the bill.

This is correct because there are *two* (2) senators. Here's another example:

There are too many questions about this issue.

In this sentence, the word *too* refers to an amount ("too many questions"). Now here's another example:

Senator Wilson is supporting this legislation, too.

In this sentence, the word *also* can be substituted for the word *too*, so it's also correct. Finally, one last example:

I look forward to signing this bill into law.

In this sentence, the tests for *two* and *too* don't work. Thus the word *to* fits the bill!

Other Common Writing Confusions

In addition to all of the above, there are other words that writers often misuse. This doesn't happen because the words sound alike, but because the writer is not aware of the proper way to use them.

Logical Comparison

Writers often make comparisons in their writing. However, it's easy to make mistakes in sentences that involve comparisons, and those mistakes are difficult to spot. Try to find the error in the following sentence:

Senator Wilson's proposed seat belt legislation was similar to Senator Abernathy.

Can't find it? First, ask what two things are actually being compared. It seems like the writer *wants* to compare two different types of legislation, but the sentence actually compares legislation ("Senator Wilson's proposed seat belt legislation") to a person ("Senator Abernathy"). This is a strange and illogical comparison to make.

So how can the writer correct this mistake? The answer is to make sure that the second half of the sentence logically refers back to the first half. The most obvious way to do this is to repeat words:

> Senator Wilson's proposed seat belt legislation was similar to Senator Abernathy's seat belt legislation.

Now the sentence is logically correct, but it's a little wordy and awkward. A better solution is to eliminate the word-for-word repetition by using suitable replacement words:

> Senator Wilson's proposed seat belt legislation was similar to that of Senator Abernathy.

> Senator Wilson's proposed seat belt legislation was similar to the bill offered by Senator Abernathy.

Here's another similar example:

> More lives in the U.S. are saved by seat belts than Japan.

The writer probably means to compare lives saved by seat belts in the U.S. to lives saved by seat belts in Japan. Unfortunately, the sentence's meaning is garbled by an illogical comparison, and instead refers to U.S. lives saved *by Japan* rather than *in Japan.* To resolve this issue, first repeat the words and phrases needed to make an identical comparison:

> More lives in the U.S. are saved by seat belts than lives in Japan are saved by seat belts.

Then, use a replacement word to clean up the repetitive text:

> More lives in the U.S. are saved by seat belts than in Japan.

Punctuation

On the test there may be a sentence where all the words are correct, but the writer uses *punctuation* incorrectly. It probably won't be something as simple as a missing period or question mark. Instead it could be one of the commonly misunderstood punctuation marks.

Colons
Colons can be used in the following situations and examples:

- To introduce lists

  - Carmakers have three choices: improve seat belt design, pay financial penalties, or go out of business.

- To introduce new ideas

  - There is only one person who can champion this legislation: Senator Wilson.

59

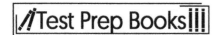

- To separate titles and subtitles

  o Show Some Restraint: The History of Seat Belts

Semicolons

Semicolons can be used in the following situations:

- To separate two related independent clauses

  o The proposed bill was voted down; opponents were concerned about the tax implications.

  Note: These are known as *independent clauses* because each one stands on its own as a complete sentence. Semicolons *cannot* be used to separate an independent clause from a dependent clause, nor to separate two dependent clauses.

- To separate complex items in a list

  o Joining Senator Wilson onstage were Jim Robinson, head of the NHTSA; Kristin Gabber, a consumer advocate; and Milton Webster, an accident survivor.

  Note: While items in a list are usually separated by commas, readers can easily get confused if the list items themselves contain internal commas.

Hyphens vs. Dashes

Hyphens (-) and *dashes* (–) are not the same. *Hyphens* are shorter, and they help combine or clarify words in certain situations like:

- Creating an adjective: *safety-conscious*
- Creating compound numbers: *fifty-nine*
- Avoiding confusion with another word: *re-sent* vs. *resent*
- Avoiding awkward letter combinations: *semi-intellectual* vs. *semiintellectual*

Dashes are longer and show an interruption in the flow of the sentence. In this context, they can be used much the same way as commas or parentheses:

- The legislation—which was supported by 80 percent of Americans—did not pass.

Commas

Commas are used in many different situations. Here are some of the most misunderstood examples:

- Separating simple items in a list.

  o The legislation had the support of Republicans, Democrats, and Independents.

- Separating adjectives that modify the same noun.

  o The weak, meaningless platitudes had no effect on the listeners.

- Separating independent and dependent clauses.

  o After passing the bill, the lawmakers celebrated.

    Note: "After passing the bill" is a *dependent clause* because it's not a complete sentence on its own.

- Separating quotations from introductory text.

  o Senator Wilson asked, "How can we get this bill passed?"

- Showing interruption in the flow of a sentence. In this context, commas can be used in the same way as semicolons or parentheses.

  o The legislation, which was supported by 80 percent of Americans, did not pass.

    Note: Commas cannot be used if the clause or phrase in question is essential to the meaning of the sentence.

During the test, it may be hard to remember all the rules for comma usage. Read the sentence and listen to its ebb and flow. If a particular answer looks, sounds, or feels wrong for some reason, there's probably a good reason for it. Look at another option instead.

Apostrophes

Apostrophes are often misused. For the purpose of the test, there are three things to know about using apostrophes:

- Use apostrophes to show possession

  o Senator Wilson's bill just passed committee.

- Use apostrophes in contractions to replace eliminated letters

  o Does not → Doesn't

Note: It's common to see acronyms made plural using apostrophes (RV's, DVD's, TV's), but these are incorrect. Acronyms function as words, so they are pluralized the same way (RVs, DVDs, TVs).

On the test, when an apostrophe-related question is asked, determine if it shows possession or is part of a contraction. If neither answer fits, then the apostrophe probably doesn't belong there.

Final Tips

Usage Conventions

On the test, don't overlook simple, obvious writing errors such as these:

- Is the first word in a sentence capitalized?
- Are countries, geographical features, and proper nouns capitalized?
- Conversely, are words capitalized that should *not* be?
- Do sentences end with proper punctuation marks?

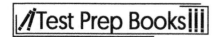

- Are commas and quotation marks used appropriately?
- Do contractions include apostrophes?
- Are apostrophes used for plurals? (Almost never!)

Look for Context

Keep in mind that the test may give several choices to replace a writing selection, and all of them may be grammatically correct. In such cases, choose the answer that makes the most sense in the context of the piece. What's the writer trying to say? What's their main idea? Look for the answer that best supports this theme.

Use Your Instincts

With the few notable exceptions above, instinct is often the best guide to spotting writing problems. If something sounds wrong, then it may very well be wrong. The good thing about a test like this is that the problem doesn't have to be labeled as an example of "faulty parallelism" or "improper noun-pronoun agreement." It's enough just to recognize that a problem exists and choose the best solution.

Take a Break

After reading and thinking about all of these aspects of grammar so intensely, the brain may start shutting down. If the words aren't making sense, or reading the same sentence several times still has no meaning, it's time to stop. Take a thirty-second vacation. Forget about grammar, syntax, and writing for half a minute to clear the mind. Take a few deep breaths and think about something to do after the test is over. It's surprising how quickly the brain refreshes itself!

Math Test

Heart of Algebra

Creating, Solving, or Interpreting a Linear Expression or Equation in One Variable

Linear expressions and equations are concise mathematical statements that can be written to model a variety of scenarios. Questions found pertaining to this topic will contain one variable only. A variable is an unknown quantity, usually denoted by a letter (x, n, p, etc.). In the case of linear expressions and equations, the power of the variable (its exponent) is 1. A variable without a visible exponent is raised to the first power.

Writing Linear Expressions and Equations

A linear expression is a statement about an unknown quantity expressed in mathematical symbols. The statement "five times a number added to forty" can be expressed as $5x + 40$. A linear equation is a statement in which two expressions (at least one containing a variable) are equal to each other. The statement "five times a number added to forty is equal to ten" can be expressed as:

$$5x + 40 = 10$$

Real-world scenarios can also be expressed mathematically. Consider the following:

> Bob had \$20 and Tom had \$4. After selling 4 ice cream cones to Bob, Tom has as much money as Bob.

The cost of an ice cream cone is an unknown quantity and can be represented by a variable. The amount of money Bob has after his purchase is four times the cost of an ice cream cone subtracted from his original \$20. The amount of money Tom has after his sale is four times the cost of an ice cream cone added to his original \$4. This can be expressed as:

$$20 - 4x = 4x + 4$$

x represents the cost of an ice cream cone.

When expressing a verbal or written statement mathematically, it is key to understand words or phrases that can be represented with symbols. The following are examples:

Symbol	Phrase
$+$	added to, increased by, sum of, more than
$-$	decreased by, difference between, less than, take away
x	multiplied by, 3 (4, 5 …) times as large, product of
$\div$	divided by, quotient of, half (third, etc.) of
$=$	is, the same as, results in, as much as
$x, t, n,$ etc.	a number, unknown quantity, value of

Evaluating and Simplifying Algebraic Expressions

Given an algebraic expression, students may be asked to evaluate for given values of variable(s). In doing so, students will arrive at a numerical value as an answer. For example:

$$\text{Evaluate } a - 2b + ab \text{ for } a = 3 \text{ and } b = -1.$$

To evaluate an expression, the given values should be substituted for the variables and simplified using the order of operations. In this case:

$$(3) - 2(-1) + (3)(-1)$$

Parentheses are used when substituting.

Given an algebraic expression, students may be asked to simplify the expression. For example:

$$\text{Simplify } 5x^2 - 10x + 2 - 8x^2 + x - 1.$$

Simplifying algebraic expressions requires combining like terms. A term is a number, variable, or product of a number and variables separated by addition and subtraction. The terms in the above expression are: $5x^2$, $-10x$, 2, $-8x^2$, x, and -1. Like terms have the same variables raised to the same powers (exponents). To combine like terms, the coefficients (numerical factor of the term including sign) are added, while the variables and their powers are kept the same. The example above simplifies to:

$$-3x^2 - 9x + 1$$

Solving Linear Equations

When asked to solve a linear equation, it requires determining a numerical value for the unknown variable. Given a linear equation involving addition, subtraction, multiplication, and division, isolation of the variable is done by working backward. Addition and subtraction are inverse operations, as are multiplication and division; therefore, they can be used to cancel each other out.

The first steps to solving linear equations are to distribute if necessary and combine any like terms that are on the same side of the equation. Sides of an equation are separated by an = sign. Next, the equation should be manipulated to get the variable on one side. Whatever is done to one side of an equation, must be done to the other side to remain equal. Then, the variable should be isolated by using inverse operations to undo the order of operations backward. Undo addition and subtraction, then undo multiplication and division.

Creating, Solving, or Interpreting Linear Inequalities in One Variable

Linear inequalities and linear equations are both comparisons of two algebraic expressions. However, unlike equations in which the expressions are equal to each other, linear inequalities compare expressions that are unequal. Linear equations typically have one value for the variable that makes the statement true. Linear inequalities generally have an infinite number of values that make the statement true. Exceptions to these last two statements are covered in Section 6.

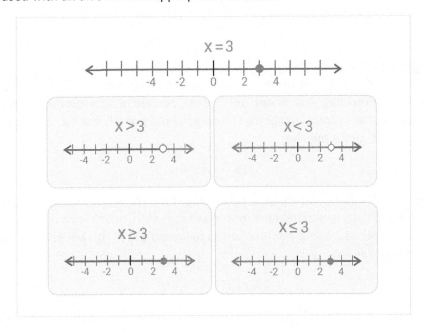

Writing Linear Inequalities

Linear inequalities are a concise mathematical way to express the relationship between unequal values. More specifically, they describe in what way the values are unequal. A value could be greater than ($>$); less than ($<$); greater than or equal to ($\geq$); or less than or equal to ($\leq$) another value. The statement "five times a number added to forty is more than sixty-five" can be expressed as:

$$5x + 40 > 65$$

Common words and phrases that express inequalities are:

Symbol	Phrase
$<$	is under, is below, smaller than, beneath
$>$	is above, is over, bigger than, exceeds
$\leq$	no more than, at most, maximum
$\geq$	no less than, at least, minimum

Solving Linear Inequalities

When solving a linear inequality, the solution is the set of all numbers that makes the statement true. The inequality $x + 2 \geq 6$ has a solution set of 4 and every number greater than 4 (4.0001, 5, 12, 107, etc.). Adding 2 to 4 or any number greater than 4 would result in a value that is greater than or equal to 6. Therefore, $x \geq 4$ would be the solution set.

Solution sets for linear inequalities often will be displayed using a number line. If a value is included in the set ($\geq$ or $\leq$), there is a shaded dot placed on that value and an arrow extending in the direction of the solutions. For a variable $>$ or $\geq$ a number, the arrow would point right on the number line (the direction where the numbers increase); and if a variable is $<$ or $\leq$ a number, the arrow would point left (where the numbers decrease). If the value is not included in the set ($>$ or $<$), an open circle on that value would be used with an arrow in the appropriate direction.

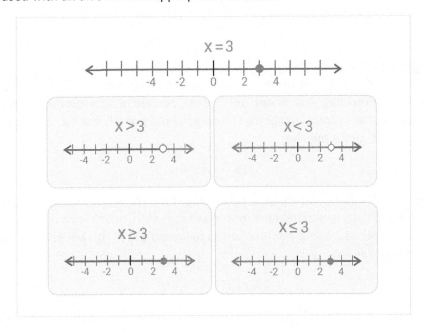

65

Students may be asked to write a linear inequality given a graph of its solution set. To do so, they should identify whether the value is included (shaded dot or open circle) and the direction in which the arrow is pointing.

In order to algebraically solve a linear inequality, the same steps should be followed as in solving a linear equation (see section on *Solving Linear Equations*). The inequality symbol stays the same for all operations EXCEPT when multiplying or dividing by a negative number. If multiplying or dividing by a negative number while solving an inequality, the relationship reverses (the sign flips). Multiplying or dividing by a positive does not change the relationship, so the sign stays the same. In other words, $>$ switches to $<$ and vice versa. An example is shown below.

Solve $-2(x + 4) \leq 22$ for the value of x.

First, distribute -2 to the binomial by multiplying:

$$-2x - 8 \leq 22$$

Next, add 8 to both sides to isolate the variable:

$$-2x \leq 30$$

Divide both sides by -2 to solve for x:

$$x \geq -15$$

Building a Linear Function that Models a Linear Relationship Between Two Quantities

Linear relationships between two quantities can be expressed in two ways: function notation or as a linear equation with two variables. The relationship is referred to as linear because its graph is represented by a line. For a relationship to be linear, both variables must be raised to the first power only.

Function/Linear Equation Notation

A relation is a set of input and output values that can be written as ordered pairs. A function is a relation in which each input is paired with exactly one output. The domain of a function consists of all inputs, and the range consists of all outputs. Graphing the ordered pairs of a linear function produces a straight line. An example of a function would be:

$$f(x) = 4x + 4$$

read "f of x is equal to four times x plus four." In this example, the input would be x and the output would be $f(x)$. Ordered pairs would be represented as $(x, f(x))$. To find the output for an input value of 3, 3 would be substituted for x into the function as follows: $f(3) = 4(3) + 4$, resulting in $f(3) = 16$. Therefore, the ordered pair:

$$(3, f(3)) = (3, 16)$$

Note $f(x)$ is a function of x denoted by f. Functions of x could be named $g(x)$, read "g of x"; $p(x)$, read "p of x"; etc.

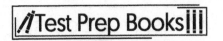
A linear function could also be written in the form of an equation with two variables. Typically, the variable x represents the inputs and the variable y represents the outputs. The variable x is considered the independent variable and y the dependent variable. The above function would be written as:

$$y = 4x + 4$$

Ordered pairs are written in the form (x, y).

Writing Linear Equations in Two Variables

When writing linear equations in two variables, the process depends on the information given. Questions will typically provide the slope of the line and its y-intercept, an ordered pair and the slope, or two ordered pairs.

Given the Slope and Y-Intercept

Linear equations are commonly written in slope-intercept form, $y = mx + b$, where m represents the slope of the line and b represents the y-intercept. The slope is the rate of change between the variables, usually expressed as a whole number or fraction. The y-intercept is the value of y when $x = 0$ (the point where the line intercepts the y-axis on a graph). Given the slope and y-intercept of a line, the values are substituted for m and b into the equation. A line with a slope of $\frac{1}{2}$ and y-intercept of -2 would have an equation:

$$y = \frac{1}{2}x - 2$$

Given an Ordered Pair and the Slope

The point-slope form of a line:

$$y - y_1 = m(x - x_1)$$

is used to write an equation when given an ordered pair (point on the equation's graph) for the function and its rate of change (slope of the line). The values for the slope, m, and the point (x_1, y_1) are substituted into the point-slope form to obtain the equation of the line. A line with a slope of 3 and an ordered pair $(4, -2)$ would have an equation:

$$y - (-2) = 3(x - 4)$$

If a question specifies that the equation be written in slope-intercept form, the equation should be manipulated to isolate y:

Solve: $y - (-2) = 3(x - 4)$

Distribute: $y + 2 = 3x - 12$

Subtract 2 from both sides: $y = 3x - 14$

Given Two Ordered Pairs

Given two ordered pairs for a function, (x_1, y_1) and (x_2, y_2), it is possible to determine the rate of change between the variables (slope of the line). To calculate the slope of the line, m, the values for the ordered pairs should be substituted into the formula:

$$m = \frac{y_2 - y_1}{x_2 - x_1}$$

The expression is substituted to obtain a whole number or fraction for the slope. Once the slope is calculated, the slope and either of the ordered pairs should be substituted into the point-slope form to obtain the equation of the line.

Creating, Solving, and Interpreting Systems of Linear Inequalities in Two Variables

Expressing Linear Inequalities in Two Variables

A linear inequality in two variables is a statement expressing an unequal relationship between those two variables. Typically written in slope-intercept form, the variable y can be greater than; less than; greater than or equal to; or less than or equal to a linear expression including the variable x. Examples include:

$$y > 3x$$

$$y \leq \frac{1}{2}x - 3$$

Questions may instruct students to model real world scenarios such as:

> You work part-time cutting lawns for $15 each and cleaning houses for $25 each. Your goal is to make more than $90 this week. Write an inequality to represent the possible pairs of lawns and houses needed to reach your goal.

This scenario can be expressed as:

$$15x + 25y > 90$$

where x is the number of lawns cut and y is the number of houses cleaned.

Graphing Solution Sets for Linear Inequalities in Two Variables

A graph of the solution set for a linear inequality shows the ordered pairs that make the statement true. The graph consists of a boundary line dividing the coordinate plane and shading on one side of the boundary. The boundary line should be graphed just as a linear equation would be graphed (see section on *Understanding Connections Between Algebraic and Graphical Representations*). If the inequality symbol is $>$ or $<$, a dashed line can be used to indicate that the line is not part of the solution set.

If the inequality symbol is $\geq$ or $\leq$, a solid line can be used to indicate that the boundary line is included in the solution set. An ordered pair (x, y) on either side of the line should be chosen to test in the inequality statement. If substituting the values for x and y results in a true statement $(15(3) + 25(2) > 90)$, that ordered pair and all others on that side of the boundary line are part of the solution set. To indicate this, that region of the graph should be shaded. If substituting the ordered pair results in a false statement, the ordered pair and all others on that side are not part of the solution set.

Therefore, the other region of the graph contains the solutions and should be shaded.

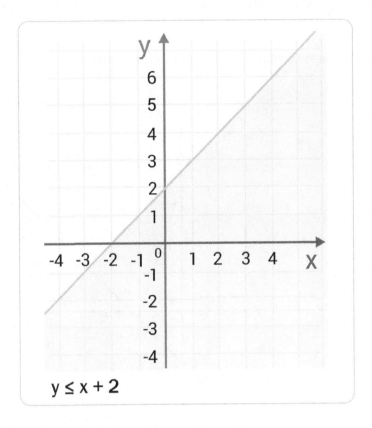

$$y \leq x + 2$$

A question may simply ask whether a given ordered pair is a solution to a given inequality. To determine this, the values should be substituted for the ordered pair into the inequality. If the result is a true statement, the ordered pair is a solution; if the result is a false statement, the ordered pair is not a solution.

Expressing Systems of Linear Inequalities in Two Variables

A system of linear inequalities consists of two linear inequalities making comparisons between two variables. Students may be given a scenario and asked to express it as a system of inequalities:

> A consumer study calls for at least 60 adult participants. It cannot use more than 25 men. Express these constraints as a system of inequalities.

This can be modeled by the system:

$$x + y \geq 60$$

$$x \leq 25$$

where x represents the number of men and y represents the number of women. A solution to the system is an ordered pair that makes both inequalities true when substituting the values for x and y.

Graphing Solution Sets for Systems of Linear Inequalities in Two Variables

The solution set for a system of inequalities is the region of a graph consisting of ordered pairs that make both inequalities true. To graph the solution set, each linear inequality should first be graphed with appropriate shading. The region of the graph should be identified where the shading for the two inequalities overlaps. This region contains the solution set for the system.

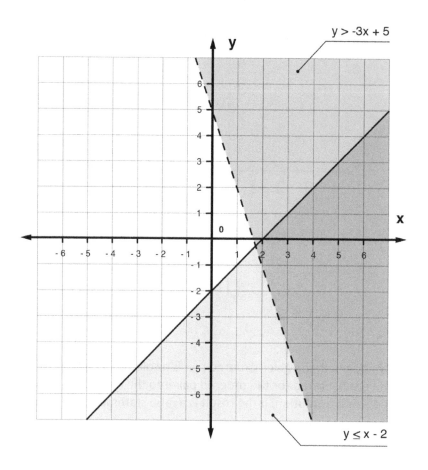

An ordered pair from the region of solutions can be selected to test in the system of inequalities.

Just as with manipulating linear inequalities in one variable, if dividing by a negative number in working with a linear inequality in two variables, the relationship reverses and the inequality sign should be flipped.

Creating, Solving, and Interpreting Systems of Two Linear Equations in Two Variables

Expressing Systems of Two Linear Equations in Two Variables

A system of two linear equations in two variables is a set of equations that use the same variables, usually x and y. Here's a sample problem:

> An Internet provider charges an installation fee and a monthly charge. It advertises that two months of its offering costs $100 and six months costs $200. Find the monthly charge and the installation fee.

70

The two unknown quantities (variables) are the monthly charge and the installation fee. There are two different statements given relating the variables: two months added to the installation fee is $100; and six months added to the installation fee is $200. Using the variable x as the monthly charge and y as the installation fee, the statements can be written as the following:

$$2x + y = 100$$

$$6x + y = 200$$

These two equations taken together form a system modeling the given scenario.

Solutions of a System of Two Linear Equations in Two Variables

A solution for a system of equations is an ordered pair that makes both equations true. One method for solving a system of equations is to graph both lines on a coordinate plane (see section on *Understanding Connections Between Algebraic and Graphical Representations*). If the lines intersect, the point of intersection is the solution to the system. Every point on a line represents an ordered pair that makes its equation true. The ordered pair represented by this point of intersection lies on both lines and therefore makes both equations true. This ordered pair should be checked by substituting its values into both of the original equations of the system. Note that given a system of equations and an ordered pair, the ordered pair can be determined to be a solution or not by checking it in both equations.

If, when graphed, the lines representing the equations of a system do not intersect, then the two lines are parallel to each other or they are the same exact line. Parallel lines extend in the same direction without ever meeting. A system consisting of parallel lines has no solution. If the equations for a system represent the same exact line, then every point on the line is a solution to the system. In this case, there would be an infinite number of solutions. A system consisting of intersecting lines is referred to as independent; a system consisting of parallel lines is referred to as inconsistent; and a system consisting of coinciding lines is referred to as dependent.

Parallel Lines	**Intersecting Lines**	**Coincident Lines**
Inconsistent	Independent	Dependent

Algebraically Solving Linear Equations (or Inequalities) in One Variable

Linear equations in one variable and linear inequalities in one variable can be solved following similar processes. Although they typically have one solution, a linear equation can have no solution or can have a solution set of all real numbers. Solution sets for linear inequalities typically consist of an infinite number of values either greater or less than a given value (where the given value may or may not be included in the set). However, a linear inequality can have no solution or can have a solution set consisting of all real numbers.

Linear Equations in One Variable – Special Cases

Solving a linear equation produces a value for the variable that makes the algebraic statement true. If there is no value for the variable that would make the statement true, there is no solution to the equation. Here's a sample equation:

$$x + 3 = x - 1$$

There is no value for x in which adding 3 to the value would produce the same result as subtracting 1 from that value. Conversely, if any value for the variable would make a true statement, the equation has an infinite number of solutions. Here's another sample equation:

$$3x + 6 = 3(x + 2)$$

Any real number substituted for x would result in a true statement (both sides of the equation are equal).

By manipulating equations similar to the two above, the variable of the equation will cancel out completely. If the constants that are left express a true statement (ex., $6 = 6$), then all real numbers are solutions to the equation. If the constants left express a false statement (ex., $3 = -1$), then there is no solution to the equation.

A question on this material may present a linear equation with an unknown value for either a constant or a coefficient of the variable and ask to determine the value that produces an equation with no solution or infinite solutions. For example:

$$3x + 7 = 3x + 10 + n$$

Find the value of n that would create an equation with an infinite number of solutions for the variable x.

To solve this problem, the equation should be manipulated so the variable x will cancel. To do this, $3x$ should be subtracted from both sides, which would leave:

$$7 = 10 + n$$

By subtracting 10 on both sides, it is determined that $n = -3$. Therefore, a value of -3 for n would result in an equation with a solution set of all real numbers.

If the same problem asked for the equation to have no solution, the value of n would be all real numbers except -3.

Linear Inequalities in One Variable – Special Cases

A linear inequality can have a solution set consisting of all real numbers or can contain no solution. When solved algebraically, a linear inequality in which the variable cancels out and results in a true statement (ex., $7 \geq 2$) has a solution set of all real numbers. A linear inequality in which the variable cancels out and results in a false statement (ex., $7 \leq 2$) has no solution.

Compound Inequalities

A compound inequality is a pair of inequalities joined by *and* or *or*. Given a compound inequality, to determine its solution set, both inequalities should be solved for the given variable. The solution set for a compound inequality containing *and* consists of all the values for the variable that make both inequalities true. If solving the compound inequality results in:

$$x \geq -2$$

$$x < 3$$

the solution set would consist of all values between -2 and 3, including 3. This may also be written as follows:

$$-2 \leq x < 3$$

Due to the graphs of their solution sets (shown below), compound inequalities such as these are referred to as conjunctions.

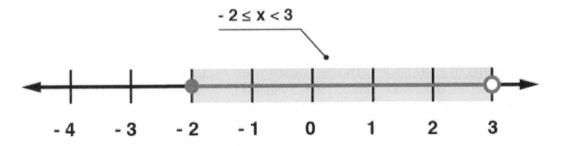

If there are no values that would make both inequalities of a compound inequality containing *and* true, then there is no solution. An example would be $x > 2$ and $x \leq 0$.

The solution set for a compound inequality containing *or* consists of all the values for the variable that make at least one of the inequalities true. The solution set for the compound inequality $x < 3$ or $x \geq 6$ consists of all values less than 3, 6, and all values greater than 6. Due to the graphs of their solution sets (shown below), compound inequalities such as these are referred to as disjunctions.

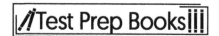
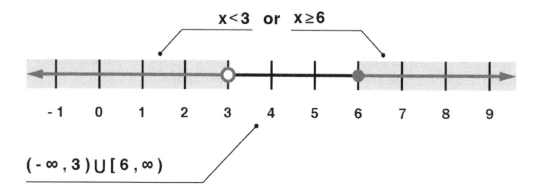

If the two inequalities for a compound inequality containing *or* "overlap," then the solution set contains all real numbers. An example would be $x > 2$ or $x < 7$. Any number would make at least one of these true.

Algebraically Solving Systems of Two Linear Equations in Two Variables

A system of two linear equations in two variables is a set of equations that use the same variables (typically x and y). A solution to the system is an ordered pair that makes both equations true. One method for solving a system is by graphing as explained in an earlier section. This method, however, is not always practical. Students may not have graph paper; or the solution may not consist of integers, making it difficult to identify the exact point of intersection on a graph. There are two methods for solving systems of equations algebraically: substitution and elimination. The method used will depend on the characteristics of the equations in the system.

Solving Systems of Equations with the Substitution Method

If one of the equations in a system has an isolated variable ($x =$ or $y =$) or a variable that can be easily isolated, the substitution method can be used. Here's a sample system:

$$x + 3y = 7$$

$$2x - 4y = 24$$

The first equation can easily be solved for x. By subtracting $3y$ on both sides, the resulting equation is:

$$x = 7 - 3y$$

When one equation is solved for a variable, the expression that it is equal can be substituted into the other equation. For this example, $(7 - 3y)$ would be substituted for x into the second equation as follows:

$$2(7 - 3y) - 4y = 24$$

Solving this equation results in $y = -1$. Once the value for one variable is known, this value should be substituted into either of the original equations to determine the value of the other variable. For the example, −1 would be substituted for y in either of the original equations. Substituting into the first equation results in:

$$x + 3(-1) = 7$$

74

and solving this equation yields $x = 10$. The solution to a system is an ordered pair, so the solution to the example is written as $(10, -1)$. The solution can be checked by substituting it into both equations of the system to ensure it results in two true statements.

Solving Systems of Equations with the Elimination Method

The elimination method for solving a system of equations involves canceling out (or eliminating) one of the variables. This method is typically used when both equations of a system are written in standard form:

$$(Ax + By = C)$$

An example is:

$$2x + 3y = 12; 5x - y = 13$$

To perform the elimination method, the equations in the system should be arranged vertically to be added together and then one or both of the equations should be multiplied so that one variable will be eliminated when the two are added. Opposites will cancel each other when added together. For example, $8x$ and $-8x$ will cancel each other when added. For the example above, writing the system vertically helps identify that the bottom equation should be multiplied by 3 to eliminate the variable y.

$$2x + 3y = 12 \quad \rightarrow \quad 2x + 3y = 12$$

$$3(5x - y = 13) \quad \rightarrow \quad 15x - 3y = 39$$

Adding the two equations together vertically results in $17x = 51$. Solving yields $x = 3$. Once the value for one variable is known, it can be substituted into either of the original equations to determine the value of the other variable. Once this is obtained, the solution can be written as an ordered pair (x, y) and checked in both equations of the system. In this example, the solution is $(3, 2)$.

Systems of Equations with No Solution or an Infinite Number of Solutions

A system of equations can have one solution, no solution, or an infinite number of solutions. If, while solving a system algebraically, both variables cancel out, then the system has either no solution or has an infinite number of solutions. If the remaining constants result in a true statement (ex., $7 = 7$), then there is an infinite number of solutions. This would indicate coinciding lines. If the remaining constants result in a false statement, then there is no solution to the system. This would indicate parallel lines.

Interpreting Variables and Constants in Expressions for Linear Functions in the Context Presented

Linear functions, also written as linear equations in two variables, can be written to model real-world scenarios. Questions on this material will provide information about a scenario and then request a linear equation to represent the scenario. The algebraic process for writing the equation will depend on the given information. The key to writing linear models is to decipher the information given to determine what it represents in the context of a linear equation (variables, slope, ordered pairs, etc.).

Identifying Variables for Linear Models

The first step to writing a linear model is to identify what the variables represent. A variable represents an unknown quantity, and in the case of a linear equation, a specific relationship exists between the two

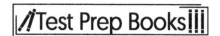
variables (usually x and y). Within a given scenario, the variables are the two quantities that are changing. The variable x is considered the independent variable and represents the inputs of a function. The variable y is considered the dependent variable and represents the outputs of a function. For example, if a scenario describes distance traveled and time traveled, distance would be represented by y and time represented by x. The distance traveled depends on the time spent traveling (time is independent). If a scenario describes the cost of a cab ride and the distance traveled, the cost would be represented by y and the distance represented by x. The cost of a cab ride depends on the distance traveled.

Identifying the Slope and Y-Intercept for Linear Models

The slope of the graph of a line represents the rate of change between the variables of an equation. In the context of a real-world scenario, the slope will tell the way in which the unknown quantities (variables) change with respect to each other. A scenario involving distance and time might state that someone is traveling at a rate of 45 miles per hour. The slope of the linear model would be 45. A scenario involving the cost of a cab ride and distance traveled might state that the person is charged $3 for each mile. The slope of the linear model would be 3.

The y-intercept of a linear function is the value of y when $x = 0$ (the point where the line intercepts the y-axis on the graph of the equation). It is sometimes helpful to think of this as a "starting point" for a linear function. Suppose for the scenario about the cab ride that the person is told that the cab company charges a flat fee of $5 plus $3 for each mile. Before traveling any distance ($x = 0$), the cost is $5. The y-intercept for the linear model would be 5.

Identifying Ordered Pairs for Linear Models

A linear equation with two variables can be written given a point (ordered pair) and the slope or given two points on a line. An ordered pair gives a set of corresponding values for the two variables (x and y). As an example, for a scenario involving distance and time, it is given that the person traveled 112.5 miles in 2 ½ hours. Knowing that x represents time and y represents distance, this information can be written as the ordered pair (2.5, 112.5).

Understanding Connections Between Algebraic and Graphical Representations

The solution set to a linear equation in two variables can be represented visually by a line graphed on the coordinate plane. Every point on this line represents an ordered pair (x, y), which makes the equation true. The process for graphing a line depends on the form in which its equation is written: slope-intercept form or standard form.

Graphing a Line in Slope-Intercept Form

When an equation is written in slope-intercept form, $y = mx + b$, m represents the slope of the line and b represents the y-intercept. The y-intercept is the value of y when $x = 0$ and the point at which the graph of the line crosses the y-axis. The slope is the rate of change between the variables, expressed as a fraction. The fraction expresses the change in y compared to the change in x. If the slope is an integer, it should be written as a fraction with a denominator of 1. For example, 5 would be written as 5/1.

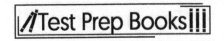

To graph a line given an equation in slope-intercept form, the y-intercept should first be plotted. For example, to graph:

$$y = -\frac{2}{3}x + 7$$

the y-intercept of 7 would be plotted on the y-axis (vertical axis) at the point $(0, 7)$. Next, the slope would be used to determine a second point for the line. Note that all that is necessary to graph a line is two points on that line. The slope will indicate how to get from one point on the line to another. The slope expresses vertical change (y) compared to horizontal change (x) and therefore is sometimes referred to as $\frac{rise}{run}$. The numerator indicates the change in the y value (move up for positive integers and move down for negative integers), and the denominator indicates the change in the x-value. For the previous example, using the slope of $-\frac{2}{3}$, from the first point at the y-intercept, the second point should be found by counting down 2 and to the right 3. This point would be located at $(3, 5)$.

If the midpoint of a line is needed, the midpoint formula can be used if the coordinates of the ends of the line segment are known. The midpoint formula is as follows:

$$M = (\frac{x_1 + x_2}{2}, \frac{y_1 + y_2}{2})$$

M is the midpoint and the coordinates of the two points are:

$$(x_1, y_1)$$

$$(x_2, y_2)$$

Graphing a Line in Standard Form
When an equation is written in standard form:

$$Ax + By = C$$

it is easy to identify the x- and y-intercepts for the graph of the line. Just as the y-intercept is the point at which the line intercepts the y-axis, the x-intercept is the point at which the line intercepts the x-axis. At the y-intercept, $x = 0$; and at the x-intercept, $y = 0$. Given an equation in standard form, $x = 0$ should be used to find the y-intercept. Likewise, $y = 0$ should be used to find the x-intercept. For example, to graph $3x + 2y = 6$, 0 for y results in:

$$3x + 2(0) = 6$$

Solving for y yields $x = 2$; therefore, an ordered pair for the line is $(2, 0)$. Substituting 0 for x results in $3(0) + 2y = 6$. Solving for y yields $y = 3$; therefore, an ordered pair for the line is $(0, 3)$. The two ordered pairs (the x- and y-intercepts) can be plotted, and a straight line through them can be constructed.

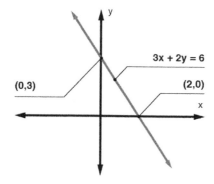

T - chart	
x	y
0	3
2	0

Intercepts

x - intercept : (2,0)

y - intercept : (0,3)

Writing the Equation of a Line Given its Graph

Given the graph of a line, its equation can be written in two ways. If the y-intercept is easily identified (is an integer), it and another point can be used to determine the slope. When determining $\frac{change\ in\ y}{change\ in\ x}$ from one point to another on the graph, the distance for $\frac{rise}{run}$ is being figured. The equation should be written in slope-intercept form, $y = mx + b$, with m representing the slope and b representing the y-intercept.

The equation of a line can also be written by identifying two points on the graph of the line. To do so, the slope is calculated and then the values are substituted for the slope and either of the ordered pairs into the point-slope form of an equation.

Vertical, Horizontal, Parallel, and Perpendicular Lines

For a vertical line, the value of x remains constant (for all ordered pairs (x, y) on the line, the value of x is the same); therefore, the equations for all vertical lines are written in the form $x = number$. For example, a vertical line that crosses the x-axis at -2 would have an equation of $x = -2$. For a horizontal line, the value of y remains constant; therefore, the equations for all horizontal lines are written in the form $y = number$.

Parallel lines extend in the same exact direction without ever meeting. Their equations have the same slopes and different y-intercepts. For example, given a line with an equation of $y = -3x + 2$, a parallel line would have a slope of -3 and a y-intercept of any value other than 2. Perpendicular lines intersect to form a right angle. Their equations have slopes that are opposite reciprocal (the sign is changed and the fraction is flipped; for example, $-\frac{2}{3}$ and $\frac{3}{2}$) and y-intercepts that may or may not be the same. For example, given a line with an equation of $y = \frac{1}{2}x + 7$, a perpendicular line would have a slope of $-\frac{2}{1}$ and any value for its y-intercept.

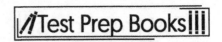

Problem-Solving and Data Analysis

Using Ratios, Rates, Proportions, and Scale Drawings to Solve Single- and Multistep Problems

Ratios, rates, proportions, and scale drawings are used when comparing two quantities. Questions on this material will include expressing relationships in simplest terms and solving for missing quantities.

Ratios

A ratio is a comparison of two quantities that represent separate groups. For example, if a recipe calls for 2 eggs for every 3 cups of milk, it can be expressed as a ratio. Ratios can be written three ways: (1) with the word "to"; (2) using a colon; or (3) as a fraction. For the previous example, the ratio of eggs to cups of milk can be written as: 2 to 3, 2:3, or $\frac{2}{3}$. When writing ratios, the order is important. The ratio of eggs to cups of milk is not the same as the ratio of cups of milk to eggs, 3:2.

In simplest form, both quantities of a ratio should be written as integers. These should also be reduced just as a fraction would be. For example, 5:10 would reduce to 1:2. Given a ratio where one or both quantities are expressed as a decimal or fraction, both should be multiplied by the same number to produce integers. To write the ratio $\frac{1}{3}$ to 2 in simplest form, both quantities should be multiplied by 3. The resulting ratio is 1 to 6.

When a problem involving ratios gives a comparison between two groups, then: (1) a total should be provided and a part should be requested; or (2) a part should be provided and a total should be requested. Consider the following:

> The ratio of boys to girls in the 11th grade is 5:4. If there is a total of 270 11th grade students, how many are girls?

To solve this, the total number of "ratio pieces" first needs to be determined. The total number of 11th grade students is divided into 9 pieces. The ratio of boys to total students is 5:9; and the ratio of girls to total students is 4:9. Knowing the total number of students, the number of girls can be determined by setting up a proportion:

$$\frac{4}{9} = \frac{x}{270}$$

Solving the proportion, it shows that there are 120 11th grade girls.

Rates

A rate is a ratio comparing two quantities expressed in different units. A unit rate is one in which the second is one unit. Rates often include the word *per*. Examples include miles per hour, beats per minute, and price per pound. The word *per* can be represented with a / symbol or abbreviated with the letter "p" and the units abbreviated. For example, miles per hour would be written mi/h. Given a rate that is not in simplest form (second quantity is not one unit), both quantities should be divided by the value of the second quantity. Suppose a patient had 99 heartbeats in 1½ minutes. To determine the heart rate, 1½ should divide both quantities. The result is 66 bpm.

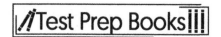

Scale Drawings

Scale drawings are used in designs to model the actual measurements of a real-world object. For example, the blueprint of a house might indicate that it is drawn at a scale of 3 inches to 8 feet. Given one value and asked to determine the width of the house, a proportion should be set up to solve the problem. Given the scale of 3in:8ft and a blueprint width of 1 ft (12 in.), to find the actual width of the building, the proportion:

$$\frac{3}{8} = \frac{12}{x}$$

should be used. This results in an actual width of 32 ft.

Proportions

A proportion is a statement consisting of two equal ratios. Proportions will typically give three of four quantities and require solving for the missing value. The key to solving proportions is to set them up properly. Here's a sample problem:

If 7 gallons of gas costs $14.70, how many gallons can you get for $20?

The information should be written as equal ratios with a variable representing the missing quantity:

$$\left(\frac{\text{gallons}}{\text{cost}} = \frac{\text{gallons}}{\text{cost}}\right) : \frac{7}{14.70} = \frac{x}{20}$$

To solve, cross multiplication (multiplying the numerator of the first ratio by the denominator of the second and vice versa) is used, and the products are set equal to each other. Cross-multiplying results in:

$$(7)(20) = (14.7)(x)$$

Solving the equation for x, it can be determined that 9.5 gallons of gas can be purchased for $20.

Indirect Proportions

The proportions described above are referred to as direct proportions or direct variation. For direct proportions, as one quantity increases, the other quantity also increases. For indirect proportions (also referred to as indirect variations, inverse proportions, or inverse variations), as one quantity increases, the other decreases. Direct proportions can be written:

$$\frac{y_1}{x_1} = \frac{y_2}{x_2}$$

Conversely, indirect proportions are written:

$$y_1 x_1 = y_2 x_2$$

Here's a sample problem:

It takes 3 carpenters 10 days to build the frame of a house. How long should it take 5 carpenters to build the same frame?

In this scenario, as one quantity increases (number of carpenters), the other decreases (number of days building); therefore, this is an inverse proportion. To solve, the products of the two variables (in this scenario, the total work performed) are set equal to each other:

$$(y_1 x_1 = y_2 x_2)$$

Using y to represent carpenters and x to represent days, the resulting equation is:

$$(3)(10) = (5)(x_2)$$

Solving for x_2, it is determined that it should take 5 carpenters 6 days to build the frame of the house.

Solving Single- and Multistep Problems Involving Percentages

The word percent means "per hundred." When dealing with percentages, it may be helpful to think of the number as a value in hundredths. For example, 15% can be expressed as "fifteen hundredths" and written as $\frac{15}{100}$ or .15.

Converting from Decimals and Fractions to Percentages

To convert a decimal to a percent, a number is multiplied by 100. To write .25 as a percent, the equation .25 × 100 yields 25%. To convert a fraction to a percent, the fraction is converted to a decimal and then multiplied by 100. To convert $\frac{3}{5}$ to a decimal, the numerator (3) is divided by the denominator (5). This results in .6, which is then multiplied by 100 to get 60%.

To convert a percent to a decimal, the number is divided by 100. For example, 150% is equal to 1.5 $\left(\frac{150}{100}\right)$. To convert a percent to a fraction, the percent sign is deleted, and the value is written as the numerator with a denominator of 100. For example:

$$2\% = \frac{2}{100}$$

Fractions should be reduced:

$$\frac{2}{100} = \frac{1}{50}$$

Percent Problems

Material on percentages can include questions such as: What is 15% of 25? What percent of 45 is 3? Five is $\frac{1}{2}$% of what number? To solve these problems, the information should be rewritten as an equation where the following helpful steps are completed: (1) "what" is represented by a variable (x); (2) "is" is represented by an = sign; and (3) "of" is represented by multiplication. Any values expressed as a percent should be written as a decimal; and if the question is asking for a percent, the answer should be converted accordingly. Here are three sample problems based on the information above:

What is 15% of 25?	What percent of 45 is 3?	Five is $\frac{1}{2}$% of what number?
$x = .15 \times 25$	$x \times 45 = 3$	$5 = .005 \times x$
$x = 3.75$	$x = 0.0\overline{6}$	$x = 1{,}000$
	$x = 6.\overline{6}\%$	

Percent Increase/Decrease

Problems dealing with percentages may involve an original value, a change in that value, and a percentage change. A problem will provide two pieces of information and ask to find the third. To do so, this formula is used:

$$\frac{change}{original\ value} \times 100 = percent\ change$$

Here's a sample problem:

> Attendance at a baseball stadium has dropped 16% from last year. Last year's average attendance was 40,000. What is this year's average attendance?

Using the formula and information, the change is unknown (x), the original value is 40,000, and the percent change is 16%. The formula can be written as:

$$\frac{x}{40,000} \times 100 = 16$$

When solving for x, it is determined the change was 6,400. The problem asked for this year's average attendance, so to calculate, the change (6,400) is subtracted from last year's attendance (40,000) to determine this year's average attendance is 33,600.

Percent More Than/Less Than

Percentage problems may give a value and what percent that given value is more than or less than an original unknown value. Here's a sample problem:

> A store advertises that all its merchandise has been reduced by 25%. The new price of a pair of shoes is $60. What was the original price?

This problem can be solved by writing a proportion. Two ratios should be written comparing the cost and the percent of the original cost. The new cost is 75% of the original cost (100% - 25%), and the original cost is 100% of the original cost. The unknown original cost can be represented by x. The proportion would be set up as:

$$\frac{60}{75} = \frac{x}{100}$$

Solving the proportion, it is determined the original cost was $80.

Solving Single- and Multistep Problems Involving Measurement Quantities, Units, and Unit Conversion

Unit Rates

A rate is a ratio in which two terms are in different units. When rates are expressed as a quantity of one, they are considered unit rates. To determine a unit rate, the first quantity is divided by the second. Knowing a unit rate makes calculations easier than simply having a rate. Suppose someone bought a

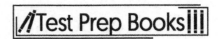

3 lbs bag of onions for $1.77. To calculate the price of 5lbs of onions, a proportion could be set up as follows:

$$\frac{3}{1.77} = \frac{5}{x}$$

However, knowing the unit rate, multiplying the value of pounds of onions by the unit price is another way to find the solution: (The unit price would be calculated $\frac{\$1.77}{3 \text{ lbs}} = \frac{\$0.59}{\text{lb}}$ or $0.59 per pound.)

$$5 \text{ lbs} \times \frac{\$.59}{\text{lb}} = \$2.95 \text{ (The "lbs" units cancel out.)}$$

Unit Conversion

Unit conversions apply to many real-world scenarios, including cooking, measurement, construction, and currency. Problems on this material can be solved similarly to those involving unit rates. Given the conversion rate, it can be written as a fraction (ratio) and multiplied by a quantity in one unit to convert it to the corresponding unit. For example, someone might want to know how many minutes are in 3½ hours. The conversion rate of 60 minutes to 1 hour can be written as:

$$\frac{60 \text{ min}}{1 \text{ h}}$$

Multiplying the quantity by the conversion rate results in:

$$3\frac{1}{2} \text{ h} \times \frac{60 \text{ min}}{1 \text{ h}} = 210 \text{ min}$$

The "h" unit is canceled. To convert a quantity in minutes to hours, the fraction for the conversion rate would be flipped (to cancel the "min" unit). To convert 195 minutes to hours, the equation:

$$195 \text{ min} \times \frac{1 \text{ h}}{60 \text{ min}}$$

would be used. The result is $\frac{195 \text{ h}}{60}$, which reduces to $3\frac{1}{4}$ hours.

Converting units may require more than one multiplication. The key is to set up the conversion rates so that units cancel out each other and the desired unit is left. Suppose someone wants to convert 3.25 yards to inches, given that 1 yd = 3 ft and 12 in = 1 ft. To calculate, the equation:

$$3.25 \text{ yd} \times \frac{3 \text{ ft}}{1 \text{ yd}} \times \frac{12 \text{ in}}{1 \text{ ft}}$$

would be used. The "yd" and "ft" units will cancel, resulting in 117 inches.

Given a Scatterplot, Using Linear, Quadratic, or Exponential Models to Describe How Variables are Related

Scatterplots can be used to determine whether a correlation exists between two variables. The horizontal (x) axis represents the independent variable and the vertical (y) axis represents the dependent variable. If when graphed, the points model a linear, quadratic, or exponential relationship, then a correlation is said to exist. If so, a line of best-fit or curve of best-fit can be drawn through the points, with the points relatively close on either side. Writing the equation for the line or curve allows for predicting values for the variables. Suppose a scatterplot displays the value of an investment as a function of years after investing. By writing an equation for the line or curve and substituting a value for one variable into the equation, the corresponding value for the other variable can be calculated.

Linear Models
If the points of a scatterplot model a linear relationship, a line of best-fit is drawn through the points. If the line of best-fit has a positive slope (y-values increase as x-values increase), then the variables have a positive correlation. If the line of best-fit has a negative slope (y-values decrease as x-values increase), then a negative correlation exists. A positive or negative correlation can also be categorized as strong or weak, depending on how closely the points are grouped around the line of best-fit.

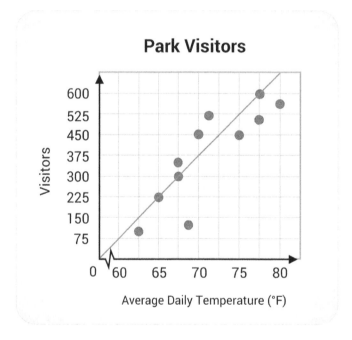

Given a line of best-fit, its equation can be written by identifying: the slope and y-intercept; a point and the slope; or two points on the line.

Quadratic Models
A quadratic function can be written in the form:

$$y = ax^2 + bx + c$$

The u-shaped graph of a quadratic function is called a parabola. The graph can either open up or open down (upside down u). The graph is symmetric about a vertical line, called the axis of symmetry. Corresponding points on the parabola are directly across from each other (same y-value) and are the same distance from the axis of symmetry (on either side). The axis of symmetry intersects the parabola at its vertex. The y-value of the vertex represents the minimum or maximum value of the function. If the

84

graph opens up, the value of a in its equation is positive, and the vertex represents the minimum of the function. If the graph opens down, the value of a in its equation is negative, and the vertex represents the maximum of the function.

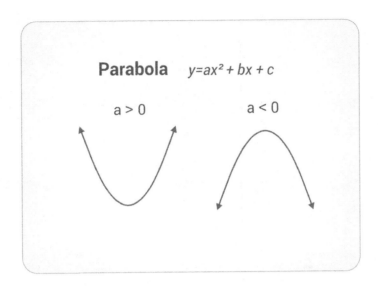

Given a curve of best-fit that models a quadratic relationship, the equation of the parabola can be written by identifying the vertex of the parabola and another point on the graph. The values for the vertex (h, k) and the point (x, y) should be substituted into the vertex form of a quadratic function:

$$y = a(x - h)^2 + k$$

to determine the value of a. To write the equation of a quadratic function with a vertex of $(4, 7)$ and containing the point $(8, 3)$, the values for h, k, x, and y should be substituted into the vertex form of a quadratic function, resulting in:

$$3 = a(8 - 4)^2 + 7$$

Solving for a, yields $a = -\frac{1}{4}$. Therefore, the equation of the function can be written as:

$$y = -\frac{1}{4}(x - 4)^2 + 7$$

The vertex form can be manipulated in order to write the quadratic function in standard form.

Exponential Models

An exponential curve can be used as a curve of best-fit for a scatterplot. The general form for an exponential function is:

$$y = ab^x$$

where b must be a positive number and cannot equal 1. When the value of b is greater than 1, the function models exponential growth (as x increases, y increases). When the value of b is less than 1, the function models exponential decay (as x increases, y decreases). If a is positive, the graph consists of points above the x-axis; if a is negative, the graph consists of points below the x-axis.

An asymptote is a line that a graph approaches.

Exponential Curve

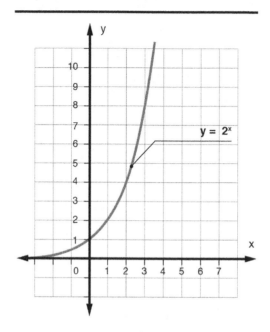

Given a curve of best-fit modeling an exponential function, its equation can be written by identifying two points on the curve. To write the equation of an exponential function containing the ordered pairs $(2, 2)$ and $(3, 4)$, the ordered pair $(2, 2)$ should be substituted in the general form and solved for a:

$$2 = a \times b^2 \rightarrow a = \frac{2}{b^2}$$

The ordered pair $(3, 4)$ and $\frac{2}{b^2}$ should be substituted in the general form and solved for b

$$4 = \frac{2}{b^2} \times b^3 \rightarrow b = 2$$

Then, 2 should be substituted for b in the equation for a and then solved for a:

$$a = \frac{2}{2^2} \rightarrow a = \frac{1}{2}$$

Knowing the values of a and b, the equation can be written as:

$$y = \frac{1}{2} \times 2^x$$

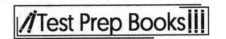
Using the Relationship Between Two Variables to Investigate Key Features of a Graph

Material on graphing relationships between two variables may include linear, quadratic, and exponential functions. Graphing linear functions is covered in a previous section.

Graphing Quadratic Functions

The standard form of a quadratic function is:

$$y = ax^2 + bx + c$$

The graph of a quadratic function is a u-shaped (or upside down u) curve, called a parabola, which is symmetric about a vertical line (axis of symmetry). To graph a parabola, its vertex (high or low point for the curve) and at least two points on each side of the axis of symmetry need to be determined.

Given a quadratic function in standard form, the axis of symmetry for its graph is the line:

$$x = -\frac{b}{2a}$$

The vertex for the parabola has an x-coordinate of $-\frac{b}{2a}$. To find the y-coordinate for the vertex, the calculated x-coordinate needs to be substituted. To complete the graph, two different x-values need to be selected and substituted into the quadratic function to obtain the corresponding y-values. This will give two points on the parabola. These two points and the axis of symmetry are used to determine the two points corresponding to these. The corresponding points are the same distance from the axis of symmetry (on the other side) and contain the same y-coordinate.

Plotting the vertex and four other points on the parabola allows for constructing the curve.

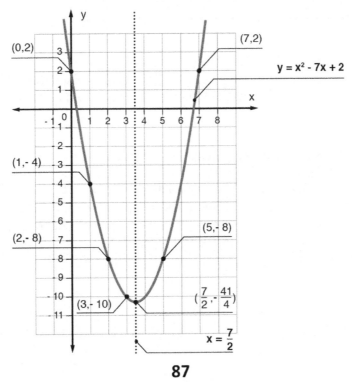

87

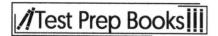
Graphing Exponential Functions

Exponential functions have a general form of:

$$y = a \times b^x$$

The graph of an exponential function is a curve that slopes upward or downward from left to right. The graph approaches a line, called an asymptote, as x or y increases or decreases. To graph the curve for an exponential function, x-values are selected and then substituted into the function to obtain the corresponding y-values. A general rule of thumb is to select three negative values, zero, and three positive values. Plotting the seven points on the graph for an exponential function should allow for constructing a smooth curve through them.

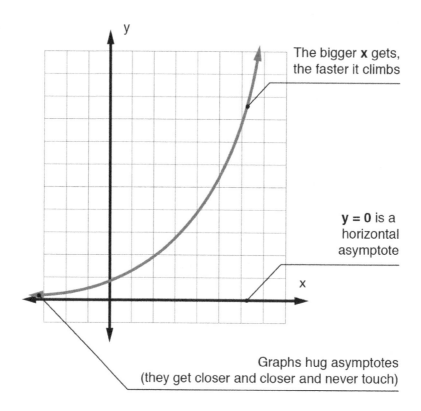

The bigger **x** gets, the faster it climbs

y = 0 is a horizontal asymptote

Graphs hug asymptotes (they get closer and closer and never touch)

Comparing Linear Growth with Exponential Growth

Both linear and exponential equations can model a relationship of growth or decay between two variables. If the dependent variable (y) increases as the independent variable (x) increases, the relationship is referred to as growth. If y decreases as x increases, the relationship is referred to as decay.

Linear Growth and Decay

A linear function can be written in the form:

$$y = mx + b$$

where x represents the inputs, y represents the outputs, b represents the y-intercept for the graph, and m represents the slope of the line. The y-intercept is the value of y when $x = 0$ and can be thought of as the "starting point." The slope is the rate of change between the variables x and y. A positive slope represents growth; a negative slope represents decay. Given a table of values for inputs (x) and outputs (y), a linear function would model the relationship if: x and y change at a constant rate per unit interval—for every two inputs a given distance apart, the distance between their corresponding outputs is constant. Here are some sample ordered pairs:

x	0	1	2	3
y	-7	-4	-1	2

For every 1 unit increase in x, y increases by 3 units. Therefore, the change is constant and thus represents linear growth.

Given a scenario involving growth or decay, determining if there is a constant rate of change between inputs (x) and outputs (y) will identify if a linear model is appropriate. A scenario involving distance and time might state that someone is traveling at a rate of 45 miles per hour. For every hour traveled (input), the distance traveled (output) increases by 45 miles. This is a constant rate of change.

The process for writing the equation to represent a linear model is covered in the section *Writing Linear Equations in Two Variables*.

Exponential Growth and Decay

An exponential function can be written in the form:

$$y = a \times b^x$$

The x- variable represents the inputs, y represents the outputs, a represents the y-intercept for the graph, and b represents the growth rate. The y-intercept is the value of y when $x = 0$ and can be thought of as the "starting point." If b is greater than 1, the function describes exponential growth; and if b is less than 1, the function describes exponential decay. Given a table of values for inputs (x) and outputs (y), an exponential function would model the relationship if the variables change by a common ratio over given intervals—for every two inputs a given distance apart, the quotients of their corresponding outputs is constant. Here are some sample ordered pairs:

x	0	1	2	3
y	3	6	12	24

For every 1 unit increase in x, the quotient of the corresponding y-values equals 2 (e.g., $\frac{6}{3}, \frac{12}{6}, \frac{24}{12}$). Therefore, the table represents exponential growth.

Given a scenario describing an exponential function, the growth or decay is expressed using multiplication. Words such as "doubling" and "halving" will often be used. A problem might indicate that

the value of an investment triples every year or that every decade the population of an insect is halved. These indicate exponential growth and decay.

The process for writing the equation to represent an exponential model is covered in a previous section.

Using Two-Way Tables to Summarize Categorical Data and Relative Frequencies, and Calculate Conditional Probability

Categorical data consists of numerical values found by dividing the entire set into subsets based on variables that represent categories. An example would be the survey results of high school seniors, specifying gender and asking whether they consume alcohol. The data can be arranged in a two-way frequency table (also called a contingency table).

Two-Way Frequency/Contingency Tables

A contingency table presents the frequency tables of both variables simultaneously, as shown below. The levels of one variable constitute the rows of the table, and the levels of the other constitute the columns. The margins consist of the sum of cell frequencies for each row and each column (marginal frequencies). The lower right corner value is the sum of marginal frequencies for the rows or the sum of the marginal frequencies for the columns. Both are equal to the total sample size.

	Drink Alcohol	Do Not Drink Alcohol	Total
Male	63	51	114
Female	37	68	105
Total	100	119	219

Conditional Frequencies

To calculate a conditional relative frequency, the cell frequency is divided by the marginal frequency for the desired outcome given the conditional category. For instance, using the table to determine the relative frequency that a female drinks, the number of females who drink (desired outcome) is divided by the total number of females (conditional category). The conditional relative frequency would equal $\frac{37}{105}$, which equals .35. If a problem asks for a conditional probability, the answer would be expressed as a fraction in simplest form. If asked for a percent, multiply the decimal by 100.

Association of Variables

An association between the variables exists if the conditional relative frequencies are different depending on condition. If the conditional relative frequencies are close to equal, then the variables are independent. For our example, 55% of senior males and 35% of senior females drink alcohol. The difference between frequencies across conditions (male or female) is enough to conclude that an association exists between the variables.

Making Inferences about Population Parameters Based on Sample Data

Statistical inference, based in probability theory, makes calculated assumptions about an entire population based on data from a sample set from that population.

Population Parameters

A population is the entire set of people or things of interest. Suppose a study is intended to determine the number of hours of sleep per night for college females in the U.S. The population would consist of

EVERY college female in the country. A sample is a subset of the population that may be used for the study. It would not be practical to survey every female college student, so a sample might consist of 100 students per school from 20 different colleges in the country. From the results of the survey, a sample statistic can be calculated. A sample statistic is a numerical characteristic of the sample data, including mean and variance. A sample statistic can be used to estimate a corresponding population parameter. A population parameter is a numerical characteristic of the entire population. Suppose the sample data had a mean (average) of 5.5. This sample statistic can be used as an estimate of the population parameter (average hours of sleep for every college female in the U.S.).

Confidence Intervals

A population parameter is usually unknown and therefore is estimated using a sample statistic. This estimate may be highly accurate or relatively inaccurate based on errors in sampling. A confidence interval indicates a range of values likely to include the true population parameter. These are constructed at a given confidence level, such as 95%. This means that if the same population is sampled repeatedly, the true population parameter would occur within the interval for 95% of the samples.

Measurement Error

The accuracy of a population parameter based on a sample statistic may also be affected by measurement error, which is the difference between a quantity's true value and its measured value. Measurement error can be divided into random error and systematic error. An example of random error for the previous scenario would be a student reporting 8 hours of sleep when she actually sleeps 7 hours per night. Systematic errors are those attributed to the measurement system. Suppose the sleep survey gave response options of 2, 4, 6, 8, or 10 hours. This would lead to systematic measurement error.

Using Statistics to Investigate Measures of Center of Data and Analyzing Shape, Center, and Spread

Descriptive statistics are used to gain an understanding of properties of a data set. This entails examining the center, spread, and shape of the sample data.

Center

The center of the sample set can be represented by its mean, median, or mode. The mean is the average of the data set, calculated by adding the data values and dividing by the sample size. The median is the value of the data point in the middle when the sample is arranged in numerical order. If the sample has an even number of data points, the mean of the two middle values is the median. The mode is the value that appears most often in a data set. It is possible to have multiple modes (if different values repeat equally as often) or no mode (if no value repeats).

Spread

Methods for determining the spread of the sample include calculating the range and standard deviation for the data. The range is calculated by subtracting the lowest value from the highest value in the set. The standard deviation of the sample can be calculated using the formula:

$$\sigma = \sqrt{\frac{\sum(x - \bar{x})^2}{n - 1}}$$

where $\bar{x}$ = sample mean and n = sample size.

Shape

The shape of the sample when displayed as a histogram or frequency distribution plot helps to determine if the sample is normally distributed (bell-shaped curve), symmetrical, or has measures of skewness (lack of symmetry) or kurtosis. Kurtosis is a measure of whether the data are heavy-tailed (high number of outliers) or light-tailed (low number of outliers).

Evaluating Reports to Make Inferences, Justify Conclusions, and Determine Appropriateness of Data Collection Methods

The presentation of statistics can be manipulated to produce a desired outcome. Here's a statement to consider: "Four out of five dentists recommend our toothpaste." Who are the five dentists? This statement is very different from the statement: "Four out of every five dentists recommend our toothpaste." Whether intentional or unintentional, statistics can be misleading. Statistical reports should be examined to verify the validity and significance of the results. The context of the numerical values allows for deciphering the meaning, intent, and significance of the survey or study. Questions on this material will require students to use critical thinking skills to justify or reject results and conclusions.

When analyzing a report, who conducted the study and their intent should be considered. Was it performed by a neutral party or by a person or group with a vested interest? A study on health risks of smoking performed by a health insurance company would have a much different intent than one performed by a cigarette company. The sampling method and the data collection method should be considered too. Was it a true random sample of the population or was one subgroup over- or underrepresented? The sleep study scenario from the previous section is one example. If all 20 schools included in the study were state colleges, the results may be biased due to a lack of private school participants. Also, the measurement system used to obtain the data should be noted. Was the system accurate and precise or was it a flawed system? If possible responses were limited for the sleep study to 2, 4, 6, 8, or 10, it could be argued that the measurement system was flawed.

Every scenario involving statistical reports will be different. The key is to examine all aspects of the study before determining whether to accept or reject the results and corresponding conclusions.

Passport to Advanced Math

Creating a Quadratic or Exponential Function

Quadratic Models
A quadratic function can be written in the standard form:

$$y = ax^2 + bx + c$$

It can be represented by a u-shaped graph called a parabola. For a quadratic function where the value of a is positive, as the inputs increase, the outputs increase until a certain value (maximum of the function) is reached. As inputs increase past the value that corresponds with the maximum output, the relationship reverses, and the outputs decrease. For a quadratic function where a is negative, as the inputs increase, the outputs (1) decrease, (2) reach a maximum, and (3) then increase.

Consider a ball thrown straight up into the air. As time passes, the height of the ball increases until it reaches its maximum height. After reaching the maximum height, as time increases, the height of the

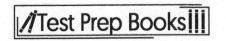

ball decreases (it is falling toward the ground). This relationship can be expressed as a quadratic function where time is the input (x), and the height of the ball is the output (y).

Given a scenario that can be modeled by a quadratic function, to write its equation, the following is needed: its vertex and any other ordered pair; or any three ordered pairs for the function. Given three ordered pairs, they should be substituted into the general form

$$(y = ax^2 + bx + c)$$

to create a system of three equations. For example, given the ordered pairs (2, 3), (3, 13), and (4, 29), it yields:

$$3 = a(2)^2 + b(2) + c \rightarrow 4a + 2b + c = 3$$

$$13 = a(3)^2 + b(3) + c \rightarrow 9a + 3b + c = 13$$

$$29 = a(4)^2 + b(4) + c \rightarrow 16a + 4b + c = 29$$

The values for a, b, and c in the system can be found and substituted into the general form to write the equation of the function. In this case, the equation is:

$$y = 3x^2 - 5x + 1$$

Exponential Models

Exponential functions can be written in the form:

$$y = a \times b^x$$

Scenarios involving growth and decay can be modeled by exponential functions.

The equation for an exponential function can be written given the y-intercept (a) and the growth rate (b). The y-intercept is the output (y) when the input (x) equals zero. It can be thought of as an "original value" or starting point. The value of b is the rate at which the original value increases ($b > 1$) or decreases ($b < 1$). Suppose someone deposits \$1,200 into a bank account that accrues 1% interest per month. The y-intercept, a, would be \$1,200, while the growth rate, b, would be 1.01 (100% of the original value + 1% interest). This scenario could be written as the exponential function:

$$y = 1,200 \times 1.01^x$$

The x-variable represents the number of months since the deposit and y represents money in the account.

Given a scenario that models an exponential function, the equation can also be written when provided two ordered pairs.

Determining the Most Suitable Form of an Expression

It is possible for algebraic expressions and equations to be written that look completely different, yet are still equivalent. For instance, the expression $4(2x - 3) - 3x + 5$ is equivalent to the expression $5x - 7$. Given two algebraic expressions, it can be determined if they are equivalent by writing them in simplest form. Distribution should be used, if applicable, and like terms should be combined. Given two

93

algebraic equations, it can be determined if they are equivalent by solving each for the same variable. Here are two sample equations to consider:

$$3x - 4y = 7$$

and

$$x + 2 = \frac{4}{3}y + 4\frac{1}{3}$$

To determine if they are equivalent, solving for x is required.

$$3x - 4y = 7 \qquad\qquad x + 2 = \frac{4}{3}y + 4\frac{1}{3}$$

$$3x = 4y + 7 \qquad\qquad x = \frac{4}{3}y + 2\frac{1}{3}$$

$$x = \frac{4}{3}y + \frac{7}{3} \qquad\qquad x = \frac{4}{3}y + 2\frac{1}{3}$$

The equations are equivalent.

Equivalent Forms of Functions

Equations in two variables can often be written in different forms to easily recognize a given trait of the function or its graph. Linear equations written in slope-intercept form allow for recognition of the slope and y-intercept; linear equations written in standard form allow for identification of the x and y-intercepts. Quadratic functions written in standard form allow for identification of the y-intercept and for easy calculation of outputs; quadratic functions written in vertex form allow for identification of the function's minimum or maximum output and its graph's vertex. Polynomial functions written in factored form allow for identification of the zeros of the function.

The method of substituting the same inputs (x-values) into functions to determine if they produce the same outputs can reveal if functions are not equivalent (different outputs). However, corresponding inputs and outputs do not necessarily indicate equivalent functions.

Create Equivalent Expressions Involving Rational Exponents

Converting To and From Radical Form

Algebraic expressions involving radicals ($\sqrt{}$, $\sqrt[3]{}$, etc.) can be written without the radical by using rational (fraction) exponents. For radical expressions, the value under the root symbol is called the radicand, and the type of root determines the index. For example, the expression $\sqrt{6x}$ has a radicand of $6x$ and an index of 2 (it is a square root). If the exponent of the radicand is 1, then:

$$\sqrt[n]{a} = a^{\frac{1}{n}}$$

The n-variable is the index. A number or variable without a power has an implied exponent of 1.

For example:

$$\sqrt{6} = 6^{\frac{1}{2}}$$

and

$$125^{\frac{1}{3}} = \sqrt[3]{125}$$

For any exponent of the radicand:

$$\sqrt[n]{a^m} = \left(\sqrt[n]{a}\right)^m = a^{\frac{m}{n}}$$

For example:

$$64^{\frac{5}{3}} = \sqrt[3]{64^5} \text{ or } \left(\sqrt[3]{64}\right)^5$$

and

$$(xy)^{\frac{2}{3}} = \sqrt[3]{(xy)^2} \text{ or } \left(\sqrt[3]{xy}\right)^2$$

Simplifying Expressions with Rational Exponents

When simplifying expressions with rational exponents, all basic properties for exponents hold true. When multiplying powers of the same base (same value with or without the same exponent), the exponents are added. For example:

$$x^{\frac{2}{7}} \times x^{\frac{3}{14}} = x^{\frac{1}{2}} \left(\frac{2}{7} + \frac{3}{14} = \frac{1}{2}\right)$$

When dividing powers of the same base, the exponents are subtracted. For example:

$$\frac{5^{\frac{2}{3}}}{5^{\frac{1}{2}}} = 5^{\frac{1}{6}} \left(\frac{2}{3} - \frac{1}{2} = \frac{1}{6}\right)$$

When raising a power to a power, the exponents are multiplied. For example:

$$\left(5^{\frac{1}{2}}\right)^4 = 5^2 \left(\frac{1}{2} \times 4 = 2\right)$$

When simplifying expressions with exponents, a number should never be raised to a power or a negative exponent. If a number has an integer exponent, its value should be determined. If the number has a rational exponent, it should be rewritten as a radical and the value determined if possible. A base with a negative exponent moves from the numerator to the denominator of a fraction (or vice versa) and is written with a positive exponent.

For example:

$$x^{-3} = \frac{1}{x^3}$$

and

$$\frac{2}{5x^{-2}} = \frac{2x^2}{5}$$

The exponent of 5 is 1, and therefore the 5 does not move.

Here's a sample expression:

$$(27x^{-9})^{\frac{1}{3}}$$

After the implied exponents are noted, a power should be raised to a power by multiplying exponents, which yields $27^{\frac{1}{3}}x^{-3}$. Next, the negative exponent is eliminated by moving the base and power:

$$\frac{27^{\frac{1}{3}}}{x^3}$$

Then the value of the number is determined to a power by writing it in radical form:

$$\frac{\sqrt[3]{27}}{x^3}$$

Simplifying yields $\frac{3}{x^3}$.

Creating an Equivalent Form of an Algebraic Expression

There are many different ways to write algebraic expressions and equations that are equivalent to each other. Converting expressions from standard form to factored form and vice versa are skills commonly used in advanced mathematics. Standard form of an expression arranges terms with variables powers in descending order (highest exponent to lowest and then constants). Factored form displays an expression as the product of its factors (what can be multiplied to produce the expression).

Converting Standard Form to Factored Form

To factor an expression, a greatest common factor needs to be factored out first. Then, if possible, the remaining expression needs to be factored into the product of binomials. A binomial is an expression with two terms.

Greatest Common Factor

The greatest common factor (GCF) of a monomial (one term) consists of the largest number that divides evenly into all coefficients (number part of a term), and if all terms contain the same variable, the variable with the lowest exponent. The GCF of $3x^4 - 9x^3 + 12x^2$ would be $3x^2$. To write the factored expression, every term needs to be divided by the GCF, then the product of the resulting quotient and

96

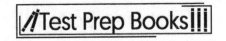

the GCF (using parentheses to show multiplication) should be written. For the previous example, the factored expression would be:

$$3x^2(x^2 - 3x + 4)$$

Factoring Ax² + Bx + C When A = 1

To factor a quadratic expression in standard form when the value of a is not equal to 1, the factors that multiply to equal the value of $a \times c$ should be found and then added to equal the value of b. Next, the expression splitting the bx term should be rewritten using those factors. Instead of three terms, there will now be four. Then the first two terms should be factored using GCF, and a common binomial should be factored from the last two terms. The factored form will be: (common binomial) (2 terms out of binomials). In the sample expression $2x^2 + 11x + 12$, the value of $a \times c$ (or 2×12) equals 24.

Two factors that multiply to 24 and added together to yield b (11) are 8 and 3. The bx term ($11x$) can be rewritten by splitting it into the factors:

$$2x^2 + 8x + 3x + 12$$

A GCF from the first two terms can be factored as:

$$2x(x + 4) + 3x + 12$$

A common binomial from the last two terms can then be factored as:

$$2x(x + 4) + 3(x + 4)$$

The factored form can be written as a product of binomials:

$$(x + 4)(2x + 3)$$

Converting Factored Form to Standard Form

To convert an expression from factored form to standard form, the factors are multiplied.

Solving a Quadratic Equation

A quadratic equation is one in which the highest exponent of the variable is 2. A quadratic equation can have two, one, or zero real solutions. Depending on its structure, a quadratic equation can be solved by (1) factoring, (2) taking square roots, or (3) using the quadratic formula.

Solving Quadratic Equations by Factoring

To solve a quadratic equation by factoring, the equation should first be manipulated to set the quadratic expression equal to zero. Next, the quadratic expression should be factored using the appropriate method(s). Then each factor should be set equal to zero. If two factors multiply to equal zero, then one or both factors must equal zero. Finally, each equation should be solved. Here's a sample:

$$x^2 - 10 = 3x - 6$$

The expression should be set equal to zero:

$$x^2 - 3x - 4 = 0$$

The expression should be factored:

$$(x - 4)(x + 1) = 0$$

Each factor should be set equal to zero: $x - 4 = 0$; $x + 1 = 0$. Solving yields $x = 4$ or $x = -1$.

Completing the Square

Completing the square is one way to find zeros when factoring is not an option. The following equation cannot be factored:

$$x^2 + 10x - 9 = 0$$

The first step in this method is to move the constant to the right side of the equation, making it:

$$x^2 + 10x = 9$$

Then, the coefficient of x is divided by 2 and squared. This number is then added to both sides of the equation, to make the equation still true. For this example:

$$\left(\frac{10}{2}\right)^2 = 25$$

is added to both sides of the equation to obtain:

$$x^2 + 10x + 25 = 9 + 25$$

This expression simplifies to $x^2 + 10x + 25 = 34$, which can then be factored into:

$$(x + 5)^2 = 34$$

Solving for x then involves taking the square root of both sides and subtracting 5. This leads to two zeros of the function:

$$x = \pm\sqrt{34} - 5$$

Depending on the type of answer the question seeks, a calculator may be used to find exact numbers.

Solving Quadratic Equations by Taking Square Roots

If a quadratic equation does not have a linear term (variable to the first power), it can be solved by taking square roots. This means x^2 needs to be isolated and then the square root of both sides of the equation should be isolated. There will be two solutions because square roots can be positive or negative. ($\sqrt{4} = 2$ or -2 because $2 \times 2 = 4$ and $-2 \times -2 = 4$.) Here's a sample equation:

$$3x^2 - 12 = 0$$

Isolating x^2 yields $x^2 = 4$. The square root of both sides is then solved: $x = 2$ or -2.

The Quadratic Formula

When a quadratic expression cannot be factored or is difficult to factor, the quadratic formula can be used to solve the equation. To do so, the equation must be in the form:

$$ax^2 + bx + c = 0$$

98

The quadratic formula is:

$$x = \frac{-b \pm \sqrt{b^2 - 4ac}}{2a}$$

(The $\pm$ symbol indicates that two calculations are necessary, one using $+$ and one using $-$.) Here's a sample equation:

$$3x^2 - 2x = 3x + 2$$

First, the quadratic expression should be set equal to zero:

$$3x^2 - 5x - 2 = 0$$

Then the values are substituted for a (3), b (-5), and c (-2) into the formula:

$$x = \frac{-(-5) \pm \sqrt{(-5)^2 - 4(3)(-2)}}{2(3)}$$

Simplification yields:

$$x = \frac{5 \pm \sqrt{49}}{6} \rightarrow x = \frac{5 \pm 7}{6}$$

Calculating two values for x using $+$ and $-$ yields:

$$x = \frac{5 + 7}{6} ; x = \frac{5 - 7}{6}$$

Simplification yields:

$$x = 2 \text{ or } -\frac{1}{3}$$

Just as with any equation, solutions should be checked by substituting the value into the original equation.

Adding, Subtracting, and Multiplying Polynomial Expressions

A polynomial expression is a monomial (one term) or the sum of monomials (more than one term separated by addition or subtraction). A polynomial in standard form consists of terms with variables written in descending exponential order and with any like terms combined.

Adding/Subtracting Polynomials
When adding or subtracting polynomials, each polynomial should be written in parenthesis; the negative sign should be distributed when necessary, and like terms need to be combined. Here's a sample equation: add $3x^3 + 4x - 3$ to $x^3 - 3x^2 + 2x - 2$. The sum is set as follows:

$$(x^3 - 3x^2 + 2x - 2) + (3x^3 + 4x - 3)$$

In front of each set of parentheses is an implied positive 1, which, when distributed, does not change any of the terms. Therefore, the parentheses should be dropped and like terms should be combined:

$$x^3 - 3x^2 + 2x - 2 + 3x^3 + 4x - 3$$

$$4x^3 - 3x^2 + 6x - 5$$

Here's another sample equation: subtract $3x^3 + 4x - 3$ from $x^3 - 3x^2 + 2x - 2$. The difference should be set as follows:

$$(x^3 - 3x^2 + 2x - 2) - (3x^3 + 4x - 3)$$

The implied $+1$ in front of the first set of parentheses will not change those four terms; however, distributing the implied -1 in front of the second set of parentheses will change the sign of each of those three terms:

$$x^3 - 3x^2 + 2x - 2 - 3x^3 - 4x + 3$$

Combining like terms yields:

$$-2x^3 - 3x^2 - 2x + 1$$

Multiplying Polynomials

When multiplying monomials, the coefficients are multiplied, and exponents of the same variable are added. For example:

$$-5x^3y^2z \times 2x^2y^5z^3 = -10x^5y^7z^4$$

When multiplying polynomials, the monomials should be distributed and multiplied, then any like terms should be combined and written in standard form. Here's a sample equation:

$$2x^3(3x^2 + 2x - 4)$$

First, $2x^3$ should be multiplied by each of the three terms in parentheses:

$$2x^3 \times 3x^2 + 2x^3 \times 2x + 2x^3 \times -4$$

$$6x^5 + 4x^4 - 8x^3$$

Multiplying binomials will sometimes be taught using the FOIL method (where the products of the first, outside, inside, and last terms are added together). However, it may be easier and more consistent to think of it in terms of distributing. Both terms of the first binomial should be distributed to both terms of the second binomial. For example, the product of binomials $(2x + 3)(x - 4)$ can be calculated by distributing $2x$ and distributing 3:

$$2x \times x + 2x \times -4 + 3 \times x + 3 \times -4$$

$$2x^2 - 8x + 3x - 12$$

Combining like terms yields:

$$2x^2 - 5x - 12$$

100

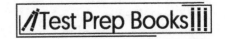

The general principle of distributing each term can be applied when multiplying polynomials of any size. To multiply $(x^2 + 3x - 1)(5x^3 - 2x^2 + 2x + 3)$, all three terms should be distributed from the first polynomial to each of the four terms in the second polynomial and then any like terms should be combined. If a problem requires multiplying more than two polynomials, two at a time can be multiplied and combined until all have been multiplied. To multiply $(x + 3)(2x - 1)(x + 5)$, two polynomials should be chosen to multiply together first. Multiplying the last two results in:

$$(2x - 1)(x + 5) = 2x^2 + 9x - 5$$

That product should then be multiplied by the third polynomial:

$$(x + 3)(2x^2 + 9x - 5)$$

The final answer should equal:

$$2x^3 + 15x^2 + 22x - 15$$

Solving an Equation in One Variable that Contains Radicals or Contains the Variable in the Denominator of a Fraction

Equations with radicals containing numbers only as the radicand are solved the same way that an equation without a radical would be. For example:

$$3x + \sqrt{81} = 45$$

would be solved using the same steps as if solving:

$$2x + 4 = 12$$

Radical equations are those in which the variable is part of the radicand. For example:

$$\sqrt{5x + 1} - 6 = 0$$

and

$$\sqrt{x - 3} + 5 = x$$

would be considered radical equations.

Radical Equations

To solve a radical equation, the radical should be isolated and both sides of the equation should be raised to the same power to cancel the radical. Raising both sides to the second power will cancel a square root, raising to the third power will cancel a cube root, etc. To solve $\sqrt{5x + 1} - 6 = 0$, the radical should be isolated first:

$$\sqrt{5x + 1} = 6$$

Then both sides should be raised to the second power:

$$(\sqrt{5x + 1})^2 = (6)^2 \rightarrow 5x + 1 = 36$$

Lastly, the linear equation should be solved: $x = 7$.

Radical Equations with Extraneous Solutions

If a radical equation contains a variable in the radicand and a variable outside of the radicand, it must be checked for extraneous solutions. An extraneous solution is one obtained by following the proper process for solving an equation but does not "check out" when substituted into the original equation. Here's a sample equation:

$$\sqrt{x-3} + 5 = x$$

Isolating the radical yields:

$$\sqrt{x-3} = x - 5$$

Next, both sides should be squared to cancel the radical:

$$(\sqrt{x-3})^2 = (x-5)^2 \rightarrow x - 3 = (x-5)(x-5)$$

The binomials should be multiplied:

$$x - 3 = x^2 - 10x + 25$$

The quadratic equation is then solved:

$$0 = x^2 - 11x + 28$$

$$0 = (x-7)(x-4)$$

$$x - 7 = 0; x - 4 = 0$$

$$x = 7 \text{ or } x = 4$$

To check for extraneous solutions, each answer can be substituted, one at a time, into the original equation. Substituting 7 for x, results in $7 = 7$. Therefore, 7 is a solution. Substituting 4 for x results in $6 = 4$. This is false; therefore, 4 is an extraneous solution.

Equations with a Variable in the Denominator of a Fraction

For equations with variables in the denominator, if the equation contains two rational expressions (on opposite sides of the equation, or on the same side and equal to zero), it can be solved like a proportion. Here's an equation to consider:

$$\frac{5}{2x - 2} = \frac{15}{x^2 - 1}$$

First, cross-multiplying yields:

$$5(x^2 - 1) = 15(2x - 2)$$

Distributing yields:

$$5x^2 - 5 = 30x - 30$$

102

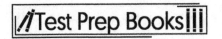
In solving the quadratic equation (see section *Solving a Quadratic Equation*), it is determined that $x = 1$ or $x = 5$. Solutions must be checked to see if they are extraneous. Extraneous solutions either produce a false statement when substituted into the original equation or create a rational expression with a denominator of zero (dividing by zero is undefined). Substituting 5 into the original equation produces $\frac{5}{8} = \frac{5}{8}$; therefore, 5 is a solution. Substituting 1 into the original equation results in both denominators equal to zero; therefore, 1 is an extraneous solution.

If an equation contains three or more rational expressions: the least common denominator (LCD) needs to be found for all the expressions, then both sides of the equation should be multiplied by the LCD. The LCD consists of the lowest number that all coefficients divide evenly into and for every variable, the highest power of that variable. Here's a sample equation:

$$\frac{3}{5x} - \frac{4}{3x} = \frac{1}{3}$$

The LCD would be $15x$. Both sides of the equation should be multiplied by $15x$:

$$15x\left(\frac{3}{5x} - \frac{4}{3x}\right) = 15x\left(\frac{1}{3}\right)$$

$$\frac{45x}{5x} - \frac{60x}{3x} = \frac{15x}{3}$$

$$9 - 20 = 5x$$

$$x = -2\frac{1}{5}$$

Any extraneous solutions should be identified.

Solving a System of One Linear Equation and One Quadratic Equation

A system of equations consists of two variables in two equations. A solution to the system is an ordered pair (x, y) that makes both equations true. When displayed graphically, a solution to a system is a point of intersection between the graphs of the equations. When a system consists of one linear equation and one quadratic equation, there may be one, two, or no solutions. If the line and parabola intersect at two points, there are two solutions to the system; if they intersect at one point, there is one solution; if they do not intersect, there is no solution.

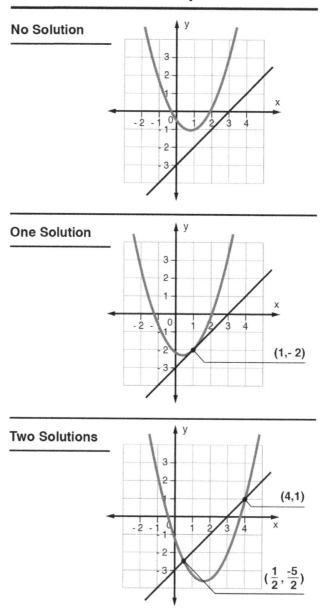

Systems with One Linear Equation and One Quadratic Equation

No Solution

One Solution

$(1, -2)$

Two Solutions

$(4, 1)$

$(\frac{1}{2}, \frac{-5}{2})$

One method for solving a system of one linear equation and one quadratic equation is to graph both functions and identify point(s) of intersection. This, however, is not always practical. Graph paper may not be available, or the intersection points may not be easily identified. Solving the system algebraically involves using the substitution method. Consider the following system:

$$y = x^2 + 9x + 11$$

$$y = 2x - 1$$

The equivalent value of y should be substituted from the linear equation ($2x - 1$) into the quadratic equation.

The resulting equation is:

$$2x - 1 = x^2 + 9x + 11$$

Next, this quadratic equation should be solved using the appropriate method: factoring, taking square roots, or using the quadratic formula (see section *Solving a Quadratic Equation*). Solving this quadratic equation by factoring results in $x = -4$ or $x = -3$. Next, the corresponding y-values should be found by substituting the x-values into the original linear equation:

$$y = 2(-4) - 1$$

$$y = 2(-3) - 1$$

The solutions should be written as ordered pairs: $(-4, -9)$ and $(-3, -7)$. Finally, the possible solutions should be checked by substituting each into both of the original equations. In this case, both solutions "check out."

Rewriting Simple Rational Expressions

A rational expression is an algebraic expression including variables that look like a fraction. In simplest form, the numerator and denominator of a rational expression do not have common divisors (factors). To simplify a rational expression, the numerator and denominator (see Section 4) should be factored; then any common factors in the numerator and denominator should be canceled. To simplify, the numerator and denominator should be written as a product of its factors:

$$\frac{3x^2 y}{12xy^3}$$

$$\frac{3 \times x \times x \times y}{2 \times 2 \times 3 \times x \times x \times y \times y \times y}$$

Canceling common factors leaves:

$$\frac{x}{2 \times 2 \times y \times y}$$

Multiplying the remaining factors results in:

$$\frac{x}{4y^2}$$

Here's a rational expression:

$$\frac{x^2 - 1}{x^2 - x - 2}$$

Factoring the numerator and denominator produces:

$$\frac{(x + 1)(x - 1)}{(x - 2)(x + 1)}$$

Each binomial in parentheses is a factor and only the exact same binomial would cancel that factor. By canceling factors, the expression is simplified to:

$$\frac{x - 1}{x - 2}$$

The variable x itself is not a factor. Therefore, they do not cancel each other out.

Multiplying/Dividing Rational Expressions

When multiplying or dividing rational expressions, the basic concepts of operations with fractions are used. To multiply, (1) all numerators and denominators need to be factored, (2) common factors should be canceled between any numerator and any denominator, (3) the remaining factors of the numerator and the remaining factors of the denominator should be multiplied, and (4) the expression should be checked to see whether it can be simplified further.

To multiply the following, each numerator and denominator should be written as a product of its factors:

$$\frac{4a^4}{3} \times \frac{6}{5a^2}$$

$$\frac{2 \times 2 \times a \times a \times a \times a}{3} \times \frac{3 \times 2}{5 \times a \times a}$$

After canceling common factors, the remaining expression is:

$$\frac{2 \times 2 \times a \times a}{1} \times \frac{2}{5}$$

A factor of 1 remains if all others are canceled. Multiplying remaining factors produces:

$$\frac{8a^2}{5}$$

To divide rational expressions, the expression should be changed to multiplying by the reciprocal of the divisor (just as with fractions: $\frac{1}{2} \div \frac{3}{4} = \frac{1}{2} \times \frac{4}{3}$); then follow the process for multiplying rational expressions.

106

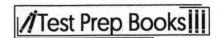

Here's a sample expression:

$$\frac{2x}{x^2 - 16} \div \frac{4x^2 + 6x}{x^2 + 6x + 8}$$

First, the division problem should be changed to a multiplication problem:

$$\frac{2x}{x^2 - 16} \times \frac{x^2 + 6x + 8}{4x^2 + 6x}$$

Then, the equation should be factored:

$$\frac{2x}{(x + 4)(x - 4)} \times \frac{(x + 4)(x + 2)}{2x(2x + 3)}$$

Canceling yields:

$$\frac{1}{(x - 4)} \times \frac{(x + 2)}{(2x + 3)}$$

Multiplying the remaining factors produces:

$$\frac{x + 2}{2x^2 - 5x - 12}$$

Adding/Subtracting Rational Expressions

Just as with adding and subtracting fractions, to add or subtract rational expressions, a common denominator is needed. (The numerator is added or subtracted, and the denominator stays the same.) If the expressions have like denominators, subtraction should be changed to add the opposite (a -1 is distributed to each term in the numerator of the expression being subtracted); the denominators should be factored and the expressions added; the numerator should then be factored; and the equation should be simplified if possible. Here's a sample expression:

$$\frac{2x^2 + 4x - 3}{x + 3} - \frac{x^2 - 2x - 12}{x + 3}$$

Changing subtraction to add the opposite yields:

$$\frac{2x^2 + 4x - 3}{x + 3} + \frac{-x^2 + 2x + 12}{x + 3}$$

The denominator cannot be factored, so the expression should be added, resulting in:

$$\frac{x^2 + 6x + 9}{x + 3}$$

Simplification is performed by factoring the numerator:

$$\frac{(x + 3)(x + 3)}{(x + 3)}$$

107

Canceling yields: $\frac{x+3}{1}$, or simply $x + 3$.

To add or subtract rational expressions with unlike denominators, the denominators must be changed by finding the least common multiple (LCM) of the expressions. To find the LCM, each expression should be factored, and the product should be formed using each factor the greatest number of times it occurs. The LCM of $12xy^2$ and $15x^3y$ would be $60x^3y^2$.

The equation $x^2 + 5x + 4$ factors to $(x + 4)(x + 1)$ and $x^2 + 2x + 1$, which factors to $(x + 1)(x + 1)$. The LCM would be $(x + 4)(x + 1)(x + 1)$.

To add or subtract expressions with unlike denominators: (1) subtraction should be changed to add the opposite; (2) the denominators are factored; (3) an LCM should be determined for the denominators; (4) the numerator and denominator of each expression should be multiplied by the missing factor(s); (5) the expressions that now have like denominators should be added; (6) the numerator should be factored; and (7) simplification should be performed if possible. Here's a sample expression:

$$\frac{x^2 + 6x + 11}{x^2 + 7x + 12} - \frac{2}{x + 3}$$

First, subtraction should be changed to addition:

$$\frac{x^2 + 6x + 11}{x^2 + 7x + 12} + \frac{-2}{x + 3}$$

Then, the denominators are factored:

$$\frac{x^2 + 6x + 11}{(x + 4)(x + 3)} + \frac{-2}{x + 3}$$

The LCM of $(x + 4)(x + 3)$ and $(x + 3)$ should be determined, which is $(x + 4)(x + 3)$. The numerator and denominator should be multiplied by the missing factor:

$$\frac{x^2 + 6x + 11}{(x + 4)(x + 3)} + \frac{-2}{x + 3} \times \frac{(x + 4)}{(x + 4)}$$

$$\frac{x^2 + 6x + 11}{(x + 4)(x + 3)} + \frac{-2x - 8}{(x + 4)(x + 3)}$$

The expressions should be added, resulting in:

$$\frac{x^2 + 4x + 3}{(x + 4)(x + 3)}$$

The numerator should be factored:

$$\frac{(x + 3)(x + 1)}{(x + 4)(x + 3)}$$

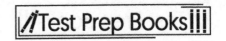

Simplifying yields:

$$\frac{x+1}{x+4}$$

Interpreting Parts of Nonlinear Expressions in Terms of Their Context

When a nonlinear function is used to model a real-life scenario, some aspects of the function may be relevant while others may not. The context of each scenario will dictate what should be used. In general, x- and y-intercepts will be points of interest. A y-intercept is the value of y when x equals zero; and an x-intercept is the value of x when y equals zero. Suppose a nonlinear function models the value of an investment (y) over the course of time (x). It would be relevant to determine the initial value (the y-intercept where time equals zero), as well as any point in time in which the value would be zero (the x-intercept).

Another aspect of a function that is typically desired is the rate of change. This tells how fast the outputs are growing or decaying with respect to given inputs. For more on rates of change regarding quadratic and exponential functions, see the earlier sections on those types of functions. For polynomial functions, the rate of change can be estimated by the highest power of the function. Polynomial functions also include absolute and/or relative minimums and maximums. Functions modeling production or expenses should be considered. Maximum and minimum values would be relevant aspects of these models.

Finally, the domain and range for a function should be considered for relevance. The domain consists of all input values, and the range consists of all output values. For instance, a function could model the volume of a container to be produced in relation to its height. Although the function that models the scenario may include negative values for inputs and outputs, these parts of the function would obviously not be relevant.

Understanding the Relationship Between Zeros and Factors of Polynomials

The zeros of a function are the x-intercepts of its graph. They are called zeros because they are the x-values for which $y = 0$.

Finding Zeros
To find the zeros of a polynomial function, it should be written in factored form, then each factor should be set equal to zero and solved. To find the zeros of the function $y = 3x^3 - 3x^2 - 36x$, the polynomial should be factored first. Factoring out a GCF results in:

$$y = 3x(x^2 - x - 12)$$

Then factoring the quadratic function yields:

$$y = 3x(x - 4)(x + 3)$$

Next, each factor should be set equal to zero: $3x = 0; x - 4 = 0; x + 3 = 0$. By solving each equation, it is determined that the function has zeros, or x-intercepts, at 0, 4, and -3.

Writing a Polynomial with Given Zeros

Given zeros for a polynomial function, to write the function, a linear factor corresponding to each zero should be written. The linear factor will be the opposite value of the zero added to x. Then the factors should be multiplied, and the function written in standard form. To write a polynomial with zeros at -2, 3, and 3, three linear factors should be written:

$$y = (x + 2)(x - 3)(x - 3)$$

Then, multiplication is used to convert the equation to standard form, producing:

$$y = x^3 - 4x^2 - 3x + 18$$

Dividing Polynomials by Linear Factors

To determine if a linear binomial is a factor of a polynomial, the polynomial should be divided by the binomial. If there is no remainder (it divides evenly), then the binomial is a factor of the polynomial. To determine if a value is a zero of a function, a binomial can be written from that zero and tested by division. To divide a polynomial by a linear factor, the terms of the dividend should be divided by the linear term of the divisor; the same process as long division of numbers (divide, multiply, subtract, drop down, and repeat) should be followed.

$$\frac{divisor\sqrt{quotient}}{dividend}$$

Remember that when subtracting a binomial, the signs of both terms should be changed. Here's a sample equation: divide $9x^3 - 18x^2 - x + 2$ by $3x + 1$. First, the problem should be set up as long division:

$$3x + 1 \overline{)\ 9x^3 - 18x^2 - x + 2}$$

Then the first term of the dividend ($9x^3$) should be divided by the linear term of the divisor ($3x$):

$$\begin{array}{r} 3x^2 \hphantom{-18x^2 - x + 2} \\ 3x + 1 \overline{)\ 9x^3 - 18x^2 - x + 2} \end{array}$$

Next, the divisor should be multiplied by that term of the quotient:

$$\begin{array}{r} 3x^2 - 7x + 2 \\ 3x + 1 \overline{)\ 9x^3 - 18x^2 - x + 2} \\ -9x^3 - 3x^2 \hphantom{- x + 2} \end{array}$$

110

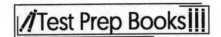

Subtraction should come next:

$$3x + 1 \overline{\smash{\big)}\ 9x^3 - 18x^2 - x + 2} \atop 3x^2 - 7x + 2$$

$$\underline{-9x^3 - 3x^2}$$
$$-21x^2$$

Now, the next term ($-x$) should be dropped down:

$$3x^2 - 7x + 2$$
$$3x + 1 \overline{\smash{\big)}\ 9x^3 - 18x^2 - x + 2}$$
$$\underline{-9x^3 - 3x^2}$$
$$-21x^2 - x$$

Then the process should be repeated, dividing $-21x^2$ by $3x$:

$$3x^2 - 7x + 2$$
$$3x + 1 \overline{\smash{\big)}\ 9x^3 - 18x^2 - x + 2}$$
$$\underline{-9x^3 - 3x^2}$$
$$-21x^2 - x$$
$$\underline{+21x^2 + 7x}$$
$$6x$$

The next term (2) should be dropped and repeated by dividing $6x$ by $3x$:

$$3x^2 - 7x + 2$$
$$3x + 1 \overline{\smash{\big)}\ 9x^3 - 18x^2 - x + 2}$$
$$\underline{-9x^3 - 3x^2}$$
$$-21x^2 - x$$
$$\underline{+21x^2 + 7x}$$
$$6x + 2$$
$$\underline{-6x - 2}$$
$$0$$

There is no remainder; therefore, $3x + 1$ is a factor of:

$$9x^3 - 18x^2 - x + 2$$

By the definition of factors:

$$(3x + 1)(3x^2 - 7x + 2) = 9x^3 - 18x^2 - x + 2$$

111

The quadratic expression can further be factored to produce:

$$(3x + 1)(3x - 1)(x - 2)$$

Understanding a Nonlinear Relationship Between Two Variables

Questions on this material will assess the ability of test takers to make connections between linear or nonlinear equations and their graphical representations. It will also require interpreting graphs in relation to systems of equations.

Graphs of Polynomial Functions

A polynomial function consists of a monomial or sum of monomials arranged in descending exponential order. The graph of a polynomial function is a smooth continuous curve that extends infinitely on both ends. From the equation of a polynomial function, the following can be determined: (1) the end behavior of the graph—does it rise or fall to the left and to the right; (2) the y-intercept and x-intercept(s) and whether the graph simply touches or passes through each x-intercept; and (3) the largest possible number of turning points, where the curve changes from rising to falling or vice versa. To graph the function, these three aspects of the graph should be determined and extra points between the intercepts should be found if necessary.

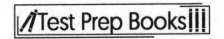

End Behavior

The end behavior of the graph of a polynomial function can be determined by the degree of the function (largest exponent) and the leading coefficient (coefficient of the term with the largest exponent). There are four possible scenarios for the end behavior: (1) if the degree is odd and the coefficient is positive, the graph falls to the left and rises to the right; (2) if the degree is odd and the coefficient is negative, the graph rises to the left and falls to the right; (3) if the degree is even and the coefficient is positive, the graph rises to the left and rises to the right, or (4) if the degree is even and the coefficient is negative, the graph falls to the left and falls to the right.

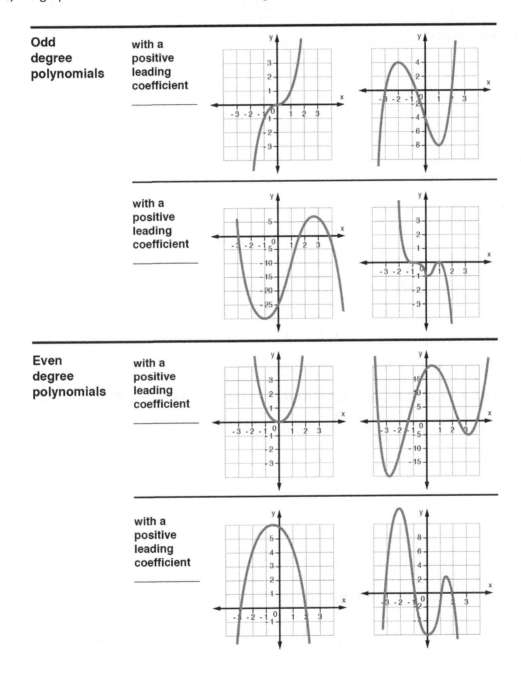

X and Y-Intercepts

The y-intercept for any function is the point at which the graph crosses the y-axis. At this point $x = 0$; therefore, to determine the y-intercept, $x = 0$ should be substituted into the function and solved for y. Finding x-intercepts, also called zeros, is covered in a previous section. For a given zero of a function, the graph can either pass through that point or simply touch that point (the graph turns at that zero). This is determined by the multiplicity of that zero. The multiplicity of a zero is the number of times its corresponding factor is multiplied to obtain the function in standard form. For example:

$$y = x^3 - 4x^2 - 3x + 18$$

can be written in factored form as:

$$y = (x + 2)(x - 3)(x - 3)$$

or

$$y = (x + 2)(x - 3)^2$$

The zeros of the function would be -2 and 3. The zero at -2 would have a multiplicity of 1, and the zero at 3 would have a multiplicity of 2. If a zero has an even multiplicity, then the graph touches the x-axis at that zero and turns around. If a zero has an odd multiplicity, then the graph crosses the x-axis at that zero.

Turning Points

The graph of a polynomial function can have, at most, a number of turning points equal to one less than the degree of the function. It is possible to have fewer turning points than this value. For example, the function:

$$y = 3x^5 + 2x^2 - 3x$$

could have no more than four turning points.

Using Function Notation, and Interpreting Statements Using Function Notation.

Function notation is covered in the *Function/Linear Equation Notation* section under *Heart of Algebra*.

Addition, Subtraction, Multiplication and Division of Functions

Functions denoted by $f(x)$, $g(x)$, etc., can be added, subtracted, multiplied, or divided. For example, the function:

$$f(x) = 15x + 100$$

represents the cost to have a catered party at a banquet hall (where *x* represents the number of guests); and the function $g(x) = 10x$ represents the cost for unlimited drinks at the party. The total cost of a catered party with unlimited drinks can be represented by adding the functions $f(x)$ and $g(x)$. In this case:

$$f(x) + g(x) = (15x + 100) + (10x)$$

Therefore:

114

$$f(x) + g(x) = 25x + 100$$

$(f(x) + g(x)$ can also be written $(f + g)(x))$. To add, subtract, multiply, or divide functions, the values of the functions should be substituted and the rules for operations with polynomials should be followed. It should be noted:

$$(f - g)(x) = f(x) - g(x); (f \times g)(x) = f(x) \times g(x)$$

and

$$\left(\frac{f}{g}\right)(x) = \frac{f(x)}{g(x)}$$

Composition of Functions

A composite function is one in which two functions are combined such that the output from the first function becomes the input for the second function (one function should be applied after another function). The composition of a function written as $(g \circ f)(x)$ or $g(f(x))$ is read "g of f of x." The inner function, $f(x)$, would be evaluated first and the answer would be used as the input of the outer function, $g(x)$. To determine the value of a composite function, the value of the inner function should be substituted for the variable of the outer function.

Here's a sample problem:

A store is offering a 20% discount on all of its merchandise. You have a coupon worth $5 off any item.

The cost of an item with the 20% discount can be modeled by the function:

$$d(x) = 0.8x$$

The cost of an item with the coupon can be modeled by the function $c(x) = x - 5$. A composition of functions to model the cost of an item applying the discount first and then the coupon would be:

$$c\big(d(x)\big)$$

Replacing $d(x)$ with its value $(0.8x)$ results in $c(0.8x)$. By evaluating the function $c(x)$ with an input of $0.8x$, it is determined that:

$$c\big(d(x)\big) = 0.8x - 5$$

To model the cost of an item if the coupon is applied first and then the discount, $d(c(x))$ should be determined. The result would be:

$$d(c(x)) = 0.8x - 4$$

Evaluating Functions

If a problem asks to evaluate with operations between functions, the new function should be determined and then the given value should be substituted as the input of the new function. To find $(f \times g)(3)$, given $f(x) = x + 1$ and $g(x) = 2x - 3$, the following should be determined:

$$(f \times g)(x)$$

$$f(x) \times g(x)$$

$$(x + 1)(2x - 3)$$

$$2x^2 - x - 3$$

Therefore:

$$(f \times g)(x) = 2x^2 - x - 3$$

To find $(f \times g)(3)$, the function $(f \times g)(x)$ needs to be evaluated for an input of 3:

$$(f \times g)(3)$$

$$2(3)^2 - (3) - 3 = 12$$

Therefore:

$$(f \times g)(3) = 12$$

Using Structure to Isolate or Identify a Quantity of Interest

Formulas are mathematical expressions that define the value of one quantity given the value of one or more different quantities. A formula or equation expressed in terms of one variable can be manipulated to express the relationship in terms of any other variable. The equation $y = 3x + 2$ is expressed in terms of the variable y. By manipulating the equation, it can be written as:

$$x = \frac{y - 2}{3}$$

This is expressed in terms of the variable x. To manipulate an equation or formula to solve for a variable of interest, how the equation would be solved if all other variables were numbers should be considered. The same steps for solving should be followed, leaving operations in terms of the variables, instead of calculating numerical values.

The formula $P = 2l + 2w$ expresses how to calculate the perimeter of a rectangle given its length and width. To write a formula to calculate the width of a rectangle given its length and perimeter, the previous formula relating the three variables should be used and the variable w should be solved. If P and l were numerical values, this would be a two-step linear equation solved by subtraction and division.

To solve the equation $P = 2l + 2w$ for w, $2l$ should be subtracted from both sides:

$$P - 2l = 2w$$

116

Then, both sides should be divided by 2:

$$\frac{P - 2l}{2} = w$$

or

$$\frac{P}{2} - l = w$$

The distance formula between two points on a coordinate plane can be found using the formula:

$$d = \sqrt{(x_2 - x_1)^2 + (y_2 - y_1)^2}$$

A problem might require determining the x-coordinate of one point (x_2), given its y-coordinate (y_2) and the distance (d) between that point and another given point (x_1, y_1). To do so, the above formula for x_1 should be solved just as a radical equation containing numerical values in place of the other variables.

Both sides should be squared; the quantity should be subtracted $(y_2 - y_1)^2$; the square root of both sides should be taken; x_1 should be subtracted to produce:

$$\sqrt{d^2 - (y_2 - y_1)^2} + x_1 = x_2$$

Additional Topics

Volume Formulas

Volume is the capacity of a three-dimensional shape. Volume is useful in determining the space within a certain three-dimensional object. Volume can be calculated for a cube, rectangular prism, cylinder, pyramid, cone, and sphere. By knowing specific dimensions of the objects, the volume of the object is computed with these figures. The units for the volumes of solids can include cubic centimeters, cubic meters, cubic inches, and cubic feet.

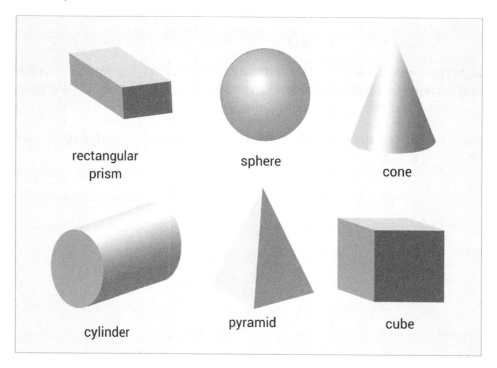

Cube

The cube is the simplest figure for which volume can be determined because all dimensions in a cube are equal. In the following example, the length, width, and height of the cube are all represented by the variable a because these measurements are equal lengths.

The volume of any rectangular, three-dimensional object is found by multiplying its length by its width by its height. In the case of a cube, the length, width, and height are all equal lengths, represented by the variable a. Therefore, the equation used to calculate the volume is $(a \times a \times a)$ or a^3. In a real-world example of this situation, if the length of a side of the cube is 3 centimeters, the volume is calculated by utilizing the formula:

$$(3 \times 3 \times 3) = 27 \text{ cm}^3$$

Rectangular Prism

The dimensions of a rectangular prism are not necessarily equal as those of a cube. Therefore, the formula for a rectangular prism recognizes that the dimensions vary and use different variables to represent these lengths. The length, width, and height of a rectangular prism can be represented with the variables a, b, and c.

The equation used to calculate volume is length times width times height. In a real-world application of this situation, if $a = 2$ cm, $b = 3$ cm, and $c = 4$ cm, the volume is calculated by utilizing the formula:

$$2 \times 3 \times 4 = 24 \text{ cm}^3$$

Cylinder

Discovering a cylinder's volume requires the measurement of the cylinder's base, length of the radius, and height. The height of the cylinder can be represented with variable h, and the radius can be represented with variable r.

The formula to find the volume of a cylinder is $\pi r^2 h$. Notice that πr^2 is the formula for the area of a circle. This is because the base of the cylinder is a circle. To calculate the volume of a cylinder, the slices of circles needed to build the entire height of the cylinder are added together. For example, if the radius is 5 feet and the height of the cylinder is 10 feet, the cylinder's volume is calculated by using the following equation:

$$\pi 5^2 \times 10$$

Substituting 3.14 for π, the volume is 785 ft³.

Pyramid

To calculate the volume of a pyramid, the area of the base of the pyramid is multiplied by the pyramid's height by $\frac{1}{3}$. The area of the base of the pyramid is found by multiplying the base length by the base width.

Therefore, the formula to calculate a pyramid's volume is:

$$(L \times W \times H) \div 3$$

Cone

The formula to calculate the volume of a circular cone is similar to the formula for the volume of a pyramid. The primary difference in determining the area of a cone is that a circle serves as the base of a cone. Therefore, the area of a circle is used for the cone's base.

The variable r represents the radius, and the variable h represents the height of the cone. The formula used to calculate the volume of a cone is:

$$\frac{1}{3}\pi r^2 h$$

Essentially, the area of the base of the cone is multiplied by the cone's height. In a real-life example where the radius of a cone is 2 meters and the height of a cone is 5 meters, the volume of the cone is calculated by utilizing the formula:

$$\frac{1}{3}\pi 2^2 \times 5 = 21$$

After substituting 3.14 for π, the volume is 21 m³.

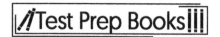
Sphere

The volume of a sphere uses π due to its circular shape.

The length of the radius, r, is the only variable needed to determine the sphere's volume. The formula to calculate the volume of a sphere is $\frac{4}{3}\pi r^3$. Therefore, if the radius of a sphere is 8 centimeters, the volume of the sphere is calculated by utilizing the formula:

$$\frac{4}{3}\pi(8)^3 = 2{,}144 \text{ cm}^3$$

Right Triangles: Pythagorean Theorem and Trigonometric Ratio

The value of a missing side of a right triangle may be determined two ways. The first way is to apply the Pythagorean Theorem, and the second way is to apply Trigonometric Ratios. The Pythagorean Theorem states that for every right triangle, the square of the length of the hypotenuse is equal to the sum of the squares of the lengths of the remaining two sides. The hypotenuse is the longest side of a right triangle and is also the side opposite the right angle.

According to the diagram $a^2 + b^2 = c^2$ where c represents the hypotenuse, and a and b represent the lengths of the remaining two sides of the right triangle.

The Pythagorean Theorem may be applied a multitude of ways. For example, a person wishes to build a garden in the shape of a rectangle, having the dimensions of 5 feet by 8 feet. The garden's design includes a diagonal board to separate various types of plants. The Pythagorean Theorem can be used to determine the length of the diagonal board.

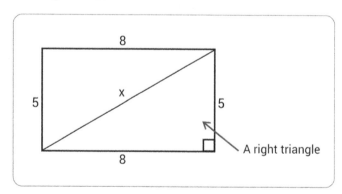

Given that side $a = 5$, side $b = 8$, and side c is unknown, use the following equation:

$$a^2 + b^2 = c^2$$

$$5^2 + 8^2 = c^2$$

$$25 + 64 = c^2$$

$$c = \sqrt{89}$$

$$c = 9.43$$

To solve for unknown sides of a right triangle using trigonometric ratios, the sine, cosine, and tangent are required.

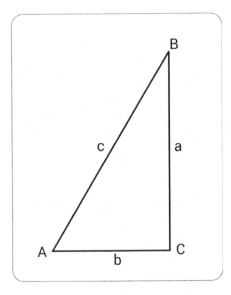

In the image above, angles are denoted by capital letters, and sides are denoted by lowercase letters. When examining angle A, b is the adjacent side, a is the opposite side, and c is the hypotenuse side. The various ratios of the lengths of the sides of the right triangle are used to find the sine, cosine, and tangent of angle A.

Thus:

$$\sin(A) = \frac{opposite}{hypotenuse}$$

$$\cos(A) = \frac{adjacent}{hypotenuse}$$

$$\tan(A) = \frac{opposite}{adjacent}$$

After substituting variables for the sides of the right triangle, $sin(A) = \frac{a}{c}$, $cos(A) = \frac{b}{c}$, and $tan(A) = \frac{a}{b}$.

As a real-world example, the height of a tree can be discovered by using the information above. Surveying equipment can determine the tree's angle of inclination is 55.3 degrees, and the distance from the tree is 10 feet.

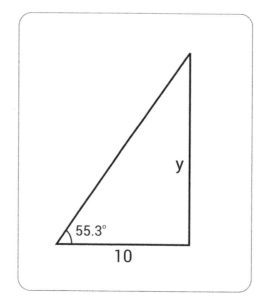

To find the height of the tree, substitute the known values into the trigonometric ratio of tangent:

$$\tan(55.3) = \frac{y}{10}$$

$$10 \times \tan(55.3) = y$$

$$10 \times 1.44418 = y$$

$$y = 14.4418$$

Operations with Complex Numbers

Complex numbers are numbers that have a real component and an imaginary component. An example of a complex number is $3 + 4i$. The real part of this complex number is 3, and the imaginary part of this complex number is $4i$. It is important to note that the imaginary number i is $\sqrt{-1}$. Complex numbers can be added, subtracted, multiplied, and divided.

Adding complex numbers together is similar to adding like terms. If given two complex numbers, students should first add the real components together and then add the imaginary components together. In this way, i is treated like a variable because it is only added or subtracted with other terms that contain i.

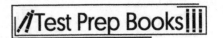

For example, if asked to simplify:

$$(2 + 4i) + (3 - 5i)$$

students should first add the real components together and then add the imaginary components together:

$$(2 + 4i) + (3 - 5i)$$

$$(2 + 3) + (4i + -5i) = 5 - i$$

In addition, if asked to subtract two complex numbers, students should first subtract the real components and then subtract the imaginary components: $(3 + 4i) - (1 + 2i)$ simplifies to:

$$(3 - 1) + (4i - 2i) = 2 + 2i$$

The examples below demonstrate how the imaginary number i is treated when it is raised to a power:

$i^1 = i$

$i^2 = -1$

$i^3 = i \times -1 = -i$

$i^4 = -1 \times -1 = 1$

To multiply complex numbers, students should use the FOIL distribution method and combine like terms. FOIL stands for first, outer, inner, and last. For example, when given two expressions of:

$$(2 + 4i)(3 + 2i)$$

the student multiplies the first term in each expression (2×3) to get 6. Next, the student multiplies the two outer terms together $(2 \times 2i)$ to get $4i$. The student multiplies the two inner terms together $(4i \times 3)$ to get $12i$. Then the student multiplies the last term of each expression together $(4i \times 2i)$ to get $8i^2$. If using the values described above, $8i^2$ can be further simplified to -8 (since $i^2 = -1$). As a final step, the student combines like terms:

$$6 + 4i + 12i + -8 = -2 + 16i$$

To find the conjugate of a complex number, the sign is changed between the two terms in the denominator. For example, given the complex number $4 + 2i$, the student should change the operation sign in the middle of the two terms from addition to subtraction. Therefore, the complex conjugate becomes $4 - 2i$.

To divide complex numbers, the student should multiply by the conjugate of the complex number. The next step is to use the FOIL method in both the numerator and the denominator with the conjugate. For example, when given:

$$\frac{2 + 2i}{3 + i}$$

the conjugate of the denominator should be found first. The conjugate of $(3 + i)$ is $(3 - i)$, because the addition sign is changed to a subtraction sign. Given the new expression:

$$\frac{2 + 2i}{3 + i} \times \frac{3 - i}{3 - i}$$

the student multiplies the two expressions in the numerator using the FOIL distribution method and the two expressions in the denominator using the FOIL distribution method. The numerator simplifies to:

$$(6 - 2i + 6i + -2i^2) = 8 + 4i$$

The denominator simplifies to:

$$(9 - 3i + 3i \pm i^2) = 10$$

As a final step, the student combines like terms: $\frac{8+4i}{10}$, which simplifies to $\frac{4+2i}{5}$.

Degrees and Radians

Degrees are used to express the size of an angle. A complete circle is represented by 360°, and a half circle is represented by 180°. In addition, a right angle fills one quarter of a circle and is represented by 90°.

Radians are another way to denote angles in terms of π, rather than degrees. A complete circle is represented by 2π radians. The formula used to convert degrees to radians is:

$$Radians = \frac{degrees \times \pi}{180}$$

For example, to convert 270 degrees to radians:

$$Radians = \frac{270 \times \pi}{180} = 4.71$$

The *arc of a circle* is the distance between two points on the circle. The length of the arc of a circle in terms of *degrees* is easily determined if the value of the central angle is known. The length of the arc is simply the value of the central angle. In this example, the length of the arc of the circle in degrees is 75°.

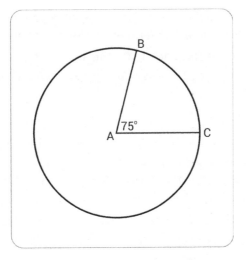

To determine the length of the arc of a circle in distance, the values for both the central angle and the radius must be known. This formula is:

$$\frac{central\ angle}{360°} = \frac{arc\ length}{2\pi r}$$

The equation is simplified by cross-multiplying to solve for the arc length.

In the following example, to solve for arc length, substitute the values of the central angle (75°) and the radius (10 inches) into the equation above.

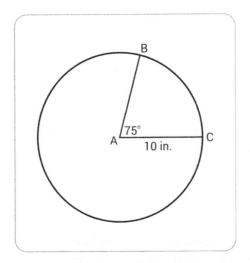

$$\frac{75°}{360°} = \frac{arc\ length}{2(3.14)(10in.)}$$

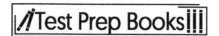
To solve the equation, first cross-multiply: $4710 = 360(arc\ length)$. Next, divide each side of the equation by 360. The result of the formula is that the arc length is 13.1 (rounded). Please note that arc length is often referred to as s.

As a special technological note for trigonometric functions, when finding the trigonometric function or an angle on the calculator, make a note using degrees or radians to get the correct value. Whether computing the sine of $\frac{\pi}{6}$ or computing the sine of 30°, the answer should come out to $\frac{1}{2}$. However, there is usually a "Mode" function on the calculator to select either radian or degree.

Circles

The equation used to find the area of a circle is $A = \pi r^2$. For example, if a circle has a radius of 5 centimeters, the area is computed by substituting 5 for the radius: $(5)^2$. Using this reasoning, to find half of the area of a circle, the formula is $A = 0.5\pi r^2$. Similarly, to find the quarter of an area of a circle, the formula is $A = 0.25\pi r^2$. To find any fractional area of a circle, a student can use the formula $A = \frac{C}{360}\pi r^2$, where C is the number of degrees of the central angle of the sector. The area of a circle can also be found by using the arc length rather than the degree of the sector. This formula is $A = rs^2$, where s is the arc length and r is the radius of the circle.

A chord is a line that connects two points on a circle's circumference. If the radius and the value of the angle subtended at the center by the chord is known, the formula to find the chord length is:

$$C = 2 \times radius \times \sin\frac{angle}{2}$$

Remember that this formula is based on half the length of the chord, so the radius is doubled to determine the full length of the chord.

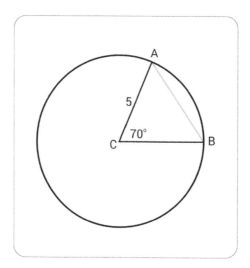

For example, the radius in the diagram above is 5 and the angle is 70 degrees. To find the chord length, plug in the values for the radius and angle to obtain the answer of 5.7.

$$5 \times \sin\frac{70}{2} = 2.87 \times 2 = 5.7$$

Chords that intersect each other at a point within a circle are related. The intersecting chord theorem states that when two chords intersect, each is cut into two portions or segments. The products of the two segments of each respective chord are equal to one another.

Other related concepts for circles include the diameter and circumference. *Circumference* is the distance around a circle. The formula for circumference is $C = 2\pi r$. The *diameter* of a circle is the distance across a circle through its center point. The formula for circumference can also be thought of as $C = d\pi$ where d is the circle's diameter, since the diameter of a circle is $2r$.

Similarity, Congruence, and Triangles

Triangles are similar if they have the same shape, the same angle measurements, and their sides are proportional to one another. Triangles are congruent if the angles of the triangles are equal in measurement and the sides of the triangles are equal in measurement.

There are five ways to show that a triangle is congruent.

- SSS (Side-Side-Side Postulate): When all three corresponding sides are equal in length, then the two triangles are congruent.

- SAS (Side-Angle-Side Postulate): If a pair of corresponding sides and the angle in between those two sides are equal, then the two triangles are congruent.

- ASA (Angle-Side-Angle Postulate): If a pair of corresponding angles are equal and the side within those angles are equal, then the two triangles are equal.

- AAS (Angle-Angle-Side Postulate): When a pair of corresponding angles for two triangles and a non-included side are equal, then the two triangles are congruent.

- HL (Hypotenuse-Leg Theorem): If two right triangles have the same hypotenuse length, and one of the other sides are also the same length, then the two triangles are congruent.

If two triangles are discovered to be similar or congruent, this information can assist in determining unknown parts of triangles, such as missing angles and sides.

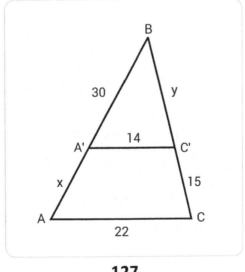

127

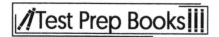

In the triangle shown above, AC and $A'C'$ are parallel lines. Therefore, BA is a transversal that intersects the two parallel lines. The corresponding angles $BA'C'$ and BAC are congruent. In a similar way, BC is also a transversal. Therefore, angle $BC'A'$ and BCA are congruent. If two triangles have two congruent angles, the triangles are similar. If the triangles are similar, their corresponding sides are proportional.

Therefore, the following equation is established:

$$\frac{30 + x}{30} = \frac{22}{14} = \frac{y + 15}{y}$$

$$\frac{30 + x}{30} = \frac{22}{14}$$

$$x = 17.1$$

$$\frac{22}{14} = \frac{y + 15}{y}$$

$$y = 26.25$$

The example below involves the question of congruent triangles. The first step is to examine whether the triangles are congruent. If the triangles are congruent, then the measure of a missing angle can be found.

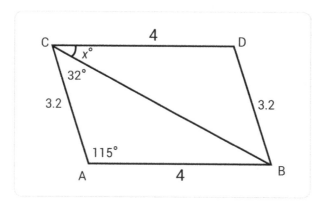

The above diagram provides values for angle measurements and side lengths in triangles CAB and CDB. Note that side CA is 3.2 and side DB is 3.2. Side CD is 4 and side AB is 4. Furthermore, line CB is congruent to itself by the reflexive property. Therefore, the two triangles are congruent by SSS (Side-Side-Side). Because the two triangles are congruent, all of the corresponding parts of the triangles are also congruent. Therefore, angle x is congruent to the inside of the angle for which a measurement is not provided in Triangle CAB. Thus:

$$115° + 32° = 147°$$

A triangle measures 180°, therefore:

$$180° - 147° = 33°$$

$Angle\ x = 33°$, because the two triangles are reversed.

128

Complementary Angle Theorem

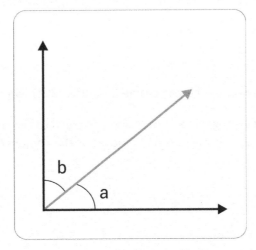

Two angles are complementary if the sum of the two angles equals 90°.

In the above diagram:

$$Angle\ a + Angle\ b = 90°$$

Therefore, the two angles are complementary. Certain trigonometric rules are also associated with complementary angles.

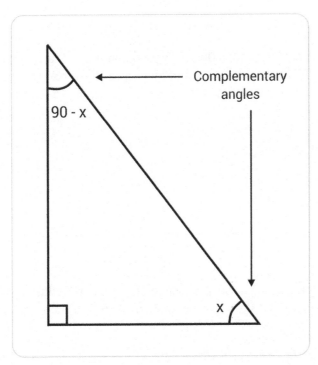

In the diagram above of a right triangle, if Angle A and Angle C are determined to be complementary angles, then certain relationships can be stated between the trigonometry of those angles.

$$sin(90° - x) = cos x$$

$$cos(90° - x) = sin x$$

For example, the sine of 80 degrees equals the cosine of $(90° - 80°)$, which is the $cos(10°)$.

This is true because the sine of an angle in a right triangle is equal to the cosine of its complement. Sine is known as the conjunction of cosine, and cosine is known as the conjunction of sine.

Examples:

1. $cos 5° = sin x°$?
2. $sin(90° - x) = ?$

For problem number 1, the student should remember that:

$$sin(90° - x) = cos x$$

$Cos 5°$ would be the same as $sin(90 - 5)°$. Therefore:

$$cos 5° = sin 85°$$

For problem number 2, the student would use the same fact that:

$$sin(90° - x)° = cos x$$

An *acute angle* is an angle that is less than 90°. If Angle A and Angle B are acute angles of a right triangle, then $sin A = cos B$. Therefore, the sine of any acute angle in a right triangle is equal to the cosine of its complement, and the cosine of any acute angle is equal to the sine of its complement.

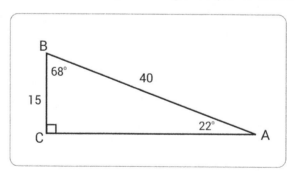

The example above is a right triangle. If only the value of angle BAC (which is 22°) was provided, the student would be able to figure out the value for angle CBA (68°) by knowing that a triangle is made up of:

$$180°(180° - 90° - 22° = 68°)$$

From the information given about acute angles on the previous page, the following statement is true:

$sin(angle\ BAC) = \frac{15}{40}$, which is equivalent to the $cos(angle\ CBA) = \frac{15}{40}$

130

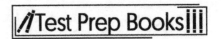

Circles on the Coordinate Plane

If a circle is placed on the coordinate plane with the center of the circle at the origin (0,0), then point (x, y) is a point on the circle. Furthermore, the line extending from the center to point (x, y) is the radius, or r. By applying the Pythagorean Theorem $(a^2 + b^2 = c^2)$ it can be stated that:

$$x^2 + y^2 = r^2$$

However, the center of the circle does not always need to be on the origin of the coordinate plane.

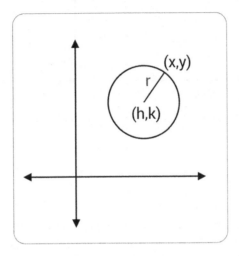

In the diagram above, the center of the circle is noted by (h, k). By applying the distance formula, the equation becomes:

$$r = \sqrt{(x - h)^2 + (y - k)^2}$$

When squaring both sides of the equation, the result is the standard form of a circle with the center (h, k) and radius r. Namely, $r^2 = (x - h)^2 + (y - k)^2$ where r equal radius and center equals (h, k). The following examples may be solved by using this information:

Example: Graph the equation:

$$-x^2 + y^2 = 25$$

To graph this equation, first note that the center of the circle is $(0, 0)$. The radius is the positive square root of 25 or 5.

Example: Find the equation for the circle below.

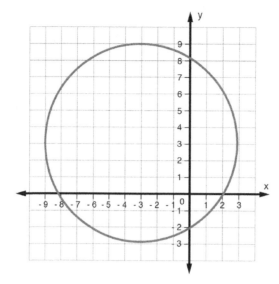

To find the equation for the circle, note that its center is not zero. Therefore, to find the circle's center, draw vertical and horizontal diameters to examine where they intersect. The center is located at point: $(-3, 3)$. Next, count the number of spaces from the center to the outside of the circle. This number is 6. Therefore, 6 is the radius. Finally, plug in the numbers that are known into the standard equation for a circle:

$$36 = \left(x - (-3)\right)^2 + (y - 3)^2$$

or

$$36 = (x + 3)^2 + (y - 3)^2$$

It is possible to determine whether a point lies on a circle or not within the coordinate plane. For example, a circle has a center of $(2, -5)$, and a radius of 6 centimeters. The first step is to apply the equation of a circle, which is $r^2 = (x - h)^2 + (y - k)^2$ where r equals radius and the center equals (h, k). Next, substitute the numbers for the center point and the number for the radius. This action simplifies the equation to:

$$36 = (x - 2)^2 + (y + 5)^2$$

Note that the radius of 6 was squared to get 36.

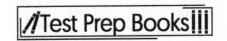

To prove that the point $(2, 1)$ lies on the circle, apply the equation of the circle that was just used and input the values of $(2, 1)$ for x and y in the equation.

$$36 = (x - 2)^2 + (y + 5)^2$$

$$36 = (2 - 2)^2 + (1 + 5)^2$$

$$36 = (0)^2 + (6)^2$$

$$36 = 36$$

Because the left side of the equation equals the right side of the equation, point $(2, 1)$ lies on the given circle.

Reading Test

Fiction

Questions 1–10 are based on the following passage:

We made it. We created it. We brought it forth from the night of the ages. We alone. Our hands. Our mind. Ours alone and only.

We know not what we are saying. Our head is reeling. We look upon the light which we have made. We shall be forgiven for anything we say tonight...

Tonight, after more days and trials than we can count, we finished building a strange thing, from the remains of the Unmentionable Times, a box of glass, devised to give forth the power of the sky of greater strength than we had ever achieved before. And when we put our wires to this box, when we closed the current—the wire glowed! It came to life, it turned red, and a circle of light lay on the stone before us.

We stood, and we held our head in our hands. We could not conceive of that which we had created. We had touched no flint, made no fire. Yet here was light, light that came from nowhere, light from the heart of metal.

We blew out the candle. Darkness swallowed us. There was nothing left around us, nothing save night and a thin thread of flame in it, as a crack in the wall of a prison. We stretched our hands to the wire, and we saw our fingers in the red glow. We could not see our body nor feel it, and in that moment nothing existed save our two hands over a wire glowing in a black abyss.

Then we thought of the meaning of that which lay before us. We can light our tunnel, and the City, and all the Cities of the world with nothing save metal and wires. We can give our brothers a new light, cleaner and brighter than any they have ever known. The power of the sky can be made to do men's bidding. There are no limits to its secrets and its might, and it can be made to grant us anything if we but choose to ask.

Then we knew what we must do. Our discovery is too great for us to waste our time in sweeping the streets. We must not keep our secret to ourselves, nor buried under the ground. We must bring it into the sight of all men. We need all our time, we need the work rooms of the Home of the Scholars, we want the help of our brother Scholars and their wisdom joined to ours. There is so much work ahead for all of us, for all the Scholars of the world.

In a month, the World Council of Scholars is to meet in our City. It is a great Council, to which the wisest of all lands are elected, and it meets once a year in the different Cities of the earth. We shall go to this Council and we shall lay before them, as our gift, this glass box with the power of the sky. We shall confess everything to them. They will see, understand and forgive. For our gift is greater than our transgression. They will explain it

to the Council of Vocations, and we shall be assigned to the Home of the Scholars. This has never been done before, but neither has a gift such as ours ever been offered to men.

We must wait. We must guard our tunnel as we had never guarded it before. For should any men save the Scholars learn of our secret, they would not understand it, nor would they believe us. They would see nothing, save our crime of working alone, and they would destroy us and our light. We care not about our body, but our light is...

Yes, we do care. For the first time do we care about our body. For this wire is as a part of our body, as a vein torn from us, glowing with our blood. Are we proud of this thread of metal, or of our hands which made it, or is there a line to divide these two?

Excerpt from *Anthem* by Ayn Rand

1. What is the overall tone of this passage?
   a. Dreary
   b. Unnerving
   c. Excited
   d. Humorous

2. Why must the invention be kept a secret?
   a. It is illegal to work alone.
   b. The Home of the Scholars will try to take credit.
   c. They were supposed to be sweeping streets.
   d. Remains from the Unmentionable Times are off limits.

3. Which literary device is used in the following sentence from paragraph five?

   Darkness swallowed us.

   a. Metaphor
   b. Synecdoche
   c. Flashback
   d. Personification

4. What does the narrator compare their discovery to?
   a. The sun
   b. A candle
   c. Prison
   d. Blood

5. Why does the narrator expect to be forgiven?
   a. Their invention will save the City money.
   b. The possibilities of the invention outweigh their crime.
   c. They will apologize to the World Council of Scholars.
   d. Their invention is part of their body.

135

6. What is the meaning of the word *transgression* mean in paragraph eight?
   a. Obedience
   b. Disruption
   c. Confession
   d. Offense

7. Which quote is an example of personification?
   a. "Our head is reeling."
   b. "Darkness swallowed us."
   c. "We stood, and we held our head in our hands."
   d. "We care not about our body, but our light is..."

8. What will NOT help advance the narrator's discovery?
   a. Using the work rooms of the Home of the Scholars
   b. Gaining wisdom from the brother Scholars
   c. Keeping the discovery a secret from the World Council of Scholars
   d. Stopping the sweeping of the streets

9. How does the narrator feel their status will change as a result of their invention?
   a. They will advance from street sweeper to the Home of the Scholars.
   b. Their status will remain the same after their confession.
   c. They will rise in status from tunnel worker to the Council of Vocations.
   d. They are not sure how their status will change due to the crime they committed.

10. Which transformation has happened by the end of the passage?
   a. The narrator has been forgiven for their transgression.
   b. The gift of electricity has been shared with all the cities of the world.
   c. The discovery has made it easier to sweep streets and light tunnels.
   d. The narrator recognizes the significance of their body.

History/Social Studies

Questions 11–18 are based upon the following passage:

Our people are losing that faith, not only in government itself but in the ability as citizens to serve as the ultimate rulers and shapers of our democracy. As a people we know our past and we are proud of it. Our progress has been part of the living history of America, even the world. We always believed that we were part of a great movement of humanity itself called democracy, involved in the search for freedom, and that belief has always strengthened us in our purpose. But just as we are losing our confidence in the future, we are also beginning to close the door on our past.

In a nation that was proud of hard work, strong families, close-knit communities, and our faith in God, too many of us now tend to worship self-indulgence and consumption. Human identity is no longer defined by what one does, but by what one owns. But we've discovered that owning things and consuming things does not satisfy our longing for meaning. We've learned that piling up material goods cannot fill the emptiness of lives which have no confidence or purpose.

136

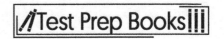

The symptoms of this crisis of the American spirit are all around us. For the first time in the history of our country a majority of our people believe that the next five years will be worse than the past five years. Two-thirds of our people do not even vote. The productivity of American workers is actually dropping, and the willingness of Americans to save for the future has fallen below that of all other people in the Western world.

As you know, there is a growing disrespect for government and for churches and for schools, the news media, and other institutions. This is not a message of happiness or reassurance, but it is the truth and it is a warning.

These changes did not happen overnight. They've come upon us gradually over the last generation, years that were filled with shocks and tragedy.

We were sure that ours was a nation of the ballot, not the bullet, until the murders of John Kennedy and Robert Kennedy and Martin Luther King, Jr. We were taught that our armies were always invincible and our causes were always just, only to suffer the agony of Vietnam. We respected the Presidency as a place of honor until the shock of Watergate.

We remember when the phrase "sound as a dollar" was an expression of absolute dependability, until ten years of inflation began to shrink our dollar and our savings. We believed that our Nation's resources were limitless until 1973, when we had to face a growing dependence on foreign oil.

These wounds are still very deep. They have never been healed. Looking for a way out of this crisis, our people have turned to the Federal Government and found it isolated from the mainstream of our Nation's life. Washington, D.C., has become an island. The gap between our citizens and our Government has never been so wide. The people are looking for honest answers, not easy answers; clear leadership, not false claims and evasiveness and politics as usual.

What you see too often in Washington and elsewhere around the country is a system of government that seems incapable of action. You see a Congress twisted and pulled in every direction by hundreds of well-financed and powerful special interests. You see every extreme position defended to the last vote, almost to the last breath by one unyielding group or another. You often see a balanced and a fair approach that demands sacrifice, a little sacrifice from everyone, abandoned like an orphan without support and without friends.

Often you see paralysis and stagnation and drift. You don't like it, and neither do I. What can we do?

First of all, we must face the truth, and then we can change our course. We simply must have faith in each other, faith in our ability to govern ourselves, and faith in the future of this Nation. Restoring that faith and that confidence to America is now the most important task we face. It is a true challenge of this generation of Americans.

Excerpt from "The Crisis of Confidence" by Jimmy Carter

11. What is the underlying message of Jimmy Carter's speech?
    a. There is no hope for the future of the United States.
    b. The American people have lost faith in their government.
    c. Finding the way again as a nation will be hard and will require facing the truth.
    d. America is not as great as other Western countries.

12. What is NOT a symptom of the crisis of the American spirit?
    a. Too many people tend to worship self-indulgence and consumption.
    b. Respect for government, churches and schools is growing.
    c. Two-thirds of American people do not vote.
    d. The willingness to save for the future has fallen.

13. Which phrase could replace "sound as a dollar" in paragraph seven?
    a. Hands down
    b. Solid as a rock
    c. Piece of cake
    d. Fair and square

14. Pointing out the shortcomings of government makes President Carter sound like he is:
    a. Unreliable as a leader
    b. Desperate for acceptance
    c. Relatable and empathetic
    d. Condescending toward citizens

15. What does Carter mean, metaphorically, when he says that "Washington, D.C. has become an island"?
    a. Members of Congress are relaxing on vacation while the people suffer.
    b. The government is using limited resources unwisely.
    c. The White House is an oasis for Americans in need.
    d. The government has isolated itself from its citizens.

16. What is the purpose of paragraphs six and seven?
    a. To point out that previous presidents have made mistakes
    b. To provide examples of why people are losing respect for government and other institutions
    c. To prove that our past is full of tragedy and our future is full of hope
    d. To suggest Americans' expectations are too high

17. How does the tone shift from the beginning to the end of the passage?
    a. The tone starts informally but ends seriously.
    b. The tone starts elevated but ends unremarkably.
    c. The tone starts bleakly but ends optimistically.
    d. The tone starts preachy but ends humbly.

18. What is Carter's proposed solution to the crisis of confidence in America?
    a. Healing the wounds, shocks, and tragedies of the past
    b. Removing special interest groups from the government
    c. Restoring faith in ourselves, democracy, and our nation
    d. Reverting back to strong families and close-knit communities

History/Social Studies

Questions 19–27 is based on the following passage:

The peoples of a number of countries of the world have recently had totalitarian regimes forced upon them against their will. The Government of the United States has made frequent protests against coercion and intimidation, in violation of the Yalta agreement, in Poland, Rumania, and Bulgaria. I must also state that in a number of other countries there have been similar developments.

At the present moment in world history nearly every nation must choose between alternative ways of life. The choice is too often not a free one.

One way of life is based upon the will of the majority, and is distinguished by free institutions, representative government, free elections, guarantees of individual liberty, freedom of speech and religion, and freedom from political oppression.

The second way of life is based upon the will of a minority forcibly imposed upon the majority. It relies upon terror and oppression, a controlled press and radio; fixed elections, and the suppression of personal freedoms.

I believe that it must be the policy of the United States to support free peoples who are resisting attempted subjugation by armed minorities or by outside pressures.

I believe that we must assist free peoples to work out their own destinies in their own way.

I believe that our help should be primarily through economic and financial aid which is essential to economic stability and orderly political processes.

The world is not static, and the status quo is not sacred. But we cannot allow changes in the status quo in violation of the Charter of the United Nations by such methods as coercion, or by such subterfuges as political infiltration. In helping free and independent nations to maintain their freedom, the United States will be giving effect to the principles of the Charter of the United Nations.

It is necessary only to glance at a map to realize that the survival and integrity of the Greek nation are of grave importance in a much wider situation. If Greece should fall under the control of an armed minority, the effect upon its neighbor, Turkey, would be immediate and serious. Confusion and disorder might well spread throughout the entire Middle East.

Moreover, the disappearance of Greece as an independent state would have a profound effect upon those countries in Europe whose peoples are struggling against great difficulties to maintain their freedoms and their independence while they repair the damages of war.

It would be an unspeakable tragedy if these countries, which have struggled so long against overwhelming odds, should lose that victory for which they sacrificed so much. Collapse of free institutions and loss of independence would be disastrous not only for

139

them but for the world. Discouragement and possibly failure would quickly be the lot of neighboring peoples striving to maintain their freedom and independence.

Should we fail to aid Greece and Turkey in this fateful hour, the effect will be far reaching to the West as well as to the East.

We must take immediate and resolute action.

I therefore ask the Congress to provide authority for assistance to Greece and Turkey in the amount of $400,000,000 for the period ending June 30, 1948. In requesting these funds, I have taken into consideration the maximum amount of relief assistance which would be furnished to Greece out of the $350,000,000 which I recently requested that the Congress authorize for the prevention of starvation and suffering in countries devastated by the war.

In addition to funds, I ask the Congress to authorize the detail of American civilian and military personnel to Greece and Turkey, at the request of those countries, to assist in the tasks of reconstruction, and for the purpose of supervising the use of such financial and material assistance as may be furnished. I recommend that authority also be provided for the instruction and training of selected Greek and Turkish personnel.

Finally, I ask that the Congress provide authority which will permit the speediest and most effective use, in terms of needed commodities, supplies, and equipment, of such funds as may be authorized.

If further funds, or further authority, should be needed for purposes indicated in this message, I shall not hesitate to bring the situation before the Congress. On this subject the Executive and Legislative branches of the Government must work together.

This is a serious course upon which we embark.

Excerpt from "The Truman Doctrine" by Harry S. Truman

19. Which quote indicates that time is of the essence?
    a. "The choice is too often not a free one."
    b. "The world is not static, and the status quo is not sacred."
    c. "This is a serious course upon which we embark."
    d. "We must take immediate and resolute action."

20. How is this speech organized?
    a. Problem and solution
    b. Chronological order
    c. Compare and contrast
    d. Categorical

21. What is the primary purpose of this speech?
    a. To persuade
    b. To describe
    c. To entertain
    d. To analyze

140

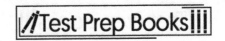

22. President Truman describes two ways of life. Which statement corresponds to his description?
    a. The first way of life is distinguished by free institutions; the second is marked by freedom of religion.
    b. The first way of life relies on terror and oppression; the second controls the press and radio.
    c. The first way of life guarantees individual liberties; the second suppresses personal freedoms.
    d. The first way of life suppresses individual liberties; the second guarantees personal freedoms.

23. What does the underlined word mean in the following sentence?

    "But we cannot allow changes in the status quo in violation of the Charter of the United Nations by such methods as coercion, or by such <u>subterfuges</u> as political infiltration."

    a. Helpful pieces of intel
    b. Tricky deceptions
    c. Time-consuming activities
    d. Underground routes

24. Based on the speech, what would be an immediate effect of Greece falling under the control of an armed minority?
    a. Turkey and the entire Middle East might experience unprecedented turmoil.
    b. The Charter of the United Nations would prevent any negative repercussions.
    c. Greece would receive hundreds of millions of dollars from the United States.
    d. Greece might become absorbed into another country and disappear off the map completely.

25. Truman states, "Should we fail to aid Greece and Turkey in this fateful hour, the effect will be far reaching to the West as well as to the East." What emotion might members of Congress feel at this moment?
    a. Disgust
    b. Astonishment
    c. Concern
    d. Eagerness

26. What is NOT one of Truman's requests to Congress?
    a. Send four million dollars in relief funds to Greece and Turkey.
    b. Overhaul the governments of Greece and Turkey.
    c. Deploy civil personnel to Greece and Turkey.
    d. Authorize the fastest and most effective use of supplies and equipment.

27. If Congress does not agree to Truman's plea, what is likely to happen?
    a. Another country will step up and offer similar relief aid.
    b. Greece and Turkey will rely on each other to avoid suppression.
    c. Most Eastern countries will experience the collapse of institutions and freedom.
    d. The United Nations will force the U.S. Congress to accept Truman's terms.

Science

Questions 28–37 are based on the following two passages:

<u>Passage 1</u>

"Insects are the flower's auxiliaries. Flies, wasps, honeybees, bumblebees, beetles, butterflies, all vie with one another in rendering aid by carrying the pollen of the stamens to the stigmas. They dive into the flower, enticed by a honeyed drop expressly prepared at the bottom of the corolla. In their efforts to obtain it they shake the stamens and daub themselves with pollen, which they carry from one flower to another. Who has not seen bumblebees coming out of the bosom of the flowers all covered with pollen? Their hairy stomachs, powdered with pollen, have only to touch a stigma in passing to communicate life to it. When in the spring you see on a blooming pear-tree, a whole swarm of flies, bees, and butterflies, hurrying, humming, and fluttering, it is a triple feast, my friends: a feast for the insect that pilfers in the depth of the flowers; a feast for the tree whose ovaries are quickened by all these merry little people; and a feast for man, to whom abundant harvest is promised. The insect is the best distributor of pollen. All the flowers it visits receive their share of quickening dust."

[...]

"To attract the insect that it needs, every flower has at the bottom of its corolla a drop of sweet liquor called nectar. From this liquor bees make their honey. To draw it from corollas shaped like a deep funnel, butterflies have a long trumpet, curled in a spiral when at rest, but which they unroll and plunge into the flower like a bore when they wish to obtain the delicious drink. The insect does not see this drop of nectar; however, it knows that it is there and finds it without hesitation. But in some flowers a grave difficulty presents itself: these flowers are closed tight everywhere. How is the treasure to be got at, how find the entrance that leads to the nectar? Well, these closed flowers have a signboard, a mark that says clearly: Enter here."

"You won't make us believe that!" cried Claire.

"I am not going to make you believe anything, my dear child; I am going to show you. Look at this snapdragon blossom. It is shut tight, its two closed lips leave no passage between. Its color is a uniform purplish red; but there, just in the middle of the lower lip, is a large spot of bright yellow. This spot, so appropriate for catching the eye, is the mark, the signboard I told you of. By its brightness it says: Here is the keyhole.

"Press your little finger on the spot. You see. The flower yawns immediately, the secret lock works. And you think the bumblebee does not know these things? Watch it in the garden and you will see how it can read the signs of the flowers. When it visits a snapdragon, it always alights on the yellow spot and nowhere else. The door opens, it enters. It twists and turns in the corolla and covers itself with pollen, with which it daubs the stigma. Having drunk the drop, it goes off to other flowers, forcing the opening of which it knows the secret thoroughly.

142

"All closed flowers have, like the snapdragon, a conspicuous point, a spot of bright color, a sign that shows the insect the entrance to the corolla and says to it: Here it is. Finally, insects whose trade it is to visit flowers and make the pollen fall from the stamens on to the stigma, have a wonderful knowledge of the significance of this spot. It is on it they use their strength to make the flower open.

"Let us recapitulate. Insects are necessary to flowers to bring pollen to the stigmas. A drop of nectar, distilled on purpose for this, attracts them to the bottom of the corolla; a bright spot shows them the road to follow. Either I am a triple idiot or we have here an admirable chain of facts. Later, my children, you will find only too many people saying: This world is the product of chance, no intelligence rules it, no Providence guides it. To those people, my friends, show the snapdragon's yellow spot. If, less clear-sighted than the burly bumblebee, they do not understand it, pity them: they have diseased brains."

Excerpt from *The Storybook of Science* by Jean-Henri Fabre

Passage 2

A very complete knowledge of the pollen-gathering behavior of the worker honeybee may be obtained by a study of the actions of bees which are working upon a plant which yields pollen in abundance. Sweet corn is an ideal plant for this purpose, and it will be used as a basis for the description which follows.

The movements of the legs and of the mouthparts are so rapid and so many members are in action at once that it is impossible for the eye to follow all at the same time. However, long-continued observation, assisted by the study of instantaneous photographs, gives confidence that the statements recorded are accurate, although some movements may have escaped notice.

To obtain pollen from corn the bee must find a tassel in the right stage of ripeness, with flowers open and stamens hanging from them. The bee alights upon a spike and crawls along it, clinging to the pendent anthers. It crawls over the anthers, going from one flower to another along the spike, being all the while busily engaged in the task of obtaining pollen. This reaches its body in several ways.

As the bee moves over the anthers it uses its mandibles and tongue, biting the anthers and licking them and securing a considerable amount of pollen upon these parts. This pollen becomes moist and sticky, since it is mingled with fluid from the mouth. A considerable amount of pollen is dislodged from the anthers as the bee moves over them. All of the legs receive a supply of this free pollen and much adheres to the hairs which cover the body, more particularly to those upon the ventral surface. This free pollen is dry and powdery and is very different in appearance from the moist pollen masses with which the bee returns to the hive. Before the return journey this pollen must be transferred to the baskets and securely packed in them.

After the bee has traversed a few flowers along the spike and has become well supplied with free pollen it begins to collect it from its body, head, and forward appendages and to transfer it to the posterior pair of legs. This may be accomplished while the bee is resting upon the flower or while it is hovering in the air before seeking additional pollen.

143

It is probably more thoroughly and rapidly accomplished while the bee is in the air, since all of the legs are then free to function in the gathering process.

If the collecting bee is seized with forceps and examined after it has crawled over the stamens of a few flowers of the corn, its legs and the ventral surface of its body are found to be thickly powdered over with pollen. If the bee hovers in the air for a few moments and is then examined very little pollen is found upon the body or upon the legs, except the masses within the pollen baskets. While in the air it has accomplished the work of collecting some of the scattered grains and of storing them in the baskets, while others have been brushed from the body.

In attempting to describe the movements by which this result is accomplished it will be best first to sketch briefly the roles of the three pairs of legs. They are as follows:

(a) The first pair of legs remove scattered pollen from the head and the region of the neck, and the pollen that has been moistened by fluid substances from the mouth.

(b) The second pair of legs remove scattered pollen from the thorax, more particularly from the ventral region, and they receive the pollen that has been collected by the first pair of legs.

(c) The third pair of legs collect a little of the scattered pollen from the abdomen and they receive pollen that has been collected by the second pair. Nearly all of this pollen is collected by the pollen combs of the hind legs, and is transferred from the combs to the pollen baskets or corbiculae in a manner to be described later.

It will thus be seen that the manipulation of pollen is a successive process, and that most of the pollen at least passes backward from the point where it happens to touch the bee until it finally reaches the corbiculae or is accidentally dislodged and falls from the rapidly moving limbs.

Excerpt from The Behavior of the Honey Bee in Pollen Collection by Dana Brackenridge Casteel

28. What do these two articles have in common?
    a. Both articles describe the roles of the bee's three different sets of legs.
    b. Both articles articulate the important role insects play in pollination.
    c. Both articles present their findings in a formal and scientific manner.
    d. Both articles discuss the methods that flowers use to attract pollinators.

29. The diction Jean-Henri Fabre uses in the first passage is:
    a. Pedantic
    b. Emotional
    c. Whimsical
    d. Ambiguous

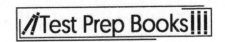

30. What does the underlined word mean in the following sentence?

"After the bee has traversed a few flowers along the spike and has become well supplied with free pollen it begins to collect it from its body, head, and forward appendages and to transfer it to the posterior pair of legs."

a. Strongest
b. Anterior
c. Ambulatory
d. Rear

31. In the first passage, what conclusion can be drawn about this character's feeling toward nature from the following sentence?

"To those people, my friends, show the snapdragon's yellow spot."

a. The character believes nature is designed with purpose and intent.
b. The character believes nature is vibrant yet random.
c. The character believes nature's most beautiful plant is the snapdragon.
d. The character believes nature is difficult to predict and understand.

32. Which entity does NOT benefit from the "triple feast?"
a. Trees
b. Insects
c. Pollen
d. Humans

33. Pollen manipulation by the honeybee is a successive process that:
a. Starts in the pollen basket and moves toward the legs
b. Starts on the body, moves to the legs, and eventually ends at the corbiculae
c. Starts on the thorax and moves toward the tongue and mandibles
d. Starts on the antennae, moves to the wings, and eventually ends at the pollen basket

34. Which kind of logical fallacy is presented in the following sentence?

"Either I am a triple idiot or we have here an admirable chain of facts."

a. Slippery slope
b. Ad hominem
c. Red herring
d. False dichotomy

35. In paragraph five of the first passage, what speaker imply when he says the "flower yawns"?
a. The petals of the flower are opening up slowly.
b. The flower is worn out from pollination and needs rest.
c. The flower is expanding its surface area to absorb more carbon dioxide.
d. The flower is having a difficult time regulating night and day.

145

36. Why does the study in the second passage use sweet corn?
    a. Honeybees are attracted to the natural sweetness of the plant.
    b. The region has an abundance of sweet corn available for study.
    c. Sweet corn does not attract any other species of pollinator, making it easier to focus on bees.
    d. Sweet corn yields a generous amount of pollen.

37. What conclusion can be drawn after reading both of these passages?
    a. To date, science has had very to say little about bees, flowers, and pollination.
    b. Honeybees and flowers have a mutually beneficial relationship.
    c. Bees are the most advanced pollinator.
    d. The process of pollination is more accidental than intentional.

Science

Questions 38–47 are based upon the following passage:

How does soap make your hands clean?

Why will gasoline take a grease spot out of your clothes?

If we were to go back to our convenient imaginary switchboard to turn off another law, we should find near the heat switches, and not far from the chemistry ones, a switch labeled Solution. Suppose we turned it off:

The fishes in the sea are among the first creatures to be surprised by our action. For instantly all the salt in the ocean drops to the bottom like so much sand, and most saltwater fishes soon perish in the freshwater.

[...]

Probably we had better let the Solution switch alone, after all. Instead, here are a couple of experiments that will help to make clear what happens when anything dissolves to make a solution.

Experiment 80. Fill a test tube one fourth full of cold water. Slowly stir in salt until no more will dissolve. Add half a teaspoonful more of salt than will dissolve. Dry the outside of the test tube and heat the salty water over the Bunsen burner. Will hot water dissolve things more readily or less readily than cold? Why do you wash dishes in hot water?

Experiment 81. Fill a test tube one fourth full of any kind of oil, and one fourth full of water. Hold your thumb over the top of the test tube and shake it hard for a minute or two. Now look at it. Pour it out, and shake some prepared cleanser into the test tube, adding a little more water. Shake the test tube thoroughly and rinse. Put it away clean.

When you shake the oil with the water, the oil breaks up into tiny droplets. These droplets are so small that they reflect the light that strikes them and so look white, or pale yellow. This milky mixture is called an emulsion. Milk is an emulsion; there are tiny droplets of butter fat and other substances scattered all through the milk. The butter fat

146

is not dissolved in the rest of the milk, and the oil is not dissolved in the water. But the droplets may be so small that an emulsion acts almost exactly like a solution.

But when you shake or stir salt or sugar in water, the particles divide up into smaller and smaller pieces, until probably each piece is just a single molecule of the salt or sugar. And these molecules get into the spaces between the water molecules and bounce around among them. They therefore act like the water and let the light through. This is a solution. The salt or sugar is dissolved in the water. Any liquid mixture which remains clear is a solution, no matter what the color. Most red ink, most blueing, clear coffee, tea, and ocean water are solutions. If a liquid is clear, no matter what the color, you can be sure that whatever things may be in it are dissolved.

Experiment 82. Pour alcohol into a test tube (square-bottomed test tubes are best for this experiment), standing the tube up beside a ruler. When the alcohol is just one inch high in the tube, stop pouring. Put exactly the same amount of water in another test tube of the same size. When you pour them together, how many inches high do you think the mixture will be? Pour the water into the alcohol, shake the mixture a little, and measure to see how high it comes in the test tube. Did you notice the warmth when you shook the tube?

If you use denatured alcohol, you are likely to have an emulsion as a result of the mixing. The alcohol part of the denatured alcohol dissolves in the water well enough, but the denaturing substance in the alcohol will not dissolve in water; so it forms tiny droplets that make the mixture of alcohol and water cloudy.

The purpose of this experiment is to show that the molecules of water get into the spaces between the molecules of alcohol. It is as if you were to add a pail of pebbles to a pail of apples. The pebbles would fill in between the apples, and the mixture would not nearly fill two pails.

Excerpt from "Common Science" by Carleton W. Washburne

38. Which title best suits this chapter?
    a. Cleaning with Science
    b. Experiments You Can Do at Home
    c. Solutions and Emulsions
    d. Solution Switchboard

39. What effect does the author achieve by presenting the scenario of the imaginary?
    a. Humor through a hypothetical situation
    b. Shock through a surprise twist
    c. Deception through misleading information
    d. Curiosity through growing suspense

40. Why does the author ask rhetorical questions?
    a. To reveal their opinion on the topic
    b. To encourage the reader to draw their own conclusions
    c. To ensure the reader is following along
    d. To convince the reader to conduct the experiments at home

147

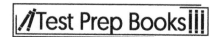
41. How are emulsions different from solutions?
   a. Emulsions are clear; solutions are cloudy.
   b. Emulsions are non-potable; solutions are potable.
   c. Emulsions have a low temperature; solutions have a high temperature.
   d. Emulsions have tiny, suspended droplets; solutions are completely dissolved.

42. What is the most likely result of Experiment 80?
   a. The heat was unable to dissolve the additional salt.
   b. Once heated, the additional salt dissolved completely.
   c. The additional salt prevented the water from heating up more than room temperature.
   d. The heated salt and water solution could be used to wash dishes.

43. When might an emulsion pass as a solution?
   a. When the scattered droplets cannot be detected because they are so small.
   b. When the substance is heated to its boiling point.
   c. When the emulsion has been stirred or shaken thoroughly.
   d. Emulsions cannot pass as solutions.

44. Which analogy makes the correct comparison?
   a. Pebbles are to apples as alcohol is to water.
   b. Water is to pebbles as alcohol is to apples.
   c. Apples are to water as pebbles are to alcohol.
   d. Alcohol and water are to emulsion as apples and pebbles are to solution.

45. What can be inferred about denatured alcohol?
   a. It can be dangerous to work with in a laboratory.
   b. It has the same basic properties as regular alcohol.
   c. It needs to be heated in order to completely dissolve.
   d. There are better alternatives to form true solutions.

46. Using deductive reasoning, how high will the mixture measure at the end of Experiment 82?
   a. Exactly two inches
   b. More than two inches
   c. Less than two inches
   d. There is no way to tell unless you conduct the experiment.

47. Which idiom could be explained using evidence from this passage?
   a. That is like comparing apples to oranges.
   b. She is going to be in hot water.
   c. They are like oil and water.
   d. No use crying over spilled milk.

Writing and Language Test

Questions 1–9 are based on the following passage:

While all dogs (1) descend through gray wolves, it's easy to notice that dog breeds come in a variety of shapes and sizes. With such a (2) drastic range of traits, appearances and body types, dogs are one of the most variable and adaptable species on the planet. (3)

148

But why so many differences. The answer is that humans have actually played a major role in altering the biology of dogs. (4) This was done through a process called selective breeding.

(5) Selective breeding which is also called artificial selection is the process in which animals with desired traits are bred in order to produce offspring that share the same traits. In natural selection, (6) animals must adapt to their environments increase their chance of survival. Over time, certain traits develop in animals that enable them to thrive in these environments. Those animals with more of these traits, or better versions of these traits, gain an (7) advantage over others of their species. Therefore, the animal's chances to mate are increased and these useful (8) genes are passed into their offspring. With dog breeding, humans select traits that are desired and encourage more of these desired traits in other dogs by breeding dogs that already have them.

The reason for different breeds of dogs is that there were specific needs that humans wanted to fill with their animals. For example, scent hounds are known for their extraordinary ability to track game through scent. These breeds are also known for their endurance in seeking deer and other prey. Therefore, early hunters took dogs that displayed these abilities and bred them to encourage these traits. Later, these generations took on characteristics that aided these desired traits. (9) For example, Bloodhounds have broad snouts and droopy ears that fall to the ground when they smell. These physical qualities not only define the look of the Bloodhound, but also contribute to their amazing tracking ability. The broad snout is able to define and hold onto scents longer than many other breeds. The long, floppy ears serve to collect and hold the scents the earth holds so that the smells are clearer and able to be distinguished.

1. Which of the following would be the best choice for this sentence (reproduced below)?

   While all dogs (1) descend through gray wolves, it's easy to notice that dog breeds come in a variety of shapes and sizes.

   a. NO CHANGE
   b. descend by gray wolves
   c. descend from gray wolves
   d. descended through gray wolves

2. Which of the following would be the best choice for this sentence (reproduced below)?

   With such a (2) drastic range of traits, appearances and body types, dogs are one of the most variable and adaptable species on the planet.

   a. NO CHANGE
   b. drastic range of traits, appearances, and body types,
   c. drastic range of traits and appearances and body types,
   d. drastic range of traits, appearances, as well as body types,

3. Which of the following would be the best choice for this sentence (reproduced below)?

(3) But why so many differences.

a. NO CHANGE
b. But are there so many differences?
c. But why so many differences are there.
d. But why so many differences?

4. Which of the following would be the best choice for this sentence (reproduced below)?

(4) This was done through a process called selective breeding.

a. NO CHANGE
b. This was done, through a process called selective breeding.
c. This was done, through a process, called selective breeding.
d. This was done through selective breeding, a process.

5. Which of the following would be the best choice for this sentence (reproduced below)?

(5) Selective breeding which is also called artificial selection is the process in which animals with desired traits are bred in order to produce offspring that share the same traits.

a. NO CHANGE
b. Selective breeding, which is also called artificial selection is the process
c. Selective breeding which is also called, artificial selection, is the process
d. Selective breeding, which is also called artificial selection, is the process

6. Which of the following would be the best choice for this sentence (reproduced below)?

In natural selection, (6) animals must adapt to their environments increase their chance of survival.

a. NO CHANGE
b. animals must adapt to their environments to increase their chance of survival.
c. animals must adapt to their environments, increase their chance of survival.
d. animals must adapt to their environments, increasing their chance of survival.

7. Which of the following would be the best choice for this sentence (reproduced below)?

Those animals with more of these traits, or better versions of these traits, gain an (7) advantage over others of their species.

a. NO CHANGE
b. advantage over others, of their species.
c. advantages over others of their species.
d. advantage over others.

150

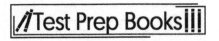

8. Which of the following would be the best choice for this sentence (reproduced below)?

> Therefore, the animal's chances to mate are increased and these useful (8) genes are passed into their offspring.

    a. NO CHANGE
    b. genes are passed onto their offspring.
    c. genes are passed on to their offspring.
    d. genes are passed within their offspring.

9. Which of the following would be the best choice for this sentence (reproduced below)?

> (9) For example, Bloodhounds have broad snouts and droopy ears that fall to the ground when they smell.

    a. NO CHANGE
    b. For example, Bloodhounds,
    c. For example Bloodhounds
    d. For example, bloodhounds

Questions 10–18 are based on the following passage:

I'm not alone when I say that it's hard to pay attention sometimes. I can't count how many times I've sat in a classroom, lecture, speech, or workshop and (10) been bored to tears or rather sleep. (11) Usually I turn to doodling in order to keep awake. This never really helps; I'm not much of an artist. Therefore, after giving up on drawing a masterpiece, I would just concentrate on keeping my eyes open and trying to be attentive. This didn't always work because I wasn't engaged in what was going on.

(12) Sometimes in particularly dull seminars, I'd imagine comical things going on in the room or with the people trapped in the room with me. Why? (13) Because I wasn't invested in what was going on I wasn't motivated to listen. I'm not going to write about how I conquered the difficult task of actually paying attention in a difficult or unappealing class—it can be done, sure. I have sat through the very epitome of boredom (in my view at least) several times and come away learning something. (14) Everyone probably has had to at one time or another do this. What I want to talk about is that profound moment when curiosity is sparked (15) in another person drawing them to pay attention to what is before them and expand their knowledge.

What really makes people pay attention? (16) Easy it's interest. This doesn't necessarily mean (17) embellishing subject matter drawing people's attention. This won't always work. However, an individual can present material in a way that is clear to understand and actually engages the audience. Asking questions to the audience or class will make them a part of the topic at hand. Discussions that make people think about the content and (18) how it applies to there lives world and future are key. If math is being discussed, an instructor can explain the purpose behind the equations or perhaps use real-world applications to show how relevant the topic is. When discussing history, a lecturer can prompt students to imagine themselves in the place of key figures and ask how they might respond. The bottom line is to explore the ideas rather than just lecture.

151

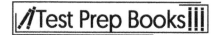
Give people the chance to explore material from multiple angles, and they'll be hungry to keep paying attention for more information.

10. Which of the following would be the best choice for this sentence (reproduced below)?

I can't count how many times I've sat in a classroom, lecture, speech, or workshop and (10) been bored to tears or rather sleep.

a. NO CHANGE
b. been bored to, tears, or rather sleep.
c. been bored, to tears or rather sleep.
d. been bored to tears or, rather, sleep.

11. Which of the following would be the best choice for this sentence (reproduced below)?

(11) Usually I turn to doodling in order to keep awake.

a. NO CHANGE
b. Usually I turn to doodling in order to keep awakened.
c. Usually I turn to doodling, in order, to keep awake.
d. Usually I turned to doodling in order to keep awake.

12. Which of the following would be the best choice for this sentence (reproduced below)?

(12) Sometimes in particularly dull seminars, I'd imagine comical things going on in the room or with the people trapped in the room with me.

a. NO CHANGE
b. Sometimes, in particularly, dull seminars,
c. Sometimes in particularly dull seminars
d. Sometimes in particularly, dull seminars,

13. Which of the following would be the best choice for this sentence (reproduced below)?

(13) Because I wasn't invested in what was going on I wasn't motivated to listen.

a. NO CHANGE
b. Because I wasn't invested, in what was going on, I wasn't motivated to listen.
c. Because I wasn't invested in what was going on. I wasn't motivated to listen.
d. I wasn't motivated to listen because I wasn't invested in what was going on.

14. Which of the following would be the best choice for this sentence (reproduced below)?

(14) Everyone probably has had to at one time or another do this.

a. NO CHANGE
b. Everyone probably has had to, at one time. Do this.
c. Everyone's probably had to do this at some time.
d. At one time or another everyone probably has had to do this.

152

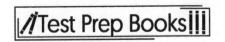

15. Which of the following would be the best choice for this sentence (reproduced below)?

What I want to talk about is that profound moment when curiosity is sparked (15) <u>in another person drawing them to pay attention to what is before them </u>and expand their knowledge.

a. NO CHANGE
b. in another person, drawing them to pay attention to what is before them
c. in another person; drawing them to pay attention to what is before them
d. in another person, drawing them to pay attention to what is before them.

16. Which of the following would be the best choice for this sentence (reproduced below)?

(16) <u>Easy it's interest.</u>

a. NO CHANGE
b. Easy it is interest.
c. Easy its interest.
d. Easy—it's interest.

17. Which of the following would be the best choice for this sentence (reproduced below)?

This doesn't necessarily mean (17) <u>embellishing subject matter drawing people's attention.</u>

a. NO CHANGE
b. embellishing subject matter which draws people's attention.
c. embellishing subject matter to draw people's attention.
d. embellishing subject matter for the purpose of drawing people's attention.

18. Which of the following would be the best choice for this sentence (reproduced below)?

Discussions that make people think about the content and (18) <u>how it applies to there lives world and future are key.</u>

a. NO CHANGE
b. how it applies to their lives, world, and future are key.
c. how it applied to there lives world and future are key.
d. how it applies to their lives, world, and future, are key.

Questions 19–27 are based on the following passage:

Since the first discovery of dinosaur bones, (19) <u>scientists has made strides in technological development and methodologies used to investigate </u>these extinct animals. We know more about dinosaurs than ever before and are still learning fascinating new things about how they looked and lived. However, one has to ask, (20) <u>how if earlier perceptions of dinosaurs </u>continue to influence people's understanding of these creatures? Can these perceptions inhibit progress towards further understanding of dinosaurs?

(21) <u>The biggest problem with studying dinosaurs is simply that there are no living dinosaurs to observe.</u> All discoveries associated with these animals are based on

153

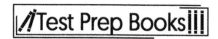

physical remains. To gauge behavioral characteristics, scientists cross-examine these (22) finds with living animals that seem similar in order to gain understanding. While this method is effective, these are still deductions. Some ideas about dinosaurs can't be tested and confirmed simply because humans can't replicate a living dinosaur. For example, a Spinosaurus has a large sail, or a finlike structure that grows from its back. Paleontologists know this sail exists and have ideas for the function of (23) the sail however they are uncertain of which idea is the true function. Some scientists believe (24) the sail serves to regulate the Spinosaurus' body temperature and yet others believe its used to attract mates. Still, other scientists think the sail is used to intimidate other predatory dinosaurs for self-defense. These are all viable explanations, but they are also influenced by what scientists know about modern animals. (25) Yet, it's quite possible that the sail could hold a completely unique function.

While it's (26) plausible, even likely that dinosaurs share many traits with modern animals, there is the danger of overattributing these qualities to a unique, extinct species. For much of the early nineteenth century, when people first started studying dinosaur bones, the assumption was that they were simply giant lizards. (27) For the longest time this image was the prevailing view on dinosaurs, until evidence indicated that they were more likely warm blooded. Scientists have also discovered that many dinosaurs had feathers and actually share many traits with modern birds.

19. Which of the following would be the best choice for this sentence (reproduced below)?

Since the first discovery of dinosaur bones, (19) scientists has made strides in technological development and methodologies used to investigate these extinct animals.

a. NO CHANGE
b. scientists has made strides in technological development, and methodologies, used to investigate
c. scientists have made strides in technological development and methodologies used to investigate
d. scientists, have made strides in technological development and methodologies used, to investigate

20. Which of the following would be the best choice for this sentence (reproduced below)?

However, one has to ask, (20) how if earlier perceptions of dinosaurs continue to influence people's understanding of these creatures?

a. NO CHANGE
b. how perceptions of dinosaurs
c. how, if, earlier perceptions of dinosaurs
d. do earlier perceptions of dinosaurs

21. Which of the following would be the best choice for this sentence (reproduced below)?

    (21) <u>The biggest problem with studying dinosaurs is simply that there are no living dinosaurs to observe.</u>

    a. NO CHANGE
    b. The biggest problem with studying dinosaurs is simple, that there are no living dinosaurs to observe.
    c. The biggest problem with studying dinosaurs is simple, there are no living dinosaurs to observe.
    d. The biggest problem with studying dinosaurs, is simply that there are no living dinosaurs to observe.

22. Which of the following would be the best choice for this sentence (reproduced below)?

    To gauge behavioral characteristics, scientists cross-examine these (22) <u>finds with living animals that seem similar in order to gain understanding.</u>

    a. NO CHANGE
    b. finds with living animals to explore potential similarities.
    c. finds with living animals to gain understanding of similarities.
    d. finds with living animals that seem similar, in order, to gain understanding.

23. Which of the following would be the best choice for this sentence (reproduced below)?

    Paleontologists know this sail exists and have ideas for the function of (23) <u>the sail however they are uncertain of which idea is the true function.</u>

    a. NO CHANGE
    b. the sail however, they are uncertain of which idea is the true function.
    c. the sail however they are, uncertain, of which idea is the true function.
    d. the sail; however, they are uncertain of which idea is the true function.

24. Which of the following would be the best choice for this sentence (reproduced below)?

    Some scientists believe (24) <u>the sail serves to regulate the Spinosaurus' body temperature and yet others believe its used to attract mates.</u>

    a. NO CHANGE
    b. the sail serves to regulate the Spinosaurus' body temperature, yet others believe it's used to attract mates.
    c. the sail serves to regulate the Spinosaurus' body temperature and yet others believe it's used to attract mates.
    d. the sail serves to regulate the Spinosaurus' body temperature however others believe it's used to attract mates.

155

25. Which of the following would be the best choice for this sentence (reproduced below)?

> (25) <u>Yet, it's quite possible</u> that the sail could hold a completely unique function.

a. NO CHANGE
b. Yet, it's quite possible,
c. It's quite possible,
d. Its quite possible

26. Which of the following would be the best choice for this sentence (reproduced below)?

> While it's (26) <u>plausible, even likely that dinosaurs share many</u> traits with modern animals, there is the danger of over attributing these qualities to a unique, extinct species.

a. NO CHANGE
b. plausible, even likely that, dinosaurs share many
c. plausible, even likely, that dinosaurs share many
d. plausible even likely that dinosaurs share many

27. Which of the following would be the best choice for this sentence (reproduced below)?

> (27) <u>For the longest time this image was the prevailing view on dinosaurs</u>, until evidence indicated that they were more likely warm blooded.

a. NO CHANGE
b. For the longest time this was the prevailing view on dinosaurs
c. For the longest time, this image, was the prevailing view on dinosaurs
d. This was the prevailing image of dinosaurs

Questions 28–36 are based on the following passage:

Everyone has heard the (28) <u>idea of the end justifying the means; that would be Weston's philosophy.</u> Weston is willing to cross any line, commit any act no matter how heinous, to achieve success in his goal. (29) <u>Ransom is repulsed by this fact, seeing total evil in Weston's plan.</u> To do an evil act in order (30) <u>to gain a result that's supposedly good would ultimately warp the final act.</u> (31) <u>This opposing viewpoints immediately distinguishes Ransom as the hero.</u> In the conflict with Un-man, Ransom remains true to his moral principles, someone who refuses to be compromised by power. Instead, Ransom makes it clear that by allowing such processes as murder and lying dictate how one attains a positive outcome, (32) <u>the righteous goal becomes corrupted.</u> The good end would not be truly good, but a twisted end that conceals corrupt deeds.

(33) <u>This idea of allowing necessary evils to happen, is very tempting, it is what Weston fell prey to.</u> (34) <u>The temptation of the evil spirit Un-man ultimately takes over Weston and he is possessed.</u> However, Ransom does not give into temptation. He remains faithful to the truth of what is right and incorrect. This leads him to directly face Un-man for the fate of Perelandra and its inhabitants.

Just as Weston was corrupted by the Un-man, (35) <u>Un-man after this seeks to tempt the Queen of Perelandra</u> to darkness. Ransom must literally (36) <u>show her the right path, to</u>

156

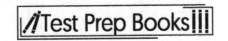

accomplish this, he does this based on the same principle as the "means to an end" argument—that good follows good, and evil follows evil. Later in the plot, Weston/Un-man seeks to use deceptive reasoning to turn the queen to sin, pushing the queen to essentially ignore Maleldil's rule to satisfy her own curiosity. In this sense, Un-man takes on the role of a false prophet, a tempter. Ransom must shed light on the truth, but this is difficult; his adversary is very clever and uses brilliant language. Ransom's lack of refinement heightens the weight of Un-man's corrupted logic, and so the Queen herself is intrigued by his logic.

Based on an excerpt from Perelandra *by C.S. Lewis*

28. Which of the following would be the best choice for this sentence (reproduced below)?

> Everyone has heard the (28) idea of the end justifying the means; that would be Weston's philosophy.

  a. NO CHANGE
  b. idea of the end justifying the means; this is Weston's philosophy.
  c. idea of the end justifying the means, this is the philosophy of Weston.
  d. idea of the end justifying the means. That would be Weston's philosophy.

29. Which of the following would be the best choice for this sentence (reproduced below)?

> (29) Ransom is repulsed by this fact, seeing total evil in Weston's plan.

  a. NO CHANGE
  b. Ransom is reviled by this fact; seeing total evil in Weston's plan.
  c. Ransom, is reviled by this fact, seeing total evil in Weston's plan.
  d. Ransom reviled by this, sees total evil in Weston's plan.

30. Which of the following would be the best choice for this sentence (reproduced below)?

> To do an evil act in order (30) to gain a result that's supposedly good would ultimately warp the final act.

  a. NO CHANGE
  b. for an outcome that's for a greater good would ultimately warp the final act.
  c. to gain a final act would warp its goodness.
  d. to achieve a positive outcome would ultimately warp the goodness of the final act.

31. Which of the following would be the best choice for this sentence (reproduced below)?

> (31) This opposing viewpoints immediately distinguishes Ransom as the hero.

  a. NO CHANGE
  b. This opposing viewpoints immediately distinguishes Ransom, as the hero.
  c. This opposing viewpoint immediately distinguishes Ransom as the hero.
  d. Those opposing viewpoints immediately distinguishes Ransom as the hero.

157

32. Which of the following would be the best choice for this sentence (reproduced below)?

> Instead, Ransom makes it clear that by allowing such processes as murder and lying dictate how one attains a positive outcome, (32) the righteous goal becomes corrupted.

a. NO CHANGE
b. the goal becomes corrupted and no longer righteous.
c. the righteous goal becomes, corrupted.
d. the goal becomes corrupted, when once it was righteous.

33. Which of the following would be the best choice for this sentence (reproduced below)?

> (33) This idea of allowing necessary evils to happen, is very tempting, it is what Weston fell prey to.

a. NO CHANGE
b. This idea of allowing necessary evils to happen, is very tempting. This is what Weston fell prey to.
c. This idea, allowing necessary evils to happen, is very tempting, it is what Weston fell prey to.
d. This tempting idea of allowing necessary evils to happen is what Weston fell prey to.

34. Which of the following would be the best choice for this sentence (reproduced below)?

> (34) The temptation of the evil spirit Un-man ultimately takes over Weston and he is possessed.

a. NO CHANGE
b. Weston gives into the temptation of the evil spirit Un-man and becomes possessed.
c. Weston is possessed as a result of the temptation of the evil spirit Un-man ultimately, who takes over.
d. The temptation of the evil spirit Un-man takes over Weston and he is possessed ultimately.

35. Which of the following would be the best choice for this sentence (reproduced below)?

> Just as Weston was corrupted by the Un-man, (35) Un-man after this seeks to tempt the Queen of Perelandra to darkness.

a. NO CHANGE
b. Un-man, after this, would tempt the Queen of Perelandra
c. Un-man, after this, seeks to tempt the Queen of Perelandra
d. Un-man then seeks to tempt the Queen of Perelandra

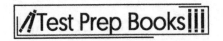
36. Which of the following would be the best choice for this sentence (reproduced below)?

> Ransom must literally (36) <u>show her the right path, to accomplish this, he does this based on the same principle as the "means to an end" argument</u>—that good follows good, and evil follows evil.

   a. NO CHANGE

   b. show her the right path. To accomplish this, he uses the same principle as the "means to an end" argument

   c. show her the right path; to accomplish this he uses the same principle as the "means to an end" argument

   d. show her the right path, to accomplish this, the same principle as the "means to an end" argument is applied

Questions 37–44 are based on the following passage:

(37) <u>What's clear about the news today is that the broader the media</u> the more ways there are to tell a story. Even if different news groups cover the same story, individual newsrooms can interpret or depict the story differently than other counterparts. Stories can also change depending on the type of (38) <u>media in question incorporating different styles and unique</u> ways to approach the news. (39) <u>It is because of these respective media types that ethical and news-related subject matter can sometimes seem different or altered.</u> But how does this affect the narrative of the new story?

I began by investigating a written newspaper article from the Baltimore Sun. Instantly striking are the bolded headlines. (40) <u>These are clearly meant for direct the viewer</u> to the most exciting and important stories the paper has to offer. What was particularly noteworthy about this edition was that the first page dealt with two major ethical issues. (41) <u>On a national level there was a story</u> on the evolving Petraeus scandal involving his supposed affair. The other article was focused locally in Baltimore, a piece questioning the city's Ethics Board and their current director. Just as a television newscaster communicates the story through camera and dialogue, the printed article applies intentional and targeted written narrative style. More so than any of the mediums, a news article seems to be focused specifically on a given story without need to jump to another. Finer details are usually expanded on (42) <u>in written articles, usually people who</u> read newspapers or go online for web articles want more than a quick blurb. The diction of the story is also more precise and can be either straightforward or suggestive (43) <u>depending in earnest on the goal of the writer.</u> However, there's still plenty of room for opinions to be inserted into the text.

Usually, all news (44) <u>outlets have some sort of bias, it's just a question of how much</u> bias clouds the reporting. As long as this bias doesn't withhold information from the reader, it can be considered credible. However, an overuse of bias, opinion, and suggestive language can rob readers of the chance to interpret the news events for themselves.

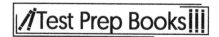

37. Which of the following would be the best choice for this sentence (reproduced below)?

> (37) What's clear about the news today is that the broader the media the more ways there are to tell a story.

   a. NO CHANGE
   b. What's clear, about the news today, is that the broader the media
   c. What's clear about today's news is that the broader the media
   d. The news today is broader than earlier media

38. Which of the following would be the best choice for this sentence (reproduced below)?

> Stories can also change depending on the type of (38) media in question incorporating different styles and unique ways to approach the news.

   a. NO CHANGE
   b. media in question; each incorporates different styles and unique
   c. media in question. To incorporate different styles and unique
   d. media in question, incorporating different styles and unique

39. Which of the following would be the best choice for this sentence (reproduced below)?

> (39) It is because of these respective media types that ethical and news-related subject matter can sometimes seem different or altered.

   a. NO CHANGE
   b. It is because of these respective media types, that ethical and news-related subject matter, can sometimes seem different or altered.
   c. It is because of these respective media types, that ethical and news-related subject matter can sometimes seem different or altered.
   d. It is because of these respective media types that ethical and news-related subject matter can sometimes seem different. Or altered.

40. Which of the following would be the best choice for this sentence (reproduced below)?

> (40) These are clearly meant for direct the viewer to the most exciting and important stories the paper has to offer.

   a. NO CHANGE
   b. These are clearly meant for the purpose of giving direction to the viewer
   c. These are clearly meant to direct the viewer
   d. These are clearly meant for the viewer to be directed

41. Which of the following would be the best choice for this sentence (reproduced below)?

> (41) <u>On a national level there was a story</u> on the evolving Petraeus scandal involving his supposed affair.

   a. NO CHANGE
   b. On a national level a story was there
   c. On a national level; there was a story
   d. On a national level, there was a story

42. Which of the following would be the best choice for this sentence (reproduced below)?

> Finer details are usually expanded on (42) <u>in written articles, usually people who</u> read newspapers or go online for web articles want more than a quick blurb.

   a. NO CHANGE
   b. in written articles. People who usually
   c. in written articles, usually, people who
   d. in written articles usually people who

43. Which of the following would be the best choice for this sentence (reproduced below)?

> The diction of the story is also more precise and can be either straightforward or suggestive (43) <u>depending in earnest on the goal of the writer.</u>

   a. NO CHANGE
   b. depending; in earnest on the goal of the writer.
   c. depending, in earnest, on the goal of the writer.
   d. the goal of the writer, in earnest, depends on the goal of the writer.

44. Which of the following would be the best choice for this sentence (reproduced below)?

> Usually, all news (44) <u>outlets have some sort of bias, it's just a question of how much</u> bias clouds the reporting.

   a. NO CHANGE
   b. outlets have some sort of bias; it's just a question of how much
   c. outlets have some sort of bias it can just be a question of how much
   d. outlets have some sort of bias, its just a question of how much

Math Test

Calculator Questions

1. Which of the following inequalities is equivalent to $3 - \frac{1}{2}x \geq 2$?

   a. $x \geq 2$
   b. $x \leq 2$
   c. $x \geq 1$
   d. $x \leq 1$

2. If $g(x) = x^3 - 3x^2 - 2x + 6$ and $f(x) = 2$, then what is $g(f(x))$?

   a. -26

   b. 6

   c. $2x^3 - 6x^2 - 4x + 12$

   d. -2

3. What are the coordinates of the focus of the parabola $y = -9x^2$?

   a. $(-3, 0)$

   b. $\left(-\frac{1}{36}, 0\right)$

   c. $(0, -3)$

   d. $\left(0, -\frac{1}{36}\right)$

4. A National Hockey League store in the state of Michigan advertises 50% off all items. Sales tax in Michigan is 6%. How much would a hat originally priced at $32.99 and a jersey originally priced at $64.99 cost during this sale? Round to the nearest penny.

   a. $97.98

   b. $103.86

   c. $51.93

   d. $48.99

5. Store brand coffee beans cost $1.23 per pound. A local coffee bean roaster charges $1.98 per $1\frac{1}{2}$ pounds. How much more would 5 pounds from the local roaster cost than 5 pounds of the store brand?

   a. $0.55

   b. $1.55

   c. $1.45

   d. $0.45

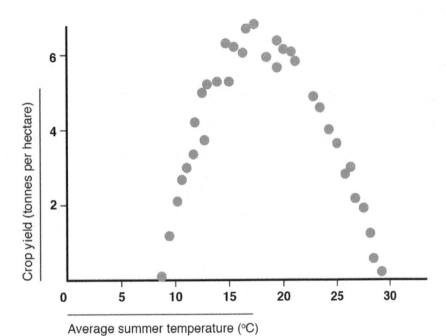
6. Which equation best represents the scatter plot below?

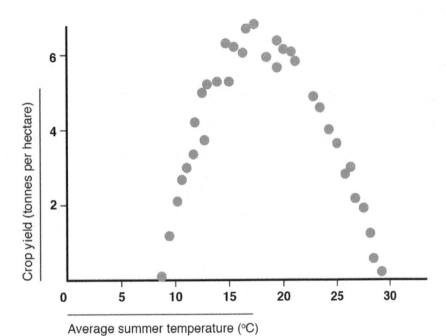

Average summer temperature (°C)

a. $y = 3x - 4$
b. $y = 2x^2 + 7x - 9$
c. $y = (3)(4^x)$
d. $y = -\frac{1}{14}x^2 + 2x - 8$

7. What is the volume of a cylinder, in terms of π, with a radius of 5 inches and a height of 10 inches?
a. $250\pi\ in^3$
b. $50\pi\ in^3$
c. $100\pi\ in^3$
d. $200\pi\ in^3$

8. What is the solution to the following system of equations?

$$x^2 - 2x + y = 8$$

$$x - y = -2$$

a. $(-2, 3)$
b. There is no solution.
c. $(-2, 0)\ (1, 3)$
d. $(-2, 0)\ (3, 5)$

9. What is the equation for the line passing through the origin and the point $(2, 1)$?
a. $y = 2x$
b. $y = \frac{1}{2}x$
c. $y = x - 2$
d. $2y = x + 1$

163

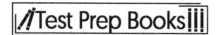

10. A rectangle was formed out of pipe cleaner. Its length was $\frac{1}{2}$ foot and its width was $\frac{11}{2}$ inches. What is its area in square inches?

    a. $\frac{11}{4}$ inches^2

    b. $\frac{11}{2}$ inches^2

    c. 22 inches^2

    d. 33 inches^2

11. What type of function is modeled by the values in the following table?

X	$f(x)$
1	2
2	4
3	8
4	16
5	32

    a. Linear
    b. Exponential
    c. Quadratic
    d. Cubic

12. A shuffled deck of 52 cards contains 4 kings. One card is drawn, and is not put back in the deck. Then a second card is drawn. What's the probability that both cards are kings?

    a. $\frac{1}{169}$

    b. $\frac{1}{221}$

    c. $\frac{1}{13}$

    d. $\frac{4}{13}$

13. Write the expression for six less than three times the sum of twice a number and one.
    a. $2x + 1 - 6$
    b. $3x + 1 - 6$
    c. $3(x + 1) - 6$
    d. $3(2x + 1) - 6$

14. $(2x - 4y)^2 =$
    a. $4x^2 - 16xy + 16y^2$
    b. $4x^2 - 8xy + 16y^2$
    c. $4x^2 - 16xy - 16y^2$
    d. $2x^2 - 8xy + 8y^2$

15. What are the zeros of $f(x) = x^2 + 4$?
   a. $x = -4$
   b. $x = \pm 2i$
   c. $x = \pm 2$
   d. $x = \pm 4i$

16. Which is the simplest form of the expression $(7n + 3n^3 + 3) + (8n + 5n^3 + 2n^4)$?
   a. $9n^4 + 15n - 2$
   b. $2n^4 + 5n^3 + 15n - 2$
   c. $9n^4 + 8n^3 + 15n$
   d. $2n^4 + 8n^3 + 15n + 3$

17. Multiply and reduce $\frac{15}{23} \times \frac{54}{127}$.
   a. $\frac{810}{2,921}$

   b. $\frac{81}{292}$

   c. $\frac{69}{150}$

   d. $\frac{810}{2929}$

18. What is the product of the following expression?

$$(4x - 8)(5x^2 + x + 6)$$

   a. $20x^3 - 36x^2 + 16x - 48$
   b. $6x^3 - 41x^2 + 12x + 15$
   c. $20x^3 + 11x^2 - 37x - 12$
   d. $2x^3 - 11x^2 - 32x + 20$

19. What is the solution for the following equation?

$$\frac{x^2 + x - 30}{x - 5} = 11$$

   a. $x = -6$
   b. There is no solution.
   c. $x = 16$
   d. $x = 5$

20. If x is not zero, then $\frac{3}{x} + \frac{5u}{2x} - \frac{u}{4} =$
   a. $\frac{12 + 10u - ux}{4x}$

   b. $\frac{3 + 5u - ux}{x}$

   c. $\frac{12x + 10u + ux}{4x}$

   d. $\frac{12 + 10u - u}{4x}$

165

21. What are the zeros of the function: $f(x) = x^3 + 4x^2 + 4x$?
   a. -2
   b. 0, -2
   c. 2
   d. 0, 2

22. Which of the following formulas would correctly calculate the perimeter of a legal-sized piece of paper that is 14 inches long and $8\frac{1}{2}$ inches wide?
   a. $P = 14 + 8\frac{1}{2}$
   b. $P = 14 + 8\frac{1}{2} + 14 + 8\frac{1}{2}$
   c. $P = 14 \times 8\frac{1}{2}$
   d. $P = 14 \times \frac{17}{2}$

23. Karen gets paid a weekly salary and a commission for every sale that she makes. The table below shows the number of sales and her pay for different weeks.

Sales	2	7	4	8
Pay	$380	$580	$460	$620

Which of the following equations represents Karen's weekly pay?
   a. $y = 90x + 200$
   b. $y = 90x - 200$
   c. $y = 40x + 300$
   d. $y = 40x - 300$

24. The square and circle have the same center. The circle has a radius of r. What is the area of the shaded region?

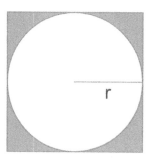

   a. $r^2 - \pi r^2$
   b. $4r^2 - 2\pi r$
   c. $(4 - \pi)r^2$
   d. $(\pi - 1)r^2$

166

25. Given the following triangle, what's the length of the missing side? Round the answer to the nearest tenth.

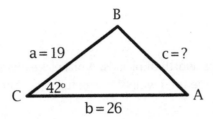

a. 17.0
b. 17.4
c. 18.0
d. 18.4

26. For the following similar triangles, what are the values of x and y (rounded to one decimal place)?

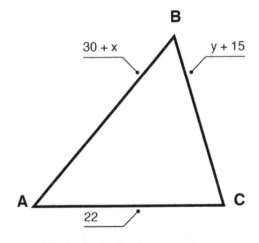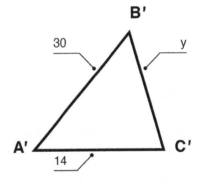

a. $x = 16.5, y = 25.1$
b. $x = 19.5, y = 24.1$
c. $x = 17.1, y = 26.3$
d. $x = 26.3, y = 17.1$

27. What are the center and radius of a circle with equation $4x^2 + 4y^2 - 16x - 24y + 51 = 0$?
a. Center $(3,2)$ and radius $\frac{1}{2}$

b. Center $(2,3)$ and radius $\frac{1}{2}$

c. Center $(3,2)$ and radius $\frac{1}{4}$

d. Center $(2,3)$ and radius $\frac{1}{4}$

28. What is the solution to $(2 \times 20) \div (7 + 1) + (6 \times 0.01) + (4 \times 0.001)$?
    a. 5.064
    b. 5.64
    c. 5.0064
    d. 48.064

29. A piggy bank contains 12 dollars' worth of nickels. A nickel weighs 5 grams, and the empty piggy bank weighs 1,050 grams. What is the total weight of the full piggy bank?
    a. 1,110 grams
    b. 1,200 grams
    c. 2,250 grams
    d. 2,200 grams

No Calculator Questions

30. Last year, the New York City area received approximately $27\frac{3}{4}$ inches of snow. The Denver area received approximately 3 times as much snow as New York City. How much snow fell in Denver?
    a. 60 inches
    b. $27\frac{1}{4}$ inches
    c. $9\frac{1}{4}$ inches
    d. $83\frac{1}{4}$ inches

31. If $-3(x + 4) \geq x + 8$, what is the value of x?
    a. $x = 4$
    b. $x \geq 2$
    c. $x \geq -5$
    d. $x \leq -5$

32. Which of the ordered pairs below is a solution to the following system of inequalities?

$$y > 2x - 3$$

$$y < -4x + 8$$

    a. $(4,5)$
    b. $(-3,-2)$
    c. $(3,-1)$
    d. $(5,2)$

33. What is the solution to $9 \times 9 \div 9 + 9 - 9 \div 9$?

34. The hospital has a nurse-to-patient ratio of $1 : 25$. If there are a maximum of 325 patients admitted at a time, how many nurses are there?

    a.   13 nurses

    b.   25 nurses

    c.   325 nurses

    d.   12 nurses

35. Solve for X: $\frac{2X}{5} - 1 = 59$.

36. Paint Inc. charges $2,000 for painting the first 1,800 feet of trim on a house and $1.00 per foot for each foot after. How much would it cost to paint a house with 3,125 feet of trim?

    a. $3,125

    b. $2,000

    c. $5,125

    d. $3,325

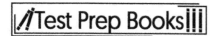

37. A bucket can hold 11.4 liters of water. A kiddie pool needs 35 gallons of water to be full. How many times will the bucket need to be filled to fill the kiddie pool?
    a. 12
    b. 35
    c. 11
    d. 45

38. In Jim's school, there are 3 girls for every 2 boys. There are 650 students in total. Using this information, how many students are girls?

39. What is the volume of a pyramid, with a square base whose side is 6 inches, and the height is 9 inches?
    a. 324 in^3
    b. 72 in^3
    c. 108 in^3
    d. 18 in^3

40. Convert $\frac{2}{9}$ to a percentage.
    a. 22%
    b. 4.5%
    c. 450%
    d. 0.22%

41. What is the volume of a cone, in terms of π, with a radius of 10 centimeters and height of 12 centimeters?
    a. $400 \pi \text{ cm}^3$
    b. $200 \pi \text{ cm}^3$
    c. $120 \pi \text{ cm}^3$
    d. $140 \pi \text{ cm}^3$

42. What is 3 out of 8 expressed as a percent?
    a. 37.5%
    b. 37%
    c. 26.7%
    d. 2.67%

43. The area of a given rectangle is 24 square centimeters. If the measure of each side is multiplied by 3, what is the area of the new figure?
    a. 48 cm^2
    b. 72 cm^2
    c. 216 cm^2
    d. 13,824 cm^2

44. If $4x - 3 = 5$, then $x =$

45. What is $4 \times 7 + (25 - 21)^2 \div 2$?

46. Solve the following:

$$\left(\sqrt{36} \times \sqrt{16}\right) - 3^2$$

47. What is the overall median of Dwayne's current test scores: 78, 92, 83, 97?

48. The total perimeter of a rectangle is 36 cm. If the length is 12 cm, what is the width?

Answer Explanations #1

Reading Test

1. C: There is a tone of excitement throughout the passage; this tone is conveyed through the narrator's account of the life-changing discovery of electricity. Mentions of tunnels and darkness could evoke a tone of dreariness, but that represents the past. This passage is looking forward to what the future will hold with this new form of light, making Choice A incorrect. Choice B is incorrect because the narrator does not feel unnerved when about the idea of confessing their crime to the Council. This passage does not use humor or lightheartedness, making Choice D incorrect.

2. A: Evidence for the correct answer can be found here: "They would see nothing, save our crime of working alone, and they would destroy us and our light." In this society, things must be done as a collective, not individually. The narrator hopes to join the Home of the Scholars, and wants their input and work space, which makes Choice B incorrect. Street sweeping is the narrator's role but it's not what makes their discovery a crime. That is why Choice C is incorrect. Besides the word *Unmentionable*, nothing indicates that remainders from former times are off-limits, making Choice D incorrect.

3. D: The sentence uses personification, whereby darkness is given a human quality—being able to swallow. There are no comparison being made, making metaphor, Choice A, incorrect. Synecdoche, which is a device that uses a part to represent a whole or vice versa is not present, making Choice B incorrect. The sentence has no interjected scenes from a previous point in the narrative, making flashback, Choice C, incorrect.

4. A: Multiple times the narrator calls their discovery "the power of the sky" which is an allusion to the sun. For example, in the third paragraph, the narrator reports, "we finished building a strange thing...a box of glass, devised to give forth the power of the sky of greater strength than we had ever achieved before." Candles were a source of light before this discovery, making Choice B incorrect. Prison represents the darkness, not the light, making Choice C incorrect. The narrator does feel that their invention is a part of their body, the way blood runs through their veins, but does not directly equate to their overall invention of electricity. This makes Choice D incorrect.

5. B: The narrator is confident their crime will be forgiven by the World Council of Scholars, because their "gift is greater than [their] transgression." The passage does not address the money their invention will save the City, making Choice A incorrect. It is not the apology alone that will grant the narrator forgiveness, making Choice C incorrect. By the end, the narrator does feel a strong connection to their invention, but the wires are only metaphorically part of their body, and the wires are not the reason the narrator believes they'll be forgiven. This makes Choice D incorrect.

6. D: *Transgression* most closely means *offense* in paragraph eight. Obedience, or following the rules, is the opposite of transgression, making Choice A incorrect. The word *transgression* has a moral or legal connotation that is lacking in the more abstract word *disruption*, making Choice B incorrect. Confession, or admitting to an offense, is what the narrator is going to do as a result of their transgression, making Choice D incorrect.

7. B: Personification is a literary device in which human characteristics are attributed to something nonhuman. So when the narrator says "darkness swallowed us," they give a human characteristic (swallowing) to something nonhuman (darkness). Choice A is incorrect because it is just an expression

174

used to indicate there are a lot of thoughts swirling around in the narrator's head. Choice *C* is refers to the human narrator's head and hands; since the narrator is a person, they cannot be personified. Choice *D* is incorrect because it is a thought that trails off using ellipsis, not personification, to indicate that the narrator has changed their opinion on the value of their body.

8. C: The narrator wants to keep their invention a secret until they are able to confess everything to the World Council of Scholars. Paragraph seven lists the resources that are necessary to advance the discovery. Those include work rooms, which makes Choice *A* incorrect. The narrator also wants help and wisdom from the brother Scholars, making Choice *B* incorrect. The narrator feels that they will need to focus all their time on their discovery, which means they will need to stop sweeping the streets, leaving Choice *D* incorrect.

9. A: Moving from street sweeper to the Home of the Scholars will be an advancement in society. This is apparent because the narrator currently lives in a tunnel with no electricity, while the wisest in all the lands are elected to the World Council of Scholars. Choice *B* is incorrect because the text indicates that being a Scholar is more desirable than being a street sweeper, so their status will not remain the same. The Council of Vocations decides what jobs people will have, and would be the group to assign the narrator to the House of Scholars. This makes Choice *C* incorrect. The narrator is not concerned with the negative consequences of their confession and is confident they will be propelled to Scholar status. This is why Choice *D* is incorrect.

10. D: The last paragraph reveals the shift in how the narrator suddenly cares about their body for the first time after they discover electricity. The passage cuts off before the author shares whether the transgression is forgiven, making Choice *A* incorrect. The plan is to share the gift of electricity with all the Cities, but the reader does not know if that plan will come to fruition. This makes Choice *B* incorrect. It's likely that electricity will make all tasks, especially those that happen at night, easier. But Choice *C* is incorrect because those benefits are not discussed in this passage.

11. C: Jimmy Carter talks about how Americans are losing confidence in their government, their ability to self-govern, and democracy. He basically says America has lost its way and must find it again. That will be hard and will require facing the truth. In the last paragraph, he says that we need to change course and restore confidence and faith. Choice *A* is incorrect because Carter believes that faith can be restored, meaning there is hope for the future. Choice *B* only addresses part of the speech, so it is not the best answer. While Carter does reference other people in the Western world, that is irrelevant to the underlying message, making Choice *D* incorrect.

12. B: Worshiping self-indulgence and consumption is cited as a symptom of the crisis of the American spirit. Additionally, Choices *C* and *D* are both listed in the third paragraph as examples of symptoms of the crisis of the American spirit, which makes them incorrect answers. Another symptom is that the majority of people believe the next five years will be worse than the last five. However, Choice *B* is wrong. Carter says, "there is a growing disrespect for government and for churches and for schools, the news media, and other institutions." Therefore, respect isn't growing, *disrespect* is,

13. B: Using context clues from the passage, a reader can infer that the saying *sound as a dollar* means something is dependable and reliable. *Solid as a rock* is another phrase that means dependability and reliability. *Hands down* refers to intensity or completeness; something that is "the best value, hands down," is absolutely the best value. The phrase *hands down* does not speak to dependability, making Choice *A* incorrect. Ease, not reliability, is the meaning behind the phrase *piece of cake*. This makes

Choice *C* incorrect. Choice *D* is incorrect because getting something fair and square means it was earned honestly.

14. C: The goal of Carter's speech is to sound relatable and capable of understanding of Americans' frustration with government. Carter emphasizes his empathy when he says, "Often you see paralysis and stagnation and drift. You don't like it, and neither do I. What can we do?" Nothing in his speech would indicate he is unqualified for the role of president, making Choice *A* incorrect. Carter may be desperate to restore faith and confidence in Americans, but not desperate for their acceptance. This makes Choice *B* incorrect. Choice *D* is incorrect because Jimmy Carter fully believes in democracy and is encouraging Americans to believe in it.

15. D: Out of context, Washington, D.C. being an island could mean many things. The meaning of the metaphor can be found in the sentences that precede and follow it, which mention isolation and a wide gap between the government and its citizens. Choice *A* is wrong because Carter is not mentioning an island to describe a vacation. This metaphor does not allude to resource, so Choice *B* is incorrect. Choice *C* implies that Americans have access to the "island" of government, but the real meaning is the opposite, that government has become unresponsive to citizens. Therefore, Choice *C* is incorrect.

16. B: According to Carter, these examples are the shocks and tragedies that have gradually caused Americans to lose their faith and confidence in government and other institutions such as schools and media. While there are references to previous presidents, it is not Carter's intention to grade their time in office, making Choice *A* incorrect. The future is not mentioned in paragraphs six and seven, rendering Choice *C* incorrect. President Carter believes Americans have very reasonable expectations, even when they're not being met. For that reason, Choice *D* is incorrect.

17. C: President Carter begins by addressing the events that have led to the crisis of confidence in America, such as the murder of Martin Luther King Jr. and the inflation and collapse of the American dollar. The last paragraph offers a message of hope for the future, ending in an optimistic tone. Since this is a presidential speech, the entire speech will be formal, making Choice *A* incorrect. The speech remains elevated and the last paragraph offers hope for the future, the opposite of unremarkable. This makes Choice *B* incorrect. Since President Carter wants to be relatable and empathetic, he avoids sounding preachy, which is why Choice *D* is wrong.

18. C: In the final paragraph, Carter answers the question of what to do; he gives a plan to face the truth and restore faith. There are wounds from the past, but Carter does not suggest healing them as a solution to the crisis. This makes Choice *A* incorrect. Choice *B* is incorrect because Carter admits special interest groups are detrimental to running a smooth government but does not propose removing them to mend the crisis. Close-knit communities are a healthy side effect of, not the solution to, restoring faith and confidence in America. This is why Choice *D* is incorrect.

19. D: The use of the phrase "immediate and resolute action" conveys a sense of urgency. Choice *A* is about the cost of safeguarding freedom; it does not refer to time, which makes it incorrect. Choice *B* focuses on how the world is always changing, but it does not mention time, making it wrong as well. Choice *C* is incorrect because while it does speak to the gravity of the situation, it does not attest to the time-sensitive nature of the matter.

20. A: The vulnerability Greece and Turkey is the problem, and the proposed three-step process that involves sharing funds and resources is the solution. Since there is only one date listed and events are not structured in a timeline, this speech is not organized chronologically. That makes Choice *B* incorrect.

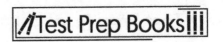

Other than a quick comparison between two ways of life, Truman's speech does not rely on comparing and contrasting, making Choice *C* incorrect. Categorical structure usually involves the classification of equally important groups or subgroups, which is not observed here, making Choice *D* incorrect.

21. A: Truman presented his argument to Congress in order to persuade it to take action to support Greece and Turkey. Truman does not rely on descriptive language, so Choice *B* is not accurate. This speech did not intend to entertain listeners, since there are no attempts at humor or amusement, making Choice *C* incorrect. This speech does analyze a situation, but analysis is not the main purpose of the speech, making Choice *D* wrong.

22. C: In the first way of life, countries ruled by a majority, with representative government, free elections, and freedom of speech. In the second way of life, the will of a small number of people is forcibly imposed upon the majority. These countries are characterized by terror and oppression. Choice *A* is wrong because both parts of the sentence describe the first way of life. Choice *B* is wrong because both qualities describe the second way of life. Choice *D* is incorrect because it is the opposite of what Truman describes; the first part describes the second way of life, and vice versa.

23. B: The word *subterfuges* could be replaced with *tricky deceptions* and the sentence would retain the same meaning. This can be gathered from nearby words like *violation*, *coercion*, and *infiltration*. *Helpful pieces of intel* would be information of military or political value, not deceit, which makes Choice *A* wrong. Political infiltration may be a time-consuming activity, but it does not address the deception of subterfuge. This leaves Choice *C* incorrect. The prefix "sub-" in the word *subterfuge* does mean "under," but it would only mean underground in a word like *subterranean*. This makes Choice *D* wrong.

24. A: President Truman argues that without interference from the United States, Greece will inevitably be oppressed by a small number of people who take up arms against the majority of the people. That will cause a ripple through Turkey, the entire Middle East, and beyond. Nothing indicates that the United Nations would step in, nor is it the responsibility of the UN to provide relief funds. This makes Choice *B* incorrect. The Truman Doctrine is a plan of preventative measures, to help Greece and Turkey recover from war. There is not a logical timeline where Truman's plan is not approved by Congress, Greece falls under the control of an armed minority, and then the United States retracts and sends hundreds of millions of dollars to Greece. This makes Choice *C* invalid. Choice *D* is incorrect because the only mention of Greece disappearing was in reference to its status as a free state.

25. C: Truman's warning about what will happen if the United States fails to help Greece and Turkey should leave his listeners with a sense of concern. Congress would feel disgusted if Truman described something revolting. This is why Choice *A* is incorrect. Choice *B* is incorrect because an audience would feel astonishment if Truman shared surprising new information. Choice *D* is not the best option because there are other sentences from the speech that would be more likely to evoke an eagerness to help (e.g., "This is a serious course upon which we embark.").

26. B: Nowhere does Truman mention overhauling the governments of Greece and Turkey. He actually believes Greece and Turkey can help themselves when they are provided with ample funds and resources. Choices *A*, *C*, and *D* can all be found directly in paragraphs fourteen, fifteen, and sixteen, which is what makes them incorrect answers.

27. C: President Truman felt the United States was the sole entity responsible for helping free people resisting a takeover from armed aggressors or outside threats. Truman does not allude to the possibility

of another country stepping in, which is why Choice A is doubtful and incorrect. Since Greece and Turkey will both be in similar states of turmoil it is unlikely they will be of any help to one another. This makes Choice B wrong. It is not the responsibility of the United Nations to intervene in these matters, and cannot force the United States to send funds to foreign countries, which renders Choice D incorrect.

28. B: Although these passages are written in completely different styles, they're both centered around the role insects play in pollination. Choice A is incorrect because only the second article breaks down the role of the three different sets of legs. The first article is not written scientifically, making Choice C wrong. Only the first passage goes into depth about nectar and the signals plants use to communicate to bees. This is why Choice D is not the best answer.

29. C: The passage by Jean-Henri Fabre was written for a children's storybook, which is why he uses whimsical language. Personifying both the bee and the flower and using terms like "signboard," "enter here," and "keyhole" evoke the mood of a fairytale or fable. Pedantic word choice suggests a pompous scholarly paper. This passage is anything but pompous and scholarly, making Choice A incorrect. This passage is light-hearted, while something emotional usually plays on deep or dark emotions. This is why Choice B is incorrect. Choice D is incorrect because, despite whimsical storytelling, the message and information are clear, not ambiguous.

30. D: The best substitution for the word *posterior* is *rear*. This answer can be drawn from realizing posterior legs means the opposite of "forward appendages." Also the prefix *post-* means behind or after. While the word *strongest* fits in the sentence nicely, nothing implies that that particular set of legs is the strongest. This makes Choice A incorrect. *Anterior*, meaning front, is actually the antonym for the word *posterior*, so Choice B is wrong. *Ambulatory* is a word that could describe any pair of functioning legs and does not differentiate the hind legs from the front or middle, which makes Choice C incorrect.

31. A: The character believes that the snapdragon's yellow spot is evidence that Providence or some higher power has designed nature. When a bee lands on the yellow spot of a closed snapdragon, the flower opens up so the bee can access the nectar and pollen. The preceding sentence confirms that the character does not believe that nature happens by chance, making Choice B incorrect. The character makes no claim that snapdragons are more beautiful than any other plant. This makes Choice C wrong. This character's speech continuously highlights the intentional behaviors between flowers and bees, so Choice D is incorrect.

32. C: The triple feast, introduced in the first paragraph of the first passage, has three beneficiaries: trees, insects, and humans. Pollen is part of the transaction between these three, but pollen not directly benefit, which is why Choices A, B, and D are incorrect.

33. B: When bees interact with the anthers of the flowers, the hairs of their bodies get covered in pollen. The bee's legs collect the pollen from all over the body and transfer it back toward the pollen baskets, also known as the corbiculae. Choice B best explains the order of the pollen manipulation process. Choices A, C, and D incorrectly describe (either by order or parts) the way bees move pollen across their bodies.

34. D: In a false dichotomy, also known as an either-or fallacy, only two alternative points are presented, even though other alternative points are available. The author is indirectly saying that if someone does not understand the relationship between the bee and the snapdragon, they are an idiot. That is a rather harsh two-option opinion. A slippery slope fallacy occurs when someone claims that a series of small events will necessarily result in one major bad event, which is not presented here, making Choice A

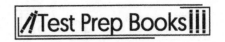
incorrect. Choice *B*, ad hominem, is incorrect because the author does not attack another person's character. There are no distractions or misleading clues that would indicate a red herring fallacy, making Choice *C* wrong.

35. A: The author means the flower's petals open up slowly like a person yawning. "To open" or "to gape" is one of the meanings of the verb "yawn." Choice *B* is incorrect because it focuses on the sleepiness of yawning, not the motion. Choice *C* is wrong because it inaccurately parallels how yawning allows people to receive more oxygen to their brains. There is no evidence to indicate the flower is having issues with regulation or time of day, making Choice D erroneous.

36. D: The researchers chose sweet corn because sweet corn produces an abundance of pollen, making it easier to observe. The passage does not mention that bees are more attracted to sweeter flowers or that sweet corn is particularly sweet to bees. This makes Choice *A* incorrect. Sweet corn was used because of its abundance of pollen, not its abundance of itself, making Choice *B* incorrect. While the article does focus on bees, it does not address other pollinators, leaving Choice *C* incorrect.

37. B: Although written in very different ways, both passages describe a mutually beneficial relationship between bees and flowers when it comes to pollination. Based on the level of detail provided, it is safe to say that the behavior of honeybees and pollen collection is well studied, making Choice *A* incorrect. Even though both passages focus their attention on honeybees, neither one states that bees are superior pollinators, making Choice *C* wrong. Both authors feel very strongly that the act of pollination is purposeful and intentional, and they feel that nothing can be attributed to randomness. This is what makes Choice *D* incorrect.

38. C: *Solution and Emulsions* is not just the correct answer, it is the exact title of the passage from *Common Science*. The title *Solutions and Emulsions* fully covers what this excerpt is about. Choice *A* is incorrect because it too narrowly focuses on the aspect of cleaning when that is only a side benefit to learning about solutions and emulsions. Choice *B* is wrong because this passage did not contain experiments about any topic other than solutions and emulsions. Choice *D* is overly focused on the opening and doesn't account for the rest of the passage, making it incorrect.

39. A: The author conjures up a world where there is an imaginary switchboard that can turn off the law of solutions, runs through an example where all saltwater fish die, and then decides the switchboard should be left alone. This is a comedic hypothetical to open the topic of solutions and emulsions. There is not an element of shock or surprise, making Choice *B* incorrect. Despite the fiction, all the information presented was logical and complete, which leaves Choice *C* incorrect. Since the author tells the reader exactly what happens when the Solutions switch is turned off, there is no element of suspense, making Choice *D* incorrect.

40. B: All of the rhetorical questions are designed to make the reader think about the results and effects of the different experiments, eventually leading them to draw their own conclusions. Science is made up of facts, not opinions, so Choice *A* is incorrect. These rhetorical questions have a greater purpose than to just ensure the readers are following along. This makes Choice *C* incorrect. There is an assumption the reader is already invested in doing the experiments and would not need prodding from rhetorical questions, which is why Choice *D* is wrong.

41. D: Evidence for this answer can be derived from the example of milk and its emulsion tendencies. Little droplets of butter and fat are suspended in milk and are not completely dissolved like sugar would

be in water when making simple syrup. Since sugar can completely dissolve into water, simple syrup is a solution. Choice *A* is incorrect because solutions are actually more likely to be clear. Both emulsions and solutions can be drinkable or non-drinkable, just depends on what components are being used. This makes Choice *B* incorrect. Choice *C* is erroneous because emulsions and solutions do not naturally have lower or higher temperatures.

42. B: After the experimenter is asked to add more salt than can be dissolved and then to use a Bunsen burner to heat the test tube, a logical result would be that the heat is an agent to dissolve the salt more readily. Choice *A* is the opposite of what result should be expected. The rhetorical question that follows the instructions implies that the salt will not impede the heating element, making Choice *C* incorrect. While the author does mention washing dishes, using the saltwater solution as soap is an inaccurate connection, leaving Choice *D* incorrect.

43. A: The passage mentions briefly that emulsions can act as solutions if their suspended droplets are so small they can't be identified. Heating can help dissolve more solute into solvent but is not the reason emulsions can act like solutions, making Choice *B* incorrect. Shaking and stirring does not change the smallest size droplets can be inside an emulsion, rendering Choice *C* incorrect. Because the passage directly says "But the droplets may be so small that an emulsion acts almost exactly like a solution," Choice *D* cannot be correct.

44. B: The last paragraph offers an analogy to better explain the results of Experiment 82. When a pail of pebbles is poured into a pail of apples, the pebbles will fill in the empty spaces between the apples. Likewise, when water is poured into alcohol, the water molecules will rest between the molecules of alcohol, meaning the combined liquids of equal measure do not quite double in size. Choice *A* and *C* both get the analogy backwards. "Pebbles are to apples" is a statement of how they relate; the pebbles fill the spaces between the apples. The second half should therefore be "as water is to alcohol." Therefore Choice *A* is incorrect. Choice *C* also incorrectly equates the apples to water molecules and the pebbles to alcohol molecules. Choice *D* is incorrect because the scenario of the pebbles and the apples is meant to explain emulsion; the apples and pebbles are not in solution, and neither are the alcohol and the water.

45. D: Even if you do not know that denatured means the alcohol has been altered in some fashion, there are context clues that imply the solution will not be pure due to the denatured substances. There is no evidence to indicate denatured alcohol is dangerous or unfit for a laboratory, making Choice *A* wrong. Choice *B* is incorrect because the author wrote an entire paragraph differentiating denatured alcohol from regular alcohol. And there is no amount of heating that will cause the denatured components to dissolve, which is what makes Choice *C* incorrect.

46. C: The apple and pebble analogy in the last paragraph explains the purpose of Experiment 82. Because the water molecules will fill the gaps between the larger alcohol molecules, it can be deduced that the mixture will measure less than two inches, which is the combined separate measurements of water and alcohol. The experiment would not prove anything if the total height measured exactly two inches, making Choice *A* incorrect. Nothing in the passage indicates the alcohol or water would expand when combined, leaving Choice *B* incorrect. There is enough surrounding evidence to make a reasonable prediction about the result of Experiment 82, which makes Choice *D* wrong.

47. C: When two people are described as oil and water it means they do not mix well or they are incompatible. This passage explains that oil and water can only be an emulsion because the two substances can never fully combine into a homogenous solution. The idiom *comparing apples to oranges*

180

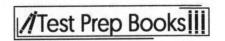

means you are comparing two unlike things, which is not explained in this passage. That makes Choice *A* incorrect. When someone is *in hot water* it means they are in trouble, which is not described in this passage, making Choice *B* wrong. When someone says *do not cry over spilled milk*, they mean advising someone not be upset over something that happened in the past and cannot be change. Choice *D* is incorrect because we learned that milk is an emulsion, but there was no advice about what to do when it is spilled.

Writing and Language Test

1. C: Choice *C* correctly uses *from* to describe the fact that dogs are related to wolves. The word *through* is incorrectly used here, so Choice *A* is incorrect. Choice *B* does not make sense. Choice *D* unnecessarily changes the verb tense in addition to incorrectly using *through*.

2. B: Choice *B* is correct because the Oxford comma is applied, clearly separating the specific terms. Choice *A* lacks this clarity. Choice *C* is correct but too wordy since commas can be easily applied. Choice *D* doesn't flow with the sentence's structure.

3. D: Choice *D* correctly uses the question mark, fixing the sentence's main issue. Thus, Choice *A* is incorrect because questions do not end with periods. Choice *B*, although correctly written, changes the meaning of the original sentence. Choice *C* is incorrect because it completely changes the direction of the sentence, disrupts the flow of the paragraph, and lacks the crucial question mark.

4. A: Choice *A* is correct since there are no errors in the sentence. Choices *B* and *C* both have extraneous commas, disrupting the flow of the sentence. Choice *D* unnecessarily rearranges the sentence.

5. D: Choice *D* is correct because the commas serve to distinguish that *artificial selection* is just another term for *selective breeding* before the sentence continues. The structure is preserved, and the sentence can flow with more clarity. Choice *A* is incorrect because the sentence needs commas to avoid being a run-on. Choice *B* is close but still lacks the required comma after *selection*, so this is incorrect. Choice *C* is incorrect because the comma to set off the aside should be placed after *breeding* instead of *called*.

6. B: Choice *B* is correct because the sentence is talking about a continuing process. Therefore, the best modification is to add the word *to* in front of *increase*. Choice *A* is incorrect because this modifier is missing. Choice *C* is incorrect because with the additional comma, the present tense of *increase* is inappropriate. Choice *D* makes more sense, but the tense is still not the best to use.

7. A: Choice *B* is incorrect because it adds an unnecessary comma. Choice *C* is incorrect because *advantage* should not be plural in this sentence without the removal of the singular *an*. Choice *D* is very tempting. While this would make the sentence more concise, this would ultimately alter the context of the sentence, which would be incorrect.

8. C: Choice *C* correctly uses *on to*, describing the way genes are passed generationally. The use of *into* is inappropriate for this context, which makes Choice *A* incorrect. Choice *B* is close, but *onto* refers to something being placed on a surface. Choice *D* doesn't make logical sense.

9. D: Choice *D* is correct, since only proper names should be capitalized. Because the name of a dog breed is not a proper name, Choice *A* is incorrect. In terms of punctuation, only one comma after *example* is needed, so Choices *B* and *C* are incorrect.

10. D: Choice *D* is the correct answer because *rather* acts as an interrupting word here and thus should be separated by commas. Choices *B* and *C* use commas incorrectly, breaking the flow of the sentence.

11. B: Since the sentence can stand on its own without *Usually*, separating it from the rest of the sentence with a comma is correct. Choice *A* needs the comma after *Usually*, while Choice *C* uses commas incorrectly. Choice *D* is tempting, but changing *turn* to past tense goes against the rest of the paragraph.

12. A: Choices *B* and *D* add unnecessary commas. Choice *C* removes the required comma after the dependent clause.

13. D: To fix the original sentence, either a comma must be added after the word *on* to separate the dependent clause from the independent clause, or the order of the clauses must be flipped. Choice *B* adds an unnecessary comma after the word *included*. Choice *C* creates an incomplete sentence by adding a period after the dependent clause.

14. C: This revision improves the awkward wording of the original sentence. Choice *B* adds an unnecessary comma and period. Choice *D* leaves out the required comma after the word *another*.

15. B: Choice *B* correctly adds a comma after the word *person*. Choice *C* inserts a semicolon where a comma is needed. Choice *D* adds a period to the middle of the sentence.

16. D: This passage is written in a very casual style, and uses some informal sentence structures (such as the use of *Why?* as a complete sentence in the first paragraph). In this case, the word *Easy* is used informally in place of the full sentence *The answer to that question is easy*. Therefore, it needs to be separated from the complete sentence It's interest. In addition to lacking this necessary punctuation, Choice *C* incorrectly changes the contraction it's to the possessive its.

17. C: Although Choice *D* is grammatically correct, it is not the best revision because to draw is simpler than for the purpose of drawing. Choice *B*, in addition to lacking a comma after the word matter, changes the intended meaning of the original sentence. We know from the sentence that follows (This won't always work.) that the writer is talking about taking the action (embellishing subject matter) in hopes of accomplishing the result (draw people's attention). The sentence Embellishing subject matter, which draws people's attention would be a definitive statement that taking the action accomplishes the result.

18. B: Choice *C* incorrectly changes *applies* to *applied*, fails to change *there* to *their*, and fails to add the necessary punctuation. Choice *D* incorrectly adds a comma between the subject (Discussions that make people think about the content and how it applies to their lives, world, and future) and the predicate (are key).

19. C: Choice *C* is correct because it fixes the core issue with this sentence: the singular has does not agree with the plural *scientists*. Choices *B* and *D* add unnecessary commas.

20. D: Choice *D* correctly conveys the writer's intention of asking if early perceptions of dinosaurs still influence people. Choice *A* does not make sense the way it is worded. Choice *B* is better, but how doesn't coincide with the context. Choice *C* adds unnecessary commas.

21. A: Choice *B* incorrectly replaces simply with simple and adds an unnecessary comma. Choice *C* uses a comma where a semicolon is needed. Choice *D* adds an unnecessary comma.

182

22. B: Choice *B* is the strongest revision, as adding *to explore* is very effective in both shortening the sentence and maintaining, even enhancing, the point of the writer. Choice *A* is not technically incorrect, but it is overcomplicated. Choice *C* is a decent revision, but the sentence could still be more condensed and sharpened. Choice *D* fails to make the sentence more concise and inserts unnecessary commas.

23. D: Choice *D* correctly applies a semicolon to introduce a new line of thought while remaining in a single sentence. The comma after *however* is also appropriately placed. Choice *A* is a run-on sentence. Choice *B* is incorrect because the single comma is not enough to fix the sentence. Choice *C* adds commas around *uncertain* which are unnecessary.

24. B: Choice *B* changes its, which is possessive, to it's, which is a contraction of "it is." It also separates the two independent clauses with a comma and streamlines the sentence by eliminating and. Choices *C* and *D* are run-on sentences.

25. A: Choices *B* and *C* add unnecessary commas, while Choice *D* uses the possessive its instead of the contraction it's.

26. C: Choice *C* is correct because the phrase *even likely* is a parenthetical element, which must be set off by commas. Choice *D* does not set off the phrase with commas. Choice *A* omits the second required comma, and Choice *B* misplaces it.

27. D: Choice *D* strengthens the overall sentence structure while condensing the words. This makes the subject of the sentence, and the emphasis of the writer, much clearer to the reader. In Choice *A*, the language is choppy and over-complicated. Choice *B* is better but lacks the reference to a specific image of dinosaurs. Choice *C* introduces unnecessary commas.

28. B: Choices *A* and *D* use the wrong verb tense in the second clause. Choice *C* uses a comma where a semicolon is needed and rephrases the second clause awkwardly.

29. A: Choices *B* and *C* employ unnecessary semicolons and commas. Choice *D* would be an ideal revision, but it lacks the comma that would be needed after Ransom.

30. D: By reorganizing the sentence, the context becomes clearer with Choice *D*. Choice *A* has an awkward sentence structure. Choice *B* offers a revision that doesn't correspond well with the original sentence's intent. Choice *C* cuts out too much of the original content, losing the full meaning.

31. C: Choice *C* fixes the disagreement between the singular this and the plural viewpoints. Choice *B* introduces an unnecessary comma. In Choice *D*, *those* agrees with *viewpoints*, but neither agrees with *distinguishes*.

32. A: Choice *A* is direct and clear, without any punctuation errors. Choice *B* is well written but too wordy. Choice *C* adds an unnecessary comma. Choice *D* is also well written but much less concise than Choice *A*.

33. D: describing idea. On its own, Choice *A* is a run-on sentence. Choice *B* is better because it separates the clauses, but it keeps the unnecessary comma. Choice *C* is also an improvement but still a run-on sentence.

34. B: Choice *B* is the best answer because it brings more clarity to the message of the sentence. Choice *A*, the original sentence, unnecessarily includes the word ultimately and leaves out a comma before the

independent clause at the end. Choices *C* and *D* are awkward and wordy; therefore, neither is the best answer.

35. D: Changing the phrase *after this* to *then* makes the sentence less complicated and captures the writer's intent, making Choice *D* correct. Choice *A* is awkwardly constructed. Choices *B* and *C* misuse their commas and do not adequately improve the clarity.

36. B: By starting a new sentence, the run-on issue is eliminated, and a new line of reasoning can be seamlessly introduced, making Choice *B* correct. While Choice *C* fixes the run-on via a semicolon, a comma is still needed after *this*. Choice *D* contains a comma splice. The independent clauses must be separated by more than just a comma, even with the rearrangement of the second half of the sentence.

37. C: Choice *C* condenses the original sentence while being more active in communicating the emphasis on changing times/media that the author is going for, so it is correct. Choice *A* is clunky because it lacks a comma after *today* to successfully transition into the second half of the sentence. Choice *B* inserts unnecessary commas. Choice *D* is a good revision of the underlined section, but not only does it not fully capture the original meaning, it also does not flow into the rest of the sentence.

38. B: Choice *B* makes it clear that "incorporating different styles and unique ways to approach the news" refers to the different types of media rather than to the stories. Choice *D* adds the missing comma before *incorporating* but doesn't clarify the meaning the way Choice *B* does. Choice *C* is incorrect because the period inserted after *question* makes the following sentence incomplete.

39. A: Choice *A* is correct: while the sentence seems long, it actually doesn't require any commas. The conjunction "that" successfully combines the two parts of the sentence without the need for additional punctuation. Choices *B* and *C* insert commas unnecessarily. Choice *D* alters the meaning of the original text by creating a new sentence, which is only a fragment.

40. C: Choice *C* correctly replaces *for* with *to*. Choice *B* is unnecessarily long and disrupts the original sentence structure. Choice *D* is also too wordy and lacks parallel structure.

41. D: Choice *D* correctly inserts a comma between the dependent and independent clauses. Choice *B* is grammatically incorrect, and Choice *C* adds a semicolon instead of a comma.

42. B: Choice *B* correctly separates the section into two sentences and changes the word order to make the second part clearer. Choice *A* is incorrect because it is a run-on. Choice *C* adds an extraneous comma, while Choice *D* makes the run-on worse and does not coincide with the overall structure of the sentence.

43. C: Choice *C* is the best answer because of how the commas are used to flank *in earnest*. This distinguishes the side thought (*in earnest*) from the rest of the sentence. Choice *A* needs punctuation. Choice *B* inserts a semicolon in a spot that doesn't make sense, resulting in a fragmented sentence and lost meaning. Choice *D* is unnecessarily repetitive and creates a run-on.

44. A: Choice *A* is correct because the sentence contains no errors. The comma after *bias* successfully links the two halves of the sentence, and the use of *it's* is correct as a contraction of *it is*. Choice *B* creates a sentence fragment, while Choice *C* creates a run-on. Choice *D* incorrectly changes *it's* to *its*.

Math Test

Calculator Questions

1. B: To simplify this inequality, subtract 3 from both sides to get $-\frac{1}{2}x \geq -1$. Then, multiply both sides by -2 (remembering this flips the direction of the inequality) to get $x \leq 2$.

2. D: This problem involves a composition function, where one function is plugged into the other function. In this case, the $f(x)$ function is plugged into the $g(x)$ function for each x value. Since f(x)=2, the composition equation become:

$$g(f(x)) = g2 = (2)^3 - 3(2)^2 - 2(2) + 6$$

Simplifying the equation gives the answer:

$$g(f(x)) = 8 - 3(4) - 2(2) + 6$$

$$g(f(x)) = 8 - 12 - 4 + 6$$

$$g(f(x)) = -2$$

3. D: A parabola of the form $y = \frac{1}{4f}x^2$ has a focus $(0, f)$. Because $y = -9x^2$, set $-9 = \frac{1}{4f}$. Solving this equation for f results in $f = -\frac{1}{36}$. Therefore, the coordinates of the focus are $\left(0, -\frac{1}{36}\right)$.

4. C: $51.93

List the givens.

$$\text{Tax} = 6.0\% = 0.06$$

$$\text{Sale} = 50\% = 0.5$$

$$\text{Hat} = \$32.99$$

$$\text{Jersey} = \$64.99$$

Calculate the sale prices.

$$\text{Hat Sale} = 0.5\,(32.99) = 16.495$$

$$\text{Jersey Sale} = 0.5\,(64.99) = 32.495$$

Total the sales prices.

$$\text{Hat sale} + \text{jersey sale} = 16.495 + 32.495 = 48.99$$

Calculate the tax and add it to the total sales prices.

$$\text{Total after tax} = 48.99 + (48.99 \times 0.06) = \$51.93$$

185

5. D: $0.45

List the givens.

$$\text{Store coffee} = \$1.23/\text{lb}$$

$$\text{Local roaster coffee} = \$1.98/1.5 \text{ lb}$$

Calculate the cost for 5 pounds of store brand.

$$\frac{\$1.23}{1 \text{ lb}} \times 5 \text{ lb} = \$6.15$$

Calculate the cost for 5 pounds of the local roaster.

$$\frac{\$1.98}{1.5 \text{ lb}} \times 5 \text{ lb} = \$6.60$$

Subtract to find the difference in price for 5 pounds.

$$\begin{array}{r} \$6.60 \\ -\$6.15 \\ \hline \$0.45 \end{array}$$

6. D: The shape of the scatter plot is a parabola (U-shaped). This eliminates Choices A (a linear equation that produces a straight line) and C (an exponential equation that produces a smooth curve upward or downward). The value of a for a quadratic function in standard form ($y = ax^2 + bx + c$) indicates whether the parabola opens up (U-shaped) or opens down (upside-down U). A negative value for a produces a parabola that opens down; therefore, Choice B can also be eliminated.

7. A: The volume of a cylinder is $\pi r^2 h$. Plugging in the given values yields:

$$\pi \times (5 \text{ in})^2 \times 10 \text{ in} = 250\pi \text{ in}^3$$

Choice B is not the correct answer because that is $5^2 \times 2\pi$. Choice C is not the correct answer since that is $10 \times 10\pi$. Choice D is not the correct answer because that is $10^2 \times 2\pi$.

8. D: This system of equations involves one quadratic function and one linear function, as seen from the degree of each equation. One way to solve this is through substitution.

Solving for y in the second equation yields:

$$y = x + 2$$

Plugging this equation in for the y of the quadratic equation yields:

$$x^2 - 2x + x + 2 = 8$$

Simplifying the equation, it becomes:

$$x^2 - x + 2 = 8$$

186

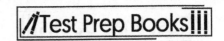

Setting this equal to zero and factoring, it becomes:

$$x^2 - x - 6 = 0 = (x - 3)(x + 2)$$

Solving these two factors for x gives the zeros:

$$x = 3, -2$$

To find the y-value for the point, each number can be plugged in to either original equation. Solving each one for y yields the points $(3, 5)$ and $(-2, 0)$.

9. B: The slope will be given by:

$$m = \frac{y_2 - y_1}{x_2 - x_1}$$

$$m = \frac{1 - 0}{2 - 0} = \frac{1}{2}$$

The y-intercept will be 0 since it passes through the origin. Using slope-intercept form, the equation for this line is:

$$y = \frac{1}{2}x$$

10. D: Recall the formula for area of a rectangle, area = length × width. The answer must be in square inches, so all values must be converted to inches. Half of a foot is equal to 6 inches. Therefore, the area of the rectangle is equal to:

$$6 \text{ in} \times \frac{11}{2} \text{ in} = \frac{66}{2} \text{in}^2 = 33 \text{ in}^2$$

11. B: The table shows values that are increasing exponentially. The differences between the inputs are the same, while the differences in the outputs are changing by a factor of 2. The values in the table can be modeled by the equation $f(x) = 2^x$.

12. B: For the first card drawn, the probability of a king being pulled is $\frac{4}{52}$. Since this card isn't replaced, if a king is drawn first, the probability of a king being drawn second is $\frac{3}{51}$. The probability of a king being drawn in both the first and second draw is the product of the two probabilities:

$$\frac{4}{52} \times \frac{3}{51} = \frac{12}{2,652}$$

To reduce this fraction, divide the top and bottom by 12 to get $\frac{1}{221}$.

13. D: "Sum" means the result of adding, so "the sum of twice a number and one" can be written as 2x+1. Next, "three times the sum of twice a number and one" would be $3(2x + 1)$. Finally, "six less than three times the sum of twice a number and one" would be $3(2x + 1) - 6$.

14. A: To expand a squared binomial, it's necessary to use the First, Outer, Inner, Last (FOIL) Method.

$$(2x - 4y)^2$$

$$(2x) \times (2x) + (2x)(-4y) + (-4y)(2x) + (-4y)(-4y)$$

$$4x^2 - 8xy - 8xy + 16y^2$$

$$4x^2 - 16xy + 16y^2$$

15. B: The zeros of this function can be found by setting: $f(x)$ equal to 0 and solving for x.

$$0 = x^2 + 4$$

$$-4 = x^2$$

$$\sqrt{-4} = x$$

Taking the square root of a negative number results in an imaginary number, so the solution is:

$$x = \pm 2i$$

16. D: The expression is simplified by collecting like terms. Terms with the same variable and exponent are like terms, and their coefficients can be added.

17. A: $\frac{810}{2921}$

Line up the fractions.

$$\frac{15}{23} \times \frac{54}{127}$$

Multiply across the top and across the bottom.

$$\frac{15 \times 54}{23 \times 127} = \frac{810}{2921}$$

18. A: Finding the product means distributing one polynomial to the other so that each term in the first is multiplied by each term in the second. Then, like terms can be collected. Multiplying the factors yields the expression:

$$20x^3 + 4x^2 + 24x - 40x^2 - 8x - 48$$

Collecting like terms means adding the x^2 terms and adding the x terms. The final answer after simplifying the expression is:

$$20x^3 - 36x^2 + 16x - 48$$

19. B: The equation can be solved by factoring the numerator into $(x + 6)(x - 5)$. Since $(x - 5)$ is on the top and bottom, that factor cancels out. This leaves the equation $x + 6 = 11$. Solving the equation gives the answer $x = 5$. When this value is plugged into the equation, it yields a zero in the denominator of the fraction. Since this is undefined, there is no solution.

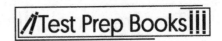
20. A: The common denominator here will be $4x$. Rewrite these fractions as

$$\frac{3}{x} + \frac{5u}{2x} - \frac{u}{4} = \frac{12}{4x} + \frac{10u}{4x} - \frac{ux}{4x} = \frac{12x + 10u - ux}{4x}$$

21. B: There are two zeros for the given function. They are $x = 0, -2$. The zeros can be found a number of ways, but this particular equation can be factored into:

$$f(x) = x(x^2 + 4x + 4) = x(x + 2)(x + 2)$$

By setting each factor equal to zero and solving for x, there are two solutions: $x = 0$ and $x = -2$. On a graph, these zeros can be seen where the line crosses the x-axis.

22. B: The perimeter of a rectangle is the sum of all four sides. Therefore, the answer is:

$$P = 14 + 8\frac{1}{2} + 14 + 8\frac{1}{2}$$

$$14 + 14 + 8 + \frac{1}{2} + 8 + \frac{1}{2} = 45 \text{ square inches}$$

23. C: $y = 40x + 300$. In this scenario, the variables are the number of sales and Karen's weekly pay. The weekly pay depends on the number of sales. Therefore, weekly pay is the dependent variable (y), and the number of sales is the independent variable (x). Each pair of values from the table can be written as an ordered pair (x, y): $(2, 380)$, $(7, 580)$, $(4, 460)$, $(8, 620)$. The ordered pairs can be substituted into the equations to see which create true statements (both sides equal) for each pair. Even if one ordered pair produces equal values for a given equation, the other three ordered pairs must be checked.

The only equation which is true for all four ordered pairs is $y = 40x + 300$:

$$380 = 40(2) + 300 \rightarrow 380 = 380$$

$$580 = 40(7) + 300 \rightarrow 580 = 580$$

$$460 = 40(4) + 300 \rightarrow 460 = 460$$

$$620 = 40(8) + 300 \rightarrow 620 = 620$$

24. C: The area of the shaded region is the area of the square minus the area of the circle. The area of the circle is πr^2. The side of the square will be $2r$, so the area of the square will be $4r^2$. Therefore, the difference is:

$$4r^2 - \pi r^2 = (4 - \pi)r^2$$

25. B: Because this isn't a right triangle, the SOHCAHTOA mnemonic can't be used. However, the law of cosines can be used:

$$c^2 = a^2 + b^2 - 2ab \cos C$$

$$c^2 = 19^2 + 26^2 - 2 \times 19 \times 26 \times \cos 42° = 302.773$$

189

Taking the square root and rounding to the nearest tenth results in $c = 17.4$.

26. C: Because the triangles are similar, the lengths of the corresponding sides are proportional. Therefore:

$$\frac{30 + x}{30} = \frac{22}{14} = \frac{y + 15}{y}$$

Using cross multiplication on the first two terms results in the equation:

$$14(30 + x) = 22 \times 30$$

When solved, this gives:

$$x \approx 17.1$$

Using cross multiplication on the last two terms results in the equation:

$$14(y + 15) = 22y$$

When solved, this gives:

$$y \approx 26.3$$

27. B: The technique of completing the square must be used to change the equation below into the standard equation of a circle:

$$4x^2 + 4y^2 - 16x - 24y + 51 = 0$$

First, the constant must be moved to the right-hand side of the equals sign and each term must be divided by the coefficient of the x^2-term (which is 4). The x- and y- terms must be grouped together to obtain:

$$x^2 - 4x + y^2 - 6y = -\frac{51}{4}$$

Then, the process of completing the square must be completed for each variable. This gives:

$$(x^2 - 4x + 4) + (y^2 - 6y + 9) = -\frac{51}{4} + 4 + 9$$

The equation can be written as:

$$(x - 2)^2 + (y - 3)^2 = \frac{1}{4}$$

Therefore, the center of the circle is $(2, 3)$ and the radius is:

$$\sqrt{\frac{1}{4}} = \frac{1}{2}$$

190

28. A: Operations within the parentheses must be completed first. Then, division is completed. Finally, addition is the last operation to complete. When adding decimals, digits within each place value are added together. Therefore, the expression is evaluated as:

$$(2 \times 20) \div (7 + 1) + (6 \times 0.01) + (4 \times 0.001) = 40 \div 8 + 0.06 + 0.004$$

$$5 + 0.06 + 0.004 = 5.064$$

29. C: A dollar contains 20 nickels. Therefore, if there are 12 dollars' worth of nickels, there are:

$$12 \times 20 = 240 \text{ nickels}$$

Each nickel weighs 5 grams. Therefore, the weight of the nickels is:

$$240 \times 5 = 1,200 \text{ grams}$$

Adding in the weight of the empty piggy bank, the filled bank weighs 2,250 grams.

No Calculator Questions

30. D: To find Denver's total snowfall, 3 must be multiplied by $27\frac{3}{4}$. In order to easily do this, the mixed number should be converted into an improper fraction.

$$27\frac{3}{4} = \frac{27 \times 4 + 3}{4} = \frac{111}{4}$$

Therefore, Denver had approximately $\frac{3 \times 111}{4} = \frac{333}{4}$ inches of snow. The improper fraction can be converted back into a mixed number through division.

$$\frac{333}{4} = 83\frac{1}{4} \text{ inches}$$

31. D: Solve a linear inequality in a similar way to solving a linear equation. First, start by distributing the -3 on the left side of the inequality.

$$-3x - 12 \geq x + 8$$

Then, add 12 to both sides.

$$-3x \geq x + 20$$

Next, subtract x from both sides.

$$-4x \geq 20$$

Finally, divide both sides of the inequality by -4. Don't forget to flip the inequality sign because you are dividing by a negative.

$$x \leq -5$$

32. B: For an ordered pair to be a solution to a system of inequalities, it must make a true statement for BOTH inequalities when substituting its values for x and y. Substituting $(-3, -2)$ into the inequalities

191

produces $(-2) > 2(-3) - 3 \rightarrow -2 > -9$ and $(-2) < -4(-3) + 8 \rightarrow -2 < 20$. Both are true statements.

33. According to the order of operations, multiplication and division must be completed first from left to right. Then, addition and subtraction are completed from left to right. Therefore:

$$9 \times 9 \div 9 + 9 - 9 \div 9$$

$$81 \div 9 + 9 - 9 \div 9$$

$$9 + 9 - 9 \div 9$$

$$9 + 9 - 1$$

$$18 - 1$$

$$17$$

34. A: Using the given information of 1 nurse to 25 patients and 325 patients, set up an equation to solve for number of nurses (N):

$$\frac{N}{325} = \frac{1}{25}$$

Multiply both sides by 325 to get N by itself on one side.

$$\frac{N}{1} = \frac{325}{25} = 13 \text{ nurses}$$

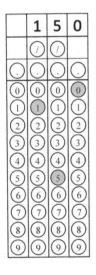
35. Set up the initial equation.

$$\frac{2x}{5} - 1 = 59$$

Add 1 to both sides.

$$\frac{2x}{5} - 1 + 1 = 59 + 1$$

$$\frac{2x}{5} = 60$$

Multiply both sides by 5/2.

$$\frac{2x}{5} \times \frac{5}{2} = 60 \times \frac{5}{2}$$

$$x = 150$$

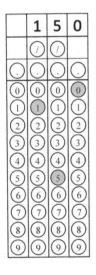

36. D: List the givens.

$$1,800 \text{ ft} = \$2,000$$

$$\text{Cost after } 1,800 \text{ ft} = \$1.00/\text{ft.}$$

Find how many feet left after the first 1,800 feet.

$$\begin{array}{r} 3,125 \text{ ft} \\ -1,800 \text{ ft} \\ \hline 1,325 \text{ ft} \end{array}$$

Calculate the cost for the feet over 1,800 feet.

$$1,325 \text{ ft} \times \frac{\$1.00}{1 \text{ ft}} = \$1,325$$

193

Add these together to find the total for the entire cost.

$$\$2,000 + \$1,325 = \$3,325$$

37. A: Calculate how many gallons the bucket holds.

$$11.4 \text{ L} \times \frac{1 \text{ gal}}{3.8 \text{ L}} = 3 \text{ gal}$$

Next, calculate how many buckets are needed to fill the 35-gallon pool.

$$\frac{35}{3} = 11.67$$

Since the amount is more than 11 but less than 12, we must fill the bucket 12 times.

38. Three girls for every two boys can be expressed as a ratio: $3:2$. This can be visualized as splitting the school into 5 groups: 3 girl groups and 2 boy groups. The number of students that are in each group can be found by dividing the total number of students by 5:

$$\frac{650 \text{ students}}{5 \text{ groups}} = \frac{130 \text{ students}}{\text{group}}$$

To find the total number of girls, multiply the number of students per group (130) by the number of girl groups in the school (3). This equals 390.

39. C: The volume of a pyramid is ($length \times width \times height$), divided by 3, and ($6 \times 6 \times 9$), divided by 3 is 108 in³. Choice *A* is incorrect because 324 in³ is ($length \times width \times height$) without dividing by 3. Choice *B* is incorrect because 6 is used for height instead of 9 (($6 \times 6 \times 6$) divided by 3) to get 72 in³. Choice *D* is incorrect because 18 in³ is (6×9), divided by 3 and leaving out a 6.

40. A: 22%

Converting from a fraction to a percentage generally involves two steps. First, the fraction needs to be converted to a decimal.

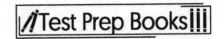

Divide 2 by 9 which results in $0.\overline{22}$. The top line indicates that the decimal actually goes on forever with an endless amount of 2's.

Second, the decimal needs to be moved two places to the right:

$$22\%$$

41. A: The volume of a cone is ($\pi r^2 h$), divided by 3, and ($\pi \times 10^2 \times 12$), divided by 3 is 400 cm³. Choice B is $10^2 \times 2$. Choice C is incorrect because it is 10×12. Choice D is also incorrect because that is $10^2 + 40$.

42. A: 37.5%

Solve this by setting up the percent formula:

$$\frac{3}{8} = \frac{\%}{100}$$

Multiply 3 by 100 to get 300. Then divide 300 by 8:

$$300 \div 8 = 37.5\%$$

Note that with the percent formula, 37.5 is automatically a percentage and does not need to have any further conversions.

43. C: Because area is a two-dimensional measurement, the dimensions are multiplied by a scale factor that is squared to determine the scale factor of the corresponding areas. The dimensions of the rectangle are multiplied by a scale factor of 3. Therefore, the area is multiplied by a scale factor of 3^2 (which is equal to 9):

$$24 \text{ cm}^2 \times 9 = 216 \text{ cm}^2$$

44. Add 3 to both sides to get $4x = 8$. Then divide both sides by 4 to get $x = 2$.

			2
	/	/	
.	.	.	.
0	0	0	0
1	1	1	1
2	2	2	②
3	3	3	3
4	4	4	4
5	5	5	5
6	6	6	6
7	7	7	7
8	8	8	8
9	9	9	9

45. To solve this correctly, keep in mind the order of operations with the mnemonic PEMDAS (Please Excuse My Dear Aunt Sally). This stands for Parentheses, Exponents, Multiplication, Division, Addition, Subtraction. Taking it step by step, solve inside the parentheses first:

$$4 \times 7 + (4)^2 \div 2$$

Then, apply the exponent:

$$4 \times 7 + 16 \div 2$$

Multiplication and division are both performed next:

$$28 + 8$$

Addition and subtraction are done last.

$$28 + 8 = 36$$

196

The solution is 36.

46. Follow the order of operations in order to solve this problem. Solve the parentheses first, being sure to follow the order of operations inside the parentheses as well. First, simplify the square roots:

$$(6 \times 4) - 3^2$$

Then, multiply inside the parentheses:

$$24 - 3^2$$

Next, simplify the exponent:

$$24 - 9$$

Finally, subtract to get 15.

47. For an even number of total values, the *median* is calculated by finding the *mean,* or average, of the two middle values once all values have been arranged in ascending order from least to greatest. In this case, $(92 + 83) \div 2$ would equal the median 87.5.

8	7	.	5
	⊘	⊘	
·	·	●	·
0	0	0	0
1	1	1	1
2	2	2	2
3	3	3	3
4	4	4	4
5	5	5	⑤
6	6	6	6
7	⑦	7	7
⑧	8	8	8
9	9	9	9

48. The formula for the perimeter of a rectangle is $P = 2L + 2W$, where P is the perimeter, L is the length, and W is the width. The first step is to substitute all of the data into the formula:

$$36 = 2(12) + 2W$$

Simplify by multiplying 2×12:

$$36 = 24 + 2W$$

Simplifying this further by subtracting 24 on each side gives:

$$36 - 24 = 24 - 24 + 2W$$

$$12 = 2W$$

Divide by 2:

$$6 = W$$

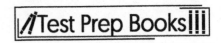

The width is 6 cm. Remember to test this answer by substituting this value into the original formula:

$$36 = 2(12) + 2(6)$$

			6
	/	/	
.	.	.	.
0	0	0	0
1	1	1	1
2	2	2	2
3	3	3	3
4	4	4	4
5	5	5	5
6	6	6	**6**
7	7	7	7
8	8	8	8
9	9	9	9

Reading Test

Fiction

Questions 1–9 are based on the following passage:

A lane was forthwith opened through the crowd of spectators. Preceded by the beadle, and attended by an irregular procession of stern-browed men and unkindly visaged women, Hester Prynne set forth towards the place appointed for her punishment. A crowd of eager and curious school-boys, understanding little of the matter in hand, except that it gave them a half-holiday, ran before her progress, turning their heads continually to stare into her face, and at the winking baby in her arms, and at the ignominious letter on her breast. It was no great distance, in those days, from the prison-door to the market-place. Measured by the prisoner's experience, however, it might be reckoned a journey of some length; for, haughty as her demeanor was, she perchance underwent an agony from every footstep of those that thronged to see her, as if her heart had been flung into the street for them all to spurn and trample upon. In our nature, however, there is a provision, alike marvelous and merciful, that the sufferer should never know the intensity of what he endures by its present torture, but chiefly by the pang that rankles after it. With almost a serene deportment, therefore, Hester Prynne passed through this portion of her ordeal, and came to a sort of scaffold, at the western extremity of the market-place. It stood nearly beneath the eaves of Boston's earliest church, and appeared to be a fixture there.

In fact, this scaffold constituted a portion of a penal machine, which now, for two or three generations past, has been merely historical and traditionary among us, but was held, in the old time, to be as effectual an agent, in the promotion of good citizenship, as ever was the guillotine among the terrorists of France. It was, in short, the platform of the pillory; and above it rose the framework of that instrument of discipline, so fashioned as to confine the human head in its tight grasp, and thus hold it up to the public gaze. The very ideal of ignominy was embodied and made manifest in this contrivance of wood and iron. There can be no outrage, methinks, against our common nature,—whatever be the delinquencies of the individual,—no outrage more flagrant than to forbid the culprit to hide his face for shame; as it was the essence of this punishment to do. In Hester Prynne's instance, however, as not unfrequently in other cases, her sentence bore, that she should stand a certain time upon the platform, but without undergoing that gripe about the neck and confinement of the head, the proneness to which was the most devilish characteristic of this ugly engine. Knowing well her part, she ascended a flight of wooden steps, and was thus displayed to the surrounding multitude, at about the height of a man's shoulders above the street.

The scene was not without a mixture of awe, such as must always invest the spectacle of guilt and shame in a fellow-creature, before society shall have grown corrupt enough to smile, instead of shuddering, at it. The witnesses of Hester Prynne's disgrace had not yet passed beyond their simplicity. They were stern enough to look upon her death, had

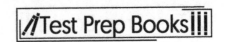

that been the sentence, without a murmur at its severity, but had none of the heartlessness of another social state, which would find only a theme for jest in an exhibition like the present. Even had there been a disposition to turn the matter into ridicule, it must have been repressed and overpowered by the solemn presence of men no less dignified than the Governor, and several of his counsellors, a judge, a general, and the ministers of the town; all of whom sat or stood in a balcony of the meeting-house, looking down upon the platform. When such personages could constitute a part of the spectacle, without risking the majesty or reverence of rank and office, it was safely to be inferred that the infliction of a legal sentence would have an earnest and effectual meaning. Accordingly, the crowd was sombre and grave. The unhappy culprit sustained herself as best a woman might, under the heavy weight of a thousand unrelenting eyes, all fastened upon her, and concentrated at her bosom. It was almost intolerable to be borne. Of an impulsive and passionate nature, she had fortified herself to encounter the stings and venomous stabs of public contumely, wreaking itself in every variety of insult; but there was a quality so much more terrible in the solemn mood of the popular mind, that she longed rather to behold all those rigid countenances contorted with scornful merriment, and herself the object. Had a roar of laughter burst from the multitude,—each man, each woman, each little shrill-voiced child, contributing their individual parts,—Hester Prynne might have repaid them all with a bitter and disdainful smile. But, under the leaden infliction which it was her doom to endure, she felt, at moments, as if she must needs shriek out with the full power of her lungs, and cast herself from the scaffold down upon the ground, or else go mad at once.

Excerpt from *The Scarlet Letter*, Nathaniel Hawthorne, 1878

1. Based on the first paragraph, what might Hester Prynne feel on her walk from prison to marketplace?
   a. Anger
   b. Fear
   c. Agony
   d. Proud

2. Based on the passage, what is the spectators' mood?
   a. Grave
   b. Amused
   c. Vengeful
   d. Outraged

3. The passage includes a description of the stockade but states it was not part of Hester's punishment. What can we infer from its inclusion?
   a. They didn't use it because she was a woman.
   b. The townspeople would have preferred its use.
   c. The threat of it was often a deterrent.
   d. The punishment could have been harsher.

4. Based on paragraph 3 of the passage, why was Prynne not mocked or ridiculed?
   a. Others had also committed crimes.
   b. She appeared too proud.
   c. Dignitaries were present.
   d. The crowd wanted to see her hanged.

5. In the final paragraph, what does the word "disdainful" mean?
   a. Admiring
   b. Contemptuous
   c. Sympathetic
   d. Mournful

6. In the first paragraph, why might a prisoner find the walk from prison to marketplace longer than the actual distance?
   a. The spectators watching cause the prisoner an emotional burden.
   b. The prisoner's ankles were shackled.
   c. Prisoners are forced to walk slowly.
   d. Kids keep running in front, taunting.

7. How did the crowd's reaction defy Prynne's expectations?
   a. She expected silence, but they cheered.
   b. She expected cheering, but they mocked her.
   c. She expected physical attacks, but they laughed.
   d. She expected verbal attacks but got none.

8. What can we conclude about Prynne's need to shriek and throw herself down or go mad?
   a. The weight of the punishment has finally hit her.
   b. Someone has attacked her.
   c. She has finally been placed in the stockade.
   d. She wants to respond to the crowd.

9. Over the course of the passage, the main point of view shifts among...
   a. A witness, the judge, and Hester Prynne
   b. Hester Prynne's experience, the crowd's experience, and Prynne's husband
   c. The narrator's viewpoint, Hester Prynne, and the crowd
   d. Hester Prynne, members of the crowd, and the town historian

History/Social Studies

Questions 10–19 are based on the following passage:

The basic problem confronting the world today, as I said in the beginning, is the preservation of human freedom for the individual and consequently for the society of which he is a part. We are fighting this battle again today as it was fought at the time of the French Revolution and as the time of the American Revolution. The issue of human liberty is as decisive now as it was then. I want to give you my conception of what is meant in my country by freedom of the individual.

Long ago in London during a discussion with Mr. Vyshinsky, he told me there was no such thing as freedom for the individual in the world. All freedom of the individual was

202

conditioned by the rights of other individuals. That of course, I granted. I said: "We approach the question from a different point of view: we here in the United Nations are trying to develop ideals which will be broader in outlook, which will consider first the rights of man, which will consider what makes man more free; not governments, but man."

The totalitarian state typically places the will of the people second to decrees promulgated by a few men at the top.

Naturally there must always be consideration of the rights of others; but in a democracy this is not a restriction. Indeed, in our democracies we make our freedoms secure because each of us is expected to respect the rights of others and we are free to make our own laws. Freedom for our peoples is not only a right, but also a tool. Freedom of speech, freedom of the press, freedom of information, freedom of assembly—these are not just abstract ideals to us; they are tools with which we create a way of life, a way of life in which we can enjoy freedom.

Sometimes the processes of democracy are slow, and I have known some of our leaders to say that a benevolent dictatorship would accomplish the ends desired in a much shorter time than it takes to go through the democratic processes of discussion and the slow formation of public opinion. But there is no way of insuring that a dictatorship will remain benevolent or that power once in the hands of a few will be returned to the people without struggle or revolution. This we have learned by experience and we accept the slow processes of democracy because we know that shortcuts compromise principles on which no compromise is possible.

The final expression of the opinion of the people with us is through free and honest elections, with valid choices on basic issues and candidates. The secret ballot is an essential to free elections but you must have a choice before you. I have heard my husband say many times that a people need never lose their freedom if they kept their right to a secret ballot and if they used that secret ballot to the full. Basic decisions of our society are made through the expressed will of the people. That is why when we see these liberties threatened, instead of falling apart, our nation becomes unified and our democracies come together as a unified group in spite of our varied backgrounds and many racial strains.

In the United States we have a capitalistic economy. That is because public opinion favors that type of economy under the conditions in which we live. But we have imposed certain restraints; for instance, we have antitrust laws. These are the legal evidence of the determination of the American people to maintain an economy of free competition and not to allow monopolies to take away the people's freedom.

Excerpt from Eleanor Roosevelt's "The Struggle for Human Rights," September 28, 1948

10. Why does Roosevelt assert that a "secret" ballot is important?
    a. Public votes were too raucous an event.
    b. It decreases the chance for bribery.
    c. Privacy secures freedom of choice.
    d. It ensures physical safety.

203

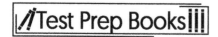

11. What does the writer say about freedom as a tool?
    a. Dictators can use it to manipulate populations.
    b. It's not just a concept; it can help achieve a desired lifestyle.
    c. It can be abused and misused by people.
    d. Only skilled individuals should be able to wield such a powerful tool.

12. According to Roosevelt, why do some people argue in favor of dictatorship?
    a. Dictatorships need not be tyrannical.
    b. Dictators come to power for a reason.
    c. Some dictators have been quite successful and popular.
    d. They believe that a dictator could achieve goals could more quickly.

13. According to the passage, what is the goal of antitrust laws?
    a. To establish trust between governments and populations
    b. To force businesses to be fair to consumers
    c. To foster economic competition
    d. To allow businesses to compete with the government

14. In the final sentence of the second paragraph, what does the word "promulgated" mean?
    a. Stifled
    b. Whispered
    c. Promoted
    d. Attacked

15. What is the main idea of this passage?
    a. We need democracy to maintain and protect individual freedom.
    b. Dictatorships can be benevolent and should be considered viable.
    c. Elections guarantee democracy and require secret ballots.
    d. Capitalism directly supports democracy and so should be encouraged.

16. Why does Roosevelt refer to both the French and American Revolutions?
    a. To demonstrate her understanding of history
    b. To draw a comparison to successful fights for freedom and democracy
    c. To highlight the fact that she is speaking to both American and French citizens
    d. To emphasize that she is speaking on the anniversary of both events

17. The tone of the passage is:
    a. Earnest
    b. Satirical
    c. Accusatory
    d. Conciliatory

18. Based on the passage, we can conclude that Roosevelt values:
    a. The relationship between France and America
    b. Capitalistic economy
    c. Knowledge of history
    d. Freedom and democracy

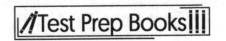
19. What is Roosevelt's concern about a "benevolent dictator"?
    a. The US has never had a dictator, so she is unfamiliar with them.
    b. The world is still recovering from World War II.
    c. There is no guarantee that a dictator will remain benevolent.
    d. There is no way a dictator will be benevolent.

History/Social Studies

Questions 20–29 are based on the following passage:

At times history and fate meet at a single time in a single place to shape a turning point in man's unending search for freedom. So it was at Lexington and Concord. So it was a century ago at Appomattox. So it was last week in Selma, Alabama. There, long-suffering men and women peacefully protested the denial of their rights as Americans. Many were brutally assaulted. One good man, a man of God, was killed.

There is no cause for pride in what has happened in Selma. There is no cause for self-satisfaction in the long denial of equal rights of millions of Americans. But there is cause for hope and for faith in our democracy in what is happening here tonight. For the cries of pain and the hymns and protests of oppressed people have summoned into convocation all the majesty of this great government—the government of the greatest nation on earth. Our mission is at once the oldest and the most basic of this country: to right wrong, to do justice, to serve man.

In our time we have come to live with the moments of great crisis. Our lives have been marked with debate about great issues—issues of war and peace, issues of prosperity and depression. But rarely in any time does an issue lay bare the secret heart of America itself. Rarely are we met with a challenge, not to our growth or abundance, or our welfare or our security, but rather to the values, and the purposes, and the meaning of our beloved nation.

The issue of equal rights for American Negroes is such an issue.

And should we defeat every enemy, and should we double our wealth and conquer the stars, and still be unequal to this issue, then we will have failed as a people and as a nation. For with a country as with a person, "What is a man profited, if he shall gain the whole world, and lose his own soul?"

There is no Negro problem. There is no Southern problem. There is no Northern problem. There is only an American problem. And we are met here tonight as Americans—not as Democrats or Republicans. We are met here as Americans to solve that problem.

This was the first nation in the history of the world to be founded with a purpose. The great phrases of that purpose still sound in every American heart, North and South: "All men are created equal," "government by consent of the governed," "give me liberty or give me death." Well, those are not just clever words, or those are not just empty theories. In their name Americans have fought and died for two centuries, and tonight around the world they stand there as guardians of our liberty, risking their lives.

205

Those words are a promise to every citizen that he shall share in the dignity of man. This dignity cannot be found in a man's possessions; it cannot be found in his power, or in his position. It really rests on his right to be treated as a man equal in opportunity to all others. It says that he shall share in freedom, he shall choose his leaders, educate his children, provide for his family according to his ability and his merits as a human being. To apply any other test—to deny a man his hopes because of his color, or race, or his religion, or the place of his birth is not only to do injustice, it is to deny America and to dishonor the dead who gave their lives for American freedom.

Except from Lyndon Johnson's "Address to Joint Session of Congress," March 15, 1965

20. Which of the following best encapsulates the purpose of this speech?
    a. To entertain
    b. To describe
    c. To teach
    d. To persuade

21. What was being protested in Selma?
    a. The closing of a bridge
    b. Denial of rights
    c. A murder
    d. Loss of wealth

22. Based on this passage, why does Johnson suggest there is hope in the events of Selma?
    a. Police responded immediately to the situation.
    b. Lots of citizens showed up to protest.
    c. It forced attention on the issue and sparked conversations about it.
    d. Despite the violence, only one life was lost.

23. How does Johnson suggest this issue is different from other debates?
    a. Other debates haven't led to protests.
    b. It is easier to solve.
    c. It is more difficult to solve.
    d. It concerns our values.

24. Based on Johnson's words, where does dignity lie?
    a. In equality
    b. In freedom to protest
    c. In American might
    d. In American abundance

25. What best describes the tone of Johnson's speech?
    a. Righteous
    b. Quixotic
    c. Scathing
    d. Vindictive

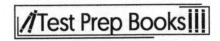
26. What does Johnson suggest will indicate failure, even among amazing successes?
    a. Failure to reach the Moon
    b. A loss of wealth
    c. Military defeat
    d. Moral or spiritual decay

27. In the second paragraph of this passage, what does the word "convocation" mean?
    a. A vocal duet
    b. A second career
    c. A gathering or assembly
    d. Closure

28. Based on the examples Johnson provides in the next to last paragraph of the passage, what can we conclude about the purpose for which America was founded?
    a. To fight wars and protect nations
    b. To lead the world
    c. To foster equality, democracy, and freedom
    d. To establish a country that others envy

29. Based on context, who are the "guardians of liberty" Johnson refers to?
    a. American citizens
    b. American troops
    c. American government
    d. Selma protestors

Science

Questions 30–37 are based on the following passage:

These community assessments conducted during the Zika outbreak, hurricane responses, and hurricane recovery in U.S. Virgin Islands (USVI) found that households were more concerned about contracting mosquito-borne diseases shortly after the Zika outbreak than during the hurricane response and hurricane recovery, even though reported mosquito biting activity increased, and environmental conditions were more favorable for mosquito breeding and exposure to bites following the hurricanes. In addition, although mosquito-borne diseases are endemic in USVI, and the population might be aware of the risk, households had concerns after the hurricanes that did not exist during the Zika outbreak, such as lack of shelter, clean water, and electricity. These differing levels of concern did not, however, change the community's support for mosquito spraying, although support for specific spray methods varied.

VIDOH used the Community Assessments for Public Health Emergency Response (CASPERs) data to make real-time outbreak and hurricane response decisions to improve mosquito bite prevention, mosquito control, and community education. For example, because the percentage of households concerned about contracting mosquito-borne diseases declined after the hurricanes compared with during the Zika outbreak response, VIDOH hurricane response education campaigns prioritized household-level mosquito bite prevention. The differing levels of support for various

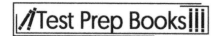
spray methods were also recognized and considered during decision making. For example, these data, along with unique environmental considerations, were used by the administration in place during the responses and recovery to determine backpack spraying to be the only acceptable option.

The CASPER is a useful tool for assessing mosquito-borne disease risk factors and creating immediately useable data to guide vector-related public health campaigns. According to CDC's internal CASPER database, a limited number of CASPERs have been conducted that assess mosquito bite prevention- and control-related factors, such as knowledge of mosquito-borne diseases; ways to protect against mosquito bites; and how to identify, quantify, and manage potential mosquito breeding sites. Even fewer CASPERs have focused solely on mosquitoes. A CASPER in Long Beach, California, during a Zika outbreak identified the need for increased mosquito abatement. In two areas of Texas, CASPERs successfully assessed the prevalence of vector-borne disease risk factors and the communities' knowledge of mosquito bite prevention and Zika virus. A CASPER conducted in American Samoa identified increased vector problems and the need for vector control after a tsunami.

Not only is CASPER an important tool for emergency response and recovery, it is also useful for collecting community public health information unrelated to an emergency. Vector control programs can use CASPERs during nonemergency situations to enhance and increase operation efficacy by evaluating the effectiveness of community campaigns and understanding community knowledge, attitudes, and practices.

Seger KR, Roth J Jr., Schnall AH, Ellis BR, Ellis EM. Community Assessments for Mosquito Prevention and Control Experiences, Attitudes, and Practices — U.S. Virgin Islands, 2017 and 2018. MMWR Morb Mortal Wkly Rep 2019;68:500–504. DOI: http://dx.doi.org/10.15585/mmwr.mm6822a3external icon.

30. Based on the passage, how did residents' self-assessment of their risk differ from the actual risk?
    a. Residents rated risk higher during the Zika outbreak than after the hurricane.
    b. Residents saw no risk at all from Zika.
    c. Residents saw no risk after the hurricane.
    d. Residents believed the risks to be equivalent.

31. The research in the first paragraph attempts to draw a correlation between which two things?
    a. Zika and hurricanes
    b. Resident concerns and Zika spread
    c. Hurricanes and mosquito spraying
    d. Basic necessities and mosquito-borne diseases

32. Based on information provided, why might other types of spraying plans be less desirable than backpack spraying?
    a. Human exposure to harmful chemicals
    b. The inability to target specific areas of mosquito proliferation
    c. Lack of community support for other methods
    d. Lack of household participation

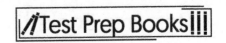
33. In non-emergency situations, which factors of disease vector control can CASPERs be helpful in understanding?
   a. Community knowledge
   b. Lack of shelter
   c. Spraying support
   d. Risk assessment

34. Based on the passage, we can conclude that:
   a. Backpack spraying will become the primary disease control mechanism.
   b. The risks associated with mosquito-borne diseases can increase with hurricanes.
   c. CASPERs will become a primary tool used by government organizations.
   d. Disease vector problems will remain isolated to island nations and the developing world.

35. What is main takeaway of the final paragraph?
   a. Mosquito-borne diseases are a serious risk for most of the developing world.
   b. Community knowledge of mosquito abatement is well below where it should be.
   c. Community action on mosquito bite prevention needs to be supported by governments.
   d. CASPERs are a vital tool for assessing the public health of communities in emergency and non-emergency situations.

36. Based on the passage, what can we say about why mosquito-borne diseases are more prevalent post-hurricane?
   a. Environmental conditions are favorable.
   b. Mosquitoes don't bite during storms.
   c. Fewer preventative drugs are available.
   d. Residents have raised awareness.

37. Based on the passage, which statement would researchers most agree with?
   a. CASPERs are best used in emergency situations.
   b. Aerial spraying is most effective to combat Zika.
   c. Hurricanes greatly increase the negative risks associated with mosquitos in the US Virgin Islands.
   d. Bite prevention is the best strategy for fighting mosquito-borne diseases.

Science

Questions 38–47 are based on the following two passages:

Passage 1

In 1992, the City of Madison, Wisconsin, found concentrations of lead in their drinking water exceeding the 90th percentile action level of 0.015 mg/L set by EPA. Lead (Pb) is a naturally occurring metal that was commonly used in household plumbing materials, such as lead service lines and leaded solder joints, before limits were set on its use in 1986.

However, in houses built before 1986, lead pipes can still be in use. Lead is rarely found in source water, but it can enter tap water as the water enters pipes with lead in older systems. Since some homes have lead service lines, the water coming into the house

may be transported via lead pipes even though there are no lead pipes inside the home. Brass plumbing fixtures can also contain small amounts of lead.

The Madison Water Utility chose to implement full lead service line replacement from 2001 through 2011 to eliminate the most significant source of lead in its water system. In 2003, sixty home taps were monitored after full lead service line replacement. They found that lead levels in the first liter of water were still high at some sites where the lead service line pipes had mostly been replaced within the previous four years. This phenomenon had been seen in other water systems, which had puzzled drinking water practitioners as to why elevated lead levels could persist for so long.

Coincident to the Madison Water Utility studies before and after the lead service line replacement program, lead service lines had been harvested from the water system and sent to EPA scientists. The EPA had the instrumentation and unique expertise to search for clues of lead release in pipe scales. That is, the materials that build up on the inside of pipes display chemical characteristics that reflect the chemical processes occurring in the water system, including the release of lead. The EPA conducted detailed analyses—color, texture, mineralogical and elemental composition—on five lead service pipe samples excavated between 2001 and 2006 from two different Madison neighborhoods.

Before the lead service line replacement program, Madison's water was delivered by an estimated 8000 lead service lines, which had been in service for 75 years or longer. The city's drinking water originated from numerous wells. The first set of lead service lines studied by EPA revealed that a highly insoluble and protective lead oxide compound had formed on the pipe walls. If all lead pipe walls had this formation, high lead releases would not be expected in the water system.

However, the second set of lead service lines came from a different neighborhood in the city. This neighborhood was fed by wells that were rich in manganese and iron. Both manganese and iron can form scales and accumulate metals, such as lead, from upstream sources, especially from upstream corroded lead pipes. EPA's results revealed that the accumulation of manganese and iron from the well water onto pipe walls had adsorbed lead and had the potential to crumble from the pipe walls and carry the lead to consumers' taps by means of the scale particulate matter entrained in the water. This finding corroborated with the results of the 2003 study where the higher lead concentration found at consumers' taps was mostly in particulate form. The presence of the manganese and iron scale on the pipe walls was the reason for high lead release in parts of the Madison water system, before and even after the lead pipes were removed.

As the 2003 residential study had shown, once the principal lead source was removed, it took more than four years in some cases for the accumulated lead to be released, which explains why lead levels remained high after the lead pipes had been replaced. Eventually, removing the source of lead did eliminate the significant lead concentration and achieved compliance with EPA's regulations.

Overall, this research showed that controlling lead exposure from water is more complicated than simply adding corrosion control chemicals to reduce the solubility of lead minerals. Buildup of manganese and iron scale in water pipes should also be considered as a source for accumulating and releasing lead, and other contaminants of

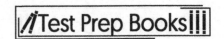

concern, into water. What happened in Madison highlights the importance of analyzing pipe scales to understand how lead accumulates and releases into the water over time.

From: "Revealing the Complicated Nature of Tap Water Lead Contamination: A Madison, Wisconsin Case Study," July 30, 2018. EPA. https://www.epa.gov/sciencematters/revealing-complicated-nature-tap-water-lead-contamination-madison-wisconsin-case

Passage 2

An estimated six to ten million older homes across the country have lead service lines. Service lines connect individual houses to the water main in the street; this means that water coming into a house may be transported via a lead service line even if no lead pipes are visible inside the home. Lead can be transferred from the lead pipe into the drinking water when the pipe materials corrode, when there are physical disturbances to the pipe, or when there are changes to the quality of water entering the home.

Given that there are many lead service lines in use across the country, limiting corrosion is a necessary step to reduce potential lead exposure from drinking water. Public water systems can control corrosion through a variety of methods including strict control of key water quality parameters and proper addition of a phosphate or silicate corrosion control inhibitor. Public water systems sometimes use modeling to inform corrosion control. EPA researchers recently looked at how well these models were predicting what is happening in the real world.

Water systems in EPA's Region 5—comprised of Minnesota, Wisconsin, Michigan, Illinois, Indiana, and Ohio—shared lead service line pipes and water quality data with EPA researchers. Actual pieces of pipe were taken out of the water systems and sent to EPA where scientists examined the pipe scales, the materials that build up on the inside of pipes. These pipe scales reveal chemical characteristics that reflect the chemical and physical processes occurring within the water system including the release of lead into drinking water.

Once EPA researchers cut open the pipes and took the scales apart, they examined each layer of scale and the minerals that were present. Different minerals have different inherent solubilities which clued researchers in to which minerals may be dissolving into the water. EPA researchers looked at which minerals were predicted to form based on the modeling, and then looked at pipe scales found on the lead service lines from those systems to see which minerals really were forming.

EPA and other outside organizations have applied predictive solubility models to try and help systems pick the right corrosion control treatment that fits their system's individual needs. These models provide guidance regarding which mineral phases are predicted to control lead release in a given environment. EPA's model uses parameters like alkalinity and pH to predict which mineral would be expected to form in the lead service lines of a water system and how much dissolved lead you would expect to find in the water.

The researchers, including EPA's Jennifer Tully, Mike DeSantis, and Mike Schock, found various lead minerals, and other non-crystalline materials forming on the inside of the pipes. They discovered that there was almost always a mix of different lead minerals

211

present in the scale. A little more than half of the lead service lines they looked at showed that the minerals present were not the same minerals that the models were predicting would be present.

Next, EPA researchers looked at water quality data from several systems that had supplied lead service lines for analysis. Since the pipe scales showed that the models were not always predicting the right mineral composition, the scientists wanted to see how well the corrosion control was working. What they found in limited sampling was that the models often have difficulty predicting real world scenarios due to the complexity of corrosion control, and this study shows the need for further evaluation and water sampling beyond just modeling to ensure that systems are using the correct treatment to keep lead out of drinking water.

From "EPA Researchers Help Water Systems Keep Lead out of Drinking Water," March 3, 2020.

38. Based on Passage 1, what complicates efforts to address lead exposure via household taps?
   a. Lack of reporting on the issue
   b. Lack of testing in many regions of the United States
   c. Inability to identify and track the sources of lead
   d. Multiple ways that lead accumulates and is released

39. Based on Passage 2, what is the public water system's role in lead contamination control?
   a. Informing residents of lead levels in their tap water
   b. Monitoring quality and corrosion control additives
   c. Replacing lead pipes in homes with safer plumbing systems
   d. Providing researchers the opportunity to track lead contamination sources

40. According to the findings in Passage 1, even if there are no lead pipes in the home, why is lead present?
   a. Some lead levels are present in all water
   b. Lead is present in the city's water source
   c. Testing is sometimes unreliable
   d. Lead service lines and accumulation leading to the home

41. According to the findings in Passage 2, why is modeling sometimes ineffective?
   a. Real-world scenarios don't always match the models.
   b. Researchers rarely have all the data to predict source points.
   c. Models are not updated to reflect new mineral presence.
   d. Changes in service lines change the outcome.

42. Based on the two passages, what would the authors most agree on?
   a. Low lead levels in water after line changes are not as concerning.
   b. Corrosion inhibitors in water source points are the most effective option.
   c. Lead is leaching from scaling in older pipes in homes.
   d. Well water is safer than municipal water.

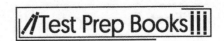
43. In Passage 1, why were lead levels still present even after the primary lead source had been removed?
    a. Accumulated lead and minerals in the system took four years to resolve.
    b. The lead was determined to be coming from the water source itself.
    c. Corrosion inhibitors had not yet been introduced.
    d. False positive tests were reported due to other minerals.

44. In the fourth paragraph of Passage 2, what does the word "solubilities" mean?
    a. Concentration levels
    b. Bonding strengths
    c. Levels of condensation
    d. Abilities to dissolve

45. Based on both passages, in older homes, what initial mitigation strategy would the researchers agree on?
    a. High-end water filtration systems
    b. Replacing lead service lines
    c. Switching water sources
    d. Corrosion additives in municipal water

46. Which statement would both research groups agree with?
    a. Replacing lead lines in homes will resolve lead levels.
    b. Addressing scaling and mineral accumulation is crucial.
    c. Scientific modeling will continue to be a fundamental tool.
    d. Source point lead pollution is the biggest concern.

47. Which statement would researchers from both passages most DISAGREE with?
    a. Low lead levels can be handled by sink filtration.
    b. Lead eradication is easier with well water.
    c. Corrosion control at water sources is our best weapon.
    d. In five years, we can control lead levels in water.

Writing and Language Test

Read the essay entitled "Education is Essential to Civilization" and answer Questions 1–15.

Early in my career, (1) <u>a master's teacher shared this thought with me "Education is the last bastion of civility."</u> While I did not completely understand the scope of those words at the time, I have since come to realize the depth, breadth, truth, and significance of what he said. (2) <u>Education provides </u>society with a vehicle for (3) <u>raising it's children to be </u>civil, decent, human beings with something valuable to contribute to the world. It is really what makes us human and what (4) <u>distinguishes </u>us as <u>civilised creatures.</u>

Being "civilized" humans means being "whole" humans. Education must address the mind, body, and soul of students. (5) <u>It would be detrimental to society, only meeting the needs of the mind, if our schools were myopic in their focus.</u> As humans, we are multi-dimensional, multi-faceted beings who need more than head knowledge to survive. (6) <u>The human heart and psyche have to be fed in order for the mind to develop</u>

properly, and the body must be maintained and exercised to help fuel the working of the brain. Education is a basic human right, and it allows us to sustain a democratic society in which participation is fundamental to its success. It should inspire students to seek better solutions to world problems and to dream of a more equitable society. Education should never discriminate on any basis, and it should create individuals who are self-sufficient, patriotic, and tolerant of (7) others' ideas.

(8) All children can learn. Although not all children learn in the same manner. All children learn best, however, when their basic physical needs are met and they feel safe, secure, and loved. Students are much more responsive to a teacher who values them and shows them respect as individual people. Teachers must model at all times the way they expect students to treat them and their peers. If teachers set high expectations for (9) there students, the students will rise to that high level. Teachers must make the well-being of students their primary focus and must not be afraid to let students learn from their own mistakes.

In the modern age of technology, a teacher's focus is no longer the "what" of the content, (10) but more importantly, the 'why.' Students are bombarded with information and have access to ANY information they need right at their fingertips. Teachers have to work harder than ever before to help students identify salient information (11) so to think critically about the information they encounter. Students have to (12) read between the lines, identify bias, and determine who they can trust in the milieu of ads, data, and texts presented to them.

Schools must work in concert with families in this important mission. While children spend most of their time in school, they are dramatically and indelibly shaped (13) with the influences of their family and culture. Teachers must not only respect this fact, (14) but must strive to include parents in the education of their children and must work to keep parents informed of progress and problems. Communication between classroom and home is essential for a child's success.

Humans have always aspired to be more, do more, and to better ourselves and our communities. This is where education lies, right at the heart of humanity's desire to be all that we can be. Education helps us strive for higher goals and better treatment of ourselves and others. I shudder to think what would become of us if education ceased to be the "last bastion of civility." (15) We must be unapologetic about expecting excellence from our students? Our very existence depends upon it.

1. What edit is needed to correct sentence 1 (reproduced below)?

Early in my career, (1) a master's teacher shared this thought with me "Education is the last bastion of civility."

a. NO CHANGE
b. a master's teacher shared this thought with me: "Education is the last bastion of civility."
c. a master's teacher shared this thought with me: "Education is the last bastion of civility".
d. a master's teacher shared this thought with me. "Education is the last bastion of civility."

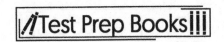

2. What edit is needed to correct sentence 2 (reproduced below)?

> (2) <u>Education provides </u>society with a vehicle for raising it's children to be civil, decent, human beings with something valuable to contribute to the world.

   a. NO CHANGE
   b. Education provide
   c. Education will provide
   d. Education providing

3. What edit is needed to correct sentence 3 (reproduced below)?

> Education provides society with a vehicle for (3) <u>raising it's children to be </u>civil, decent, human beings with something valuable to contribute to the world.

   a. NO CHANGE
   b. raises its children to be
   c. raising its' children to be
   d. raising its children to be

4. Which word, if any, is misspelled?
   a. None of these are misspelled.
   b. Distinguishes
   c. Civilised
   d. Creatures

5. What edit is needed to correct sentence 5 (reproduced below)?

> (5) <u>It would be detrimental to society, only meeting the needs of the mind, if our schools were myopic in their focus.</u>

   a. NO CHANGE
   b. It would be detrimental to society if our schools were myopic in their focus, only meeting the needs of the mind.
   c. Only meeting the needs of our mind, our schools were myopic in their focus, detrimental to society.
   d. Myopic is the focus of our schools, being detrimental to society for only meeting the needs of the mind.

6. Which of these sentences, if any, should begin a new paragraph?
   a. There should be no new paragraph.
   b. The human heart and psyche have to be fed in order for the mind to develop properly, and the body must be maintained and exercised to help fuel the working of the brain.
   c. Education is a basic human right, and it allows us to sustain a democratic society in which participation is fundamental to its success.
   d. It should inspire students to seek better solutions to world problems and to dream of a more equitable society.

215

7. What edit is needed to correct sentence 7 (reproduced below)?

> Education should never discriminate on any basis, and it should create individuals who are self-sufficient, patriotic, and tolerant of (7) others' ideas.

  a. NO CHANGE
  b. other's ideas
  c. others ideas
  d. others's ideas

8. What edit is needed to correct sentence 8 (reproduced below)?

> (8) All children can learn. Although not all children learn in the same manner. All

  a. NO CHANGE
  b. All children can learn although not all children learn in the same manner.
  c. All children can learn although, not all children learn in the same manner.
  d. All children can learn, although not all children learn in the same manner.

9. What edit is needed to correct sentence 9 (reproduced below)?

> If teachers set high expectations for (9) there students, the students will rise to that high level.

  a. NO CHANGE
  b. they're students
  c. their students
  d. thare students

10. What edit is needed to correct sentence 10 (reproduced below)?

> In the modern age of technology, a teacher's focus is no longer the "what" of the content, (10) but more importantly, the 'why.'

  a. NO CHANGE
  b. but more importantly, the "why."
  c. but more importantly, the 'why'.
  d. but more importantly, the "why".

11. What edit is needed to correct sentence 11 (reproduced below)?

> Teachers have to work harder than ever before to help students identify salient information (11) so to think critically about the information they encounter.

  a. NO CHANGE
  b. and to think critically
  c. but to think critically
  d. nor to think critically

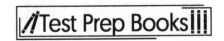
12. What edit is needed to correct sentence 12 (reproduced below)?

Students have to (12) <u>read between the lines, identify bias, and determine</u> who they can trust in the milieu of ads, data, and texts presented to them.

a. NO CHANGE
b. read between the lines, identify bias, and determining
c. read between the lines, identifying bias, and determining
d. reads between the lines, identifies bias, and determines

13. What edit is needed to correct sentence 13 (reproduced below)?

While children spend most of their time in school, they are dramatically and indelibly shaped (13) <u>with the influences</u> of their family and culture.

a. NO CHANGE
b. for the influences
c. to the influences
d. by the influences

14. What edit is needed to correct sentence 14 (reproduced below)?

Teachers must not only respect this fact, (14) <u>but must strive</u> to include parents in the education of their children and must work to keep parents informed of progress and problems.

a. NO CHANGE
b. but to strive
c. but striving
d. but strived

15. What edit is needed to correct sentence 15 (reproduced below)?

(15) <u>We must be unapologetic about expecting excellence from our students? Our very existence depends upon it.</u>

a. NO CHANGE
b. We must be unapologetic about expecting excellence from our students, our very existence depends upon it.
c. We must be unapologetic about expecting excellence from our students—our very existence depends upon it.
d. We must be unapologetic about expecting excellence from our students our very existence depends upon it.

Questions 16–24 are based on the following passage:

(16) <u>One of the icon's of romantic and science fiction literature</u> remains Mary Shelley's classic, *Frankenstein, or The Modern Prometheus*. Schools throughout the world still teach the book in literature and philosophy courses. Scientific communities also engage in discussion on the novel. But why? Besides the novel's engaging (17) <u>writing style the story's central theme</u> remains highly relevant in a world of constant discovery and moral

dilemmas. Central to the core narrative is the (18) <u>struggle between enlightenment and the cost of overusing power</u>.

The subtitle, *The Modern Prometheus*, encapsulates the inner theme of the story more than the main title of *Frankenstein*. As with many romantic writers, Shelley invokes the classical myths and (19) <u>symbolism of Ancient Greece and Rome to high light core ideas</u>. Looking deeper into the myth of Prometheus sheds light not only on the character of Frankenstein (20) <u>but also poses a psychological dilemma to the audience.</u> Prometheus is the titan who gave fire to mankind. (21) <u>However, more than just fire he gave people knowledge and power.</u> The power of fire advanced civilization. Yet, for giving fire to man, Prometheus is (22) <u>punished by the gods bound to a rock and tormented for his act</u>. This is clearly a parallel to Frankenstein—he is the modern Prometheus.

Frankenstein's quest for knowledge becomes an obsession. It leads him to literally create new life, breaking the bounds of conceivable science to illustrate that man can create life out of nothing. (23) <u>Yet he ultimately faltered as a creator,</u> abandoning his progeny in horror of what he created. Frankenstein then suffers his creature's wrath, (24) <u>the result of his pride, obsession for power and lack of responsibility.</u>

Shelley isn't condemning scientific achievement. Rather, her writing reflects that science and discovery are good things, but, like all power, it must be used wisely. The text alludes to the message that one must have reverence for nature and be mindful of the potential consequences. Frankenstein did not take responsibility or even consider how his actions would affect others. His scientific brilliance ultimately led to suffering.

16. Which of the following would be the best choice for this sentence (reproduced below)?

    (16) <u>One of the icon's of romantic and science fiction literature</u> remains Mary Shelley's classic, *Frankenstein, or The Modern Prometheus*.

    a. NO CHANGE
    b. One of the icons of romantic and science fiction literature
    c. One of the icon's of romantic, and science fiction literature,
    d. The icon of romantic and science fiction literature

17. Which of the following would be the best choice for this sentence (reproduced below)?

    Besides the novel's engaging (17) <u>writing style the story's central theme</u> remains highly relevant in a world of constant discovery and moral dilemmas.

    a. NO CHANGE
    b. writing style the central theme of the story
    c. writing style, the story's central theme
    d. the story's central theme's writing style

18. Which of the following would be the best choice for this sentence (reproduced below)?

> Central to the core narrative is the (18) <u>struggle between enlightenment and the cost of overusing power.</u>

a. NO CHANGE
b. struggle between enlighten and the cost of overusing power.
c. struggle between enlightenment's cost of overusing power.
d. struggle between enlightening and the cost of overusing power.

19. Which of the following would be the best choice for this sentence (reproduced below)?

> As with many romantic writers, Shelley invokes the classical myths and (19) <u>symbolism of Ancient Greece and Rome to high light core ideas.</u>

a. NO CHANGE
b. symbolism of Ancient Greece and Rome to highlight core ideas.
c. symbolism of ancient Greece and Rome to highlight core ideas.
d. symbolism of Ancient Greece and Rome highlighting core ideas.

20. Which of the following would be the best choice for this sentence (reproduced below)?

> Looking deeper into the myth of Prometheus sheds light not only on the character of Frankenstein (20) <u>but also poses a psychological dilemma to the audience.</u>

a. NO CHANGE
b. but also poses a psychological dilemma with the audience.
c. but also poses a psychological dilemma for the audience.
d. but also poses a psychological dilemma there before the audience.

21. Which of the following would be the best choice for this sentence (reproduced below)?

> (21) <u>However, more than just fire he gave people knowledge and power.</u>

a. NO CHANGE
b. However, more than just fire he gave people, knowledge, and power.
c. However, more than just fire, he gave people knowledge and power.
d. In addition to fire, Prometheus gave people knowledge and power.

22. Which of the following would be the best choice for this sentence (reproduced below)?

> Yet, for giving fire to man, Prometheus is (22) <u>punished by the gods bound to a rock and tormented for his act.</u>

a. NO CHANGE
b. punished by the gods, bound to a rock and tormented for his act.
c. bound to a rock and tormented by the gods as punishment.
d. punished for his act by being bound to a rock and tormented as punishment from the gods.

23. Which of the following would be the best choice for this sentence (reproduced below)?

> (23) Yet he ultimately faltered as a creator, abandoning his progeny in horror of what he created.

a. NO CHANGE
b. Yet, he ultimately falters as a creator by
c. Yet, he ultimately faltered as a creator,
d. Yet he ultimately falters as a creator by

24. Which of the following would be the best choice for this sentence (reproduced below)?

> Frankenstein then suffers his creature's wrath, (24) the result of his pride, obsession for power and lack of responsibility.

a. NO CHANGE
b. the result of his pride, obsession for power and lacking of responsibility.
c. the result of his pride, obsession for power, and lack of responsibility.
d. the result of his pride and also his obsession for power and lack of responsibility.

Questions 25–33 are based on the following passage:

The power of legends continues to enthrall our imagination, provoking us both to wonder and explore. (25) Who doesnt love a good legend? Some say legends never (26) die and this is certainly the case for the most legendary creature of all, Bigfoot. To this day, people still claim sightings of the illusive cryptid. Many think of Bigfoot as America's monster, yet many nations have legends of a similar creature. In my own research I have found that Australia has the Yowie, China has the Yerin, and Russia has the Almas. (27) Their all over the world, the Bigfoots and the legends tied to them. Does this mean they could exist?

There are many things to consider when addressing (28) this question but the chief factor is whether there is credible evidence. (29) For science to formally recognize that such a species exists, there needs to be physical proof. While people have found supposed footprints and even (30) captured photos and film of the creature, this validity of such evidence is up for debate. There is room for uncertainty. Most visual evidence is out of focus, thus (31) there is often skepticism whether such images are real. Some researchers have even claimed to have hair and blood samples, but still there is doubt in the scientific community. The reason is simple: there needs to be a body or living specimen found and actively studied in order to prove the Bigfoots' existence.

Yet, one cannot ignore the fact that (32) hundreds of witnesses continuing to describe a creature with uniform features all over the world. These Bigfoot sightings aren't a modern occurrence either. Ancient civilizations have reported (33) seeing Bigfoot as well including Native Americans. It is from Native Americans that we gained the popular term Sasquatch, which is the primary name for the North American Bigfoot. How does their testimony factor in? If indigenous people saw these animals, could they not have existed at some point? After all, when Europeans first arrived in Africa, they disbelieved the native accounts of the gorilla. But sure enough, Europeans eventually found gorillas and collected a body.

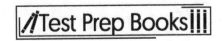

25. Which of the following would be the best choice for this sentence (reproduced below)?

    (25) Who doesnt love a good legend?

   a. NO CHANGE
   b. Who does not love a good legend?
   c. A good legend, who doesn't love one?
   d. Who doesn't love a good legend?

26. Which of the following would be the best choice for this sentence (reproduced below)?

    Some say legends never (26) die and this is certainly the case for the most legendary creature of all, Bigfoot.

   a. NO CHANGE
   b. die, and this is certainly the case
   c. die; this is certainly the case
   d. die. This is certainly the case

27. Which of the following would be the best choice for this sentence (reproduced below)?

    (27) Their all over the world, the bigfoots and the legends tied to them.

   a. NO CHANGE
   b. There all over the world, the
   c. They're all over the world, the
   d. All over the world they are, the

28. Which of the following would be the best choice for this sentence (reproduced below)?

    There are many things to consider when addressing (28) this question but the chief factor is whether there is credible evidence.

   a. NO CHANGE
   b. this question, but the chief factor
   c. this question however the chief factor
   d. this question; but the chief factor

29. Which of the following would be the best choice for this sentence (reproduced below)?

    (29) For science to formally recognize that such a species exists, there needs to be physical proof.

   a. NO CHANGE
   b. Physical proof are needed in order for science to formally recognize that such a species exists.
   c. For science to formally recognize that such a species exists there needs to be physical proof.
   d. For science, to formally recognize that such a species exists, there needs to be physical proof.

30. Which of the following would be the best choice for this sentence (reproduced below)?

> While people have found supposed footprints and even (30) <u>captured photos and film of the creature, this validity of such evidence is up for debate.</u>

  a. NO CHANGE
  b. captured photos and film of the creature. This validity of such evidence is up for debate.
  c. captured photos and film of the creature, the validities of such evidence is up for debate.
  d. captured photos and film of the creature, the validity of such evidence is up for debate.

31. Which of the following would be the best choice for this sentence (reproduced below)?

> Most visual evidence is out of focus, thus (31) <u>there is often skepticism whether such images are real.</u>

  a. NO CHANGE
  b. often skepticism whether such images are real.
  c. there is often skepticism, whether such images are real.
  d. there is often skepticism weather such images are real.

32. Which of the following would be the best choice for this sentence (reproduced below)?

> Yet, one cannot ignore the fact that (32) <u>hundreds of witnesses continuing to describe a creature</u> with uniform features all over the world.

  a. NO CHANGE
  b. hundreds of witnesses continuing to describing a creature
  c. hundreds of witnesses continue to describe a creature
  d. hundreds of the witnesses continue to described a creature

33. Which of the following would be the best choice for this sentence (reproduced below)?

> Ancient civilizations have reported (33) <u>seeing Bigfoot as well including Native Americans.</u>

  a. NO CHANGE
  b. seeing Bigfoot, Native Americans as well.
  c. seeing Bigfoot also the Native Americans.
  d. seeing Bigfoot, including Native Americans.

The next seven questions are based on the following passage:

> I have to admit that when my father bought a recreational vehicle (RV), I thought he was making a huge mistake. I didn't really know anything about RVs, but I knew that my dad was as big a "city slicker" as there was. (34) <u>In fact, I even thought he might have gone a little bit crazy.</u> On trips to the beach, he preferred to swim at the pool, and whenever he went hiking, he avoided touching any plants for fear that they might be poison ivy. Why would this man, with an almost irrational fear of the outdoors, want a 40-foot camping behemoth?

> (35) <u>The RV</u> was a great purchase for our family and brought us all closer together. Every morning (36) <u>we would wake up, eat breakfast, and broke camp.</u> We laughed at our own

comical attempts to back The Beast into spaces that seemed impossibly small. (37) <u>We rejoiced as "hackers."</u> When things inevitably went wrong and we couldn't solve the problems on our own, we discovered the incredible helpfulness and friendliness of the RV community. (38) <u>We even made some new friends in the process.</u>

(39) <u>Above all, it allowed us to share adventures. While traveling across America,</u> which we could not have experienced in cars and hotels. Enjoying a campfire on a chilly summer evening with the mountains of Glacier National Park in the background or waking up early in the morning to see the sun rising over the distant spires of Arches National Park are memories that will always stay with me and our entire family. (40) <u>Those are also memories that my siblings and me</u> have now shared with our own children.

34. Which of the following would be the best choice for this sentence (reproduced below)?

(34) <u>In fact, I even thought he might have gone a little bit crazy.</u>

a. NO CHANGE
b. Move the sentence so that it comes before the preceding sentence.
c. Move the sentence to the end of the first paragraph.
d. Omit the sentence.

35. In context, which is the best version of the underlined portion of this sentence (reproduced below)?

(35) <u>The RV</u> was a great purchase for our family and brought us all closer together.

a. NO CHANGE
b. Not surprisingly, the RV
c. Furthermore, the RV
d. As it turns out, the RV

36. Which is the best version of the underlined portion of this sentence (reproduced below)?

Every morning (36) <u>we would wake up, eat breakfast, and broke camp.</u>

a. NO CHANGE
b. we would wake up, eat breakfast, and break camp.
c. would we wake up, eat breakfast, and break camp?
d. we are waking up, eating breakfast, and breaking camp.

37. Which is the best version of the underlined portion of this sentence (reproduced below)?

(37) <u>We rejoiced as "hackers."</u>

a. NO CHANGE
b. To a nagging problem of technology, we rejoiced as "hackers."
c. We rejoiced when we figured out how to "hack" a solution to a nagging technological problem.
d. To "hack" our way to a solution, we had to rejoice.

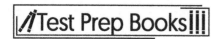

38. Which is the best version of the underlined portion of this sentence (reproduced below)?

> (38) We even made some new friends in the process.

a. NO CHANGE
b. In the process was the friends we were making.
c. We are even making some new friends in the process.
d. We will make new friends in the process.

39. Which is the best version of the underlined portion of this sentence (reproduced below)?

> (39) Above all, it allowed us to share adventures. While traveling across America, which we could not have experienced in cars and hotels.

a. NO CHANGE
b. Above all, it allowed us to share adventures while traveling across America
c. Above all, it allowed us to share adventures; while traveling across America
d. Above all, it allowed us to share adventures—while traveling across America

40. Which is the best version of the underlined portion of this sentence (reproduced below)?

> (40) Those are also memories that my siblings and me have now shared with our own children.

a. NO CHANGE
b. Those are also memories that me and my siblings
c. Those are also memories that my siblings and I
d. Those are also memories that I and my siblings

The next four questions are based on the following passage:

> We live in a savage world; that's just a simple fact. It is a time of violence, when the need for self-defense is imperative. (41) Martial arts, like Jiu-Jitsu, still play a vital role in ones survival. (42) Jiu-Jitsu, however doesn't justify kicking people around, even when being harassed or attacked. Today, laws prohibit the (43) use of unnecessary force in self-defense; these serve to eliminate beating someone to a pulp once they have been neutralized. Such laws are needed. Apart from being unnecessary to continually strike a person when (44) their down, its immoral. Such over-aggressive retaliation turns the innocent into the aggressor. Jiu-Jitsu provides a way for defending oneself while maintaining the philosophy of restraint and self-discipline. Integrated into its core philosophy, jiujitsu tempers the potential to do great physical harm with respect for that power and for life.

> Excerpt from the essay *Morality and the Warrior's Path*

41. Which of the following would be the best choice for this sentence (reproduced below)?

> (41) Martial arts, like Jiu-Jitsu, still play a vital role in ones survival.

a. NO CHANGE
b. Martial arts, like Jiu-Jitsu, still play a vital role in one's survival.
c. Martial arts, like Jiu-Jitsu still play a vital role in ones survival.
d. Martial arts, like Jiu-Jitsu, still plays a vital role in one's survival.

42. Which of the following would be the best choice for this sentence (reproduced below)?

> (42) Jiu-Jitsu, however doesn't justify kicking people around, even when being harassed or attacked.

a. NO CHANGE
b. Jiu-Jitsu, however, isn't justified by kicking people around,
c. However, Jiu-Jitsu doesn't justify kicking people around,
d. Jiu-Jitsu however doesn't justify kicking people around,

43. Which of the following would be the best choice for this sentence (reproduced below)?

> Today, laws prohibit the (43) use of unnecessary force in self-defense; these serve to eliminate beating someone to a pulp once they have been neutralized.

a. NO CHANGE
b. use of unnecessary force in self-defense serving to eliminate
c. use of unnecessary force, in self-defense, these serve to eliminate
d. use of unnecessary force. In self-defense, these serve to eliminate

44. Which of the following would be the best choice for this sentence (reproduced below)?

> Apart from being unnecessary to continually strike a person when (44) their down, its immoral.

a. NO CHANGE
b. their down, it's immoral.
c. they're down, its immoral.
d. they're down, it's immoral.

Math Test

Calculator Questions

1. If a car can travel 300 miles in 4 hours, how far can it go in an hour and a half?
   a. 100 miles
   b. 112.5 miles
   c. 135.5 miles
   d. 150 miles

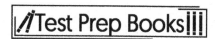

2. At the store, Jan spends $90 on apples and oranges. Apples cost $1 each and oranges cost $2 each. If Jan buys the same number of apples as oranges, how many oranges did she buy?

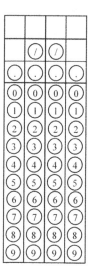

3. Where does the point $(-3, -4)$ lie in relation to the circle with the equation $(x)^2 + (y)^2 = 25$?
   a.   Inside of the circle.
   b.   Outside of the circle.
   c.   On the circle.
   d.   There is not enough information to tell.

4. A train traveling 50 miles per hour takes a trip lasting 3 hours. If a map has a scale of 1 inch per 10 miles, how many inches apart are the train's starting point and ending point on the map if it travelled in a straight line?

5. A traveler takes an hour to drive to a museum, spends 3 hours and 30 minutes there, and takes half an hour to drive home. What percentage of their time was spent driving?
   a. 15%
   b. 30%
   c. 40%
   d. 60%

6. A truck is carrying three cylindrical barrels. Their bases have a diameter of 2 feet, and they have a height of 3 feet. What is the total volume of the three barrels in cubic feet?
   a. 3π
   b. 9π
   c. 12π
   d. 15π

7. Greg buys a $10 lunch with 5% sales tax. He leaves a $2 tip after paying his bill. How much money does he spend?
   a. $12.50
   b. $12
   c. $13
   d. $13.25

8. Marty wishes to save $150 over a 4-day period. How much must Marty save each day on average?
   a. $37.50
   b. $35
   c. $45.50
   d. $41

9. Bernard can make $80 per day. If he needs to make $300 and only works full days, how many days will this take?

227

10. A couple buys a house for $150,000. They sell it for $165,000. By what percentage did the house's value increase?
    a. 10%
    b. 13%
    c. 15%
    d. 17%

11. A school has 15 teachers and 20 teaching assistants. They have 200 students. What is the ratio of faculty to students?
    a. $3 : 20$
    b. $4 : 17$
    c. $5 : 54$
    d. $7 : 40$

12. A map has a scale of 1 inch per 5 miles. A car can travel 60 miles per hour. If the distance from the start to the destination is 3 inches on the map, how many minutes will it take the car to make the trip?

13. Taylor works two jobs. The first pays $20,000 per year. The second pays $10,000 per year. She donates 15% of her income to charity. How much does she donate each year?
    a. $4,500
    b. $5,000
    c. $5,500
    d. $6,000

14. Suppose an investor deposits $1,200 into a bank account that accrues 1 percent interest per month. Assuming x represents the number of months since the deposit and y represents the money in the account, which of the following exponential functions models the scenario?
    a. $y = (0.01)(1{,}200^x)$
    b. $y = (1200)(0.01^x)$
    c. $y = (1.01)(1200^x)$
    d. $y = (1200)(1.01^x)$

15. Suppose the function $y = \frac{1}{8}x^3 + 2x - 21$ approximates the population of a given city between the years 1900 and 2000 with x representing the year (where 1900 is $x = 0$) and y representing the population (in thousands). Which of the following domains are relevant for the scenario?

a. $(-\infty, \infty)$
b. $[1900, 2000]$
c. $[0, 100]$
d. $[0, 0]$

16. If Sarah reads at an average rate of 21 pages in four nights, how long will it take her to read 140 pages?

a. 6 nights
b. 26 nights
c. 8 nights
d. 27 nights

17. Mom's car drove 72 miles in 90 minutes. There are 5,280 feet per mile. How fast did she drive in feet per second?

a. 0.8 feet per second
b. 48.9 feet per second
c. 0.009 feet per second
d. 70.4 feet per second

18. This chart indicates how many sales of CDs, vinyl records, and MP3 downloads occurred over the last year. Approximately what percentage of the total sales was from CDs?

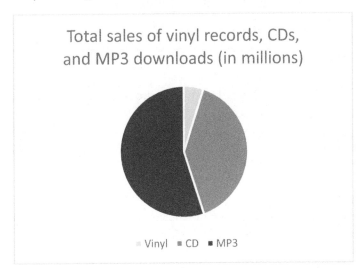

Total sales of vinyl records, CDs, and MP3 downloads (in millions)

Vinyl CD MP3

a. 55%
b. 25%
c. 40%
d. 5%

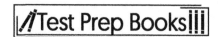

19. After a 20% sale discount, Frank purchased a new refrigerator for $850. How much did he save from the original price?
    a. $170
    b. $212.50
    c. $105.75
    d. $200

20. Which of the following is NOT a way to write 40 percent of N?
    a. $(0.4)N$

    b. $\frac{2}{5}N$

    c. $40N$

    d. $\frac{4N}{10}$

21. The graph of which function has an x-intercept of -2?
    a. $y = 2x - 3$
    b. $y = 4x + 2$
    c. $y = x^2 + 5x + 6$
    d. $y = 2x^2 + 3x - 1$

22. The table below displays the number of three-year-olds at Kids First Daycare who are potty-trained and those who still wear diapers.

	Potty-trained	Wear diapers	Total
Boys	26	22	48
Girls	34	18	52
Total	60	40	

What is the probability of a three-year-old girl from the school being potty-trained?
    a. 52%
    b. 34%
    c. 65%
    d. 57%

23. A clothing company with a target market of U.S. boys surveys 2,000 twelve-year-old boys to find their height. The average height of the boys is 61 inches. For the above scenario, 61 inches represents which of the following?
    a. Sample statistic
    b. Population parameter
    c. Confidence interval
    d. Measurement error

24. A government agency is researching the average consumer cost of gasoline throughout the United States. Which data collection method would produce the most valid results?
   a. Randomly choosing one hundred gas stations in the state of New York
   b. Randomly choosing ten gas stations from each of the fifty states
   c. Randomly choosing five hundred gas stations from across all fifty states with the number chosen proportional to the population of the state
   d. Methods A, B, and C would each produce equally valid results.

25. What is the equation of a circle whose center is (1, 5) and radius is 4?
   a. $(x-1)^2 + (y-25)^2 = 4$
   b. $(x-1)^2 + (y-25)^2 = 16$
   c. $(x+1)^2 + (y+5)^2 = 16$
   d. $(x-1)^2 + (y-5)^2 = 16$

26. What is the slope of this line?

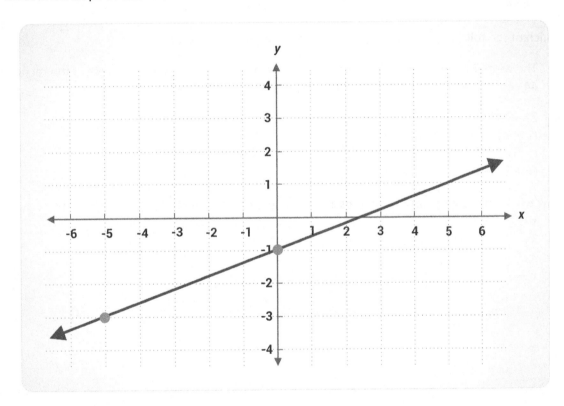

   a. 2

   b. $\frac{5}{2}$

   c. $\frac{1}{2}$

   d. $\frac{2}{5}$

27. What is the perimeter of the figure below? Note that the solid outer line is the perimeter.

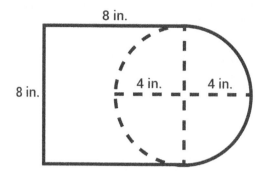

a. 48.566 ft
b. 36.566 ft
c. 19.78 ft
d. 30.566 ft

28. Which of the following equations best represents the problem below?

The width of a rectangle is 2 centimeters less than the length. If the perimeter of the rectangle is 44 centimeters, then what are the dimensions of the rectangle?

a. $2l + 2(l - 2) = 44$
b. $(l + 2) + (l + 2) + l = 48$
c. $l \times (l - 2) = 44$
d. $(l + 2) + (l + 2) + l = 44$

29. How will the following algebraic expression be simplified: $(5x^2 - 3x + 4) - (2x^2 - 7)$?
a. x^5
b. $3x^2 - 3x + 11$
c. $3x^2 - 3x - 3$
d. $x - 3$

No Calculator Questions

30. Kristen purchases $100 worth of CDs and DVDs. The CDs cost $10 each and the DVDs cost $15. If she bought four DVDs, how many CDs did she buy?

31. A student gets an 85% on a test with 20 questions. How many answers did the student solve correctly?

32. Four people split a bill. The first person pays for $\frac{1}{5}$, the second person pays for $\frac{1}{4}$, and the third person pays for $\frac{1}{3}$. What fraction of the bill does the fourth person pay?

   a. $\frac{13}{60}$

   b. $\frac{47}{60}$

   c. $\frac{1}{4}$

d. $\frac{4}{15}$

33. Five of six numbers have a sum of 25. The average of all six numbers is 6. What is the sixth number?

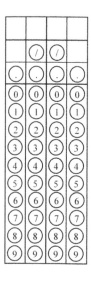

34. Kimberley earns $10 an hour babysitting, and after 10 p.m., she earns $12 an hour. The time she works is rounded to the nearest hour for pay purposes. On her last job, she worked from 5:30 p.m. to 11 p.m. In total, how much did Kimberley earn for that job?
    a. $45
    b. $57
    c. $62
    d. $42

35. A family purchases a vehicle in 2005 for $20,000. In 2010, they decide to sell it for a newer model. They are able to sell the car for $8,000. By what percentage did the value of the family's car drop?
    a. 40%
    b. 68%
    c. 60%
    d. 33%

36. In May of 2010, a couple purchased a house for $100,000. In September of 2016, the couple sold the house for $93,000 so they could purchase a bigger one to start a family. How many months did they own the house?
    a. 76
    b. 54
    c. 85
    d. 93

37. At the beginning of the day, Xavier has 20 apples. At lunch, he meets his sister Emma and gives her half of his apples. After lunch, he stops by his neighbor Jim's house and gives him 6 of his apples. He then uses $\frac{3}{4}$ of his remaining apples to make an apple pie for dessert at dinner. At the end of the day, how many apples does Xavier have left?

    a. 4
    b. 6
    c. 2
    d. 1

38. If $\frac{5}{2} \div \frac{1}{3} = n$, then n is between:

    a. 5 and 7
    b. 7 and 9
    c. 9 and 11
    d. 3 and 5

39. A closet is filled with red, blue, and green shirts. If $\frac{1}{3}$ of the shirts are green and $\frac{2}{5}$ are red, what fraction of the shirts are blue?

    a. $\frac{4}{15}$

    b. $\frac{1}{5}$

    c. $\frac{7}{15}$

    d. $\frac{1}{2}$

40. Shawna buys $2\frac{1}{2}$ gallons of paint. If she uses $\frac{1}{3}$ of it on the first day, how much does she have left?

    a. $1\frac{5}{6}$ gallons

    b. $1\frac{1}{2}$ gallons

    c. $1\frac{2}{3}$ gallons

    d. 2 gallons

41. What is the volume of a cylinder, in terms of π, with a radius of 6 centimeters and a height of 2 centimeters?

    a. $36\pi \ cm^3$
    b. $24\pi \ cm^3$
    c. $72\pi \ cm^3$
    d. $48\pi \ cm^3$

42. Keith's bakery had 252 customers go through its doors last week. This week, that number increased to 378. By what percentage did his customer volume increase?

    a. 26%
    b. 50%
    c. 35%
    d. 12%

235

43. 20 is 40% of what number?
   a. 50
   b. 8
   c. 200
   d. 5,000

44. If Danny takes 48 minutes to walk 3 miles, how many minutes should it take him to walk 5 miles maintaining the same speed?

45. The perimeter of a 6-sided polygon is 56 cm. The lengths of three sides are 9 cm each. The lengths of two other sides are 8 cm each. What is the length of the missing side?

46. If the sine of $30° = x$, the cosine of what angle, in degrees, also equals x?

47. What is the value of $x^2 - 2xy + 2y^2$ when $x = 2, y = 3$?

48. Sam is twice as old as his sister, Lisa. Their oldest brother, Ray, will be 25 in three years. If Lisa is 13 years younger than Ray, how old is Sam?

Answer Explanations #2

Reading Test

1. C: Choice *C* is the correct answer. It is easy to imagine that she may have felt either anger, Choice *A*, or fear, Choice *B*, but those are not expressed in the text. Instead, while the passage mentions that her appearance was haughty, Choice *D*, it goes on to say that she likely felt agony, Choice *C*.

2. A: Choice *A* is correct. The passage does not mention feeling vengeful, Choice *C*. Further, the passage mentions that the crowd may have been tempted to ridicule and therefore be amused, Choice *B*, but they were not. Nor are they outraged, Choice *D*, as the passage notes that the nature of the punishment wouldn't lend itself to that feeling.

3. D: Choice *D* is correct. The passage states that Prynne was only required to stand on the scaffold, not be in the stockade, though the stockade was still in use. There is no mention of the stockade's not being used because she is a woman, Choice *A*, nor that the townspeople wanted her to be in it, Choice *B*. Finally, Choice *C* is incorrect because the passage does not discuss the stockade's use as a deterrent.

4. C: Choice *C* is correct. The passage clearly mentions that if the crowd had any inclination to ridicule, it would be suppressed by the presence of the governor, a judge, and other dignitaries. There is no mention in the passage of crimes committed by others, Choice *A*. Though her demeanor was proud, this was not the reason given for the lack of ridicule, so Choice *B* is not correct. Though there is mention of a death sentence, the passage does not say that the crowd wanted to see her put to death, so Choice *D* is also not correct.

5. B: Choice *B* is correct. Based on the context of the sentence and the paired adjective in the passage ("bitter"), a reader can infer that the meaning is not a positive one; therefore, Choice *A* is incorrect. Further, Choice *C* is incorrect as there is no logical reason why Prynne would be sympathetic. Finally, the text does not say that Prynne is mourning, so Choice *D* is incorrect.

6. A: Choice *A* is correct. The passage notes the agony felt by a prisoner who is exposed to spectators and laid bare for all to see. There is no mention of shackled ankles or walking speed, so Choice *B* and Choice *C* are incorrect. While there is mention of children later in the passage, it is not connected to the walk from prison to marketplace, so Choice *D* is incorrect.

7. D: Choice *D* is correct. The final paragraph of the passage notes that she expected venomous attacks, but the event was quiet instead. Therefore, Choice *A* which suggests cheering, Choice *B*, which suggests mocking, and Choice *C*, which suggests laughter, are all incorrect.

8. A: Choice *A* is correct. The passage's final sentences suggest the weight of her sentence and its looming duration as the reason for her need for emotional release. No one attacks her, so Choice *B* is incorrect. She is never placed in the stockade, so Choice *C* is incorrect. The crowd has been solemn and does not mock or ridicule her; while she might want to respond to the silence, that is not suggested by the passage. Choice *D* is, therefore, incorrect.

9. C: Choice *C* is correct. The passage opens with the third person narrator describing the scene, then moves to Prynne's experience, then that of the crowd and moves between those over the course of the paragraphs. While the judge is mentioned, an entire crowd acts as witness so Choice *A* is incorrect.

Prynne's husband is not present in this passage, so Choice *B* is incorrect. The town historian is not identified or discussed, though we do get town history, so Choice *D* is incorrect

10. C: Choice *C* is correct. Roosevelt notes that secrecy ensures an individual's right to vote as she chooses. Choice *A* and Choice *D* may be true; public votes were known for their carnivalesque atmosphere, and private votes protect voters from violent confrontations with their political foes. However, these ideas are not stated in the passage. Choice *B* is incorrect as the opposite may be true. Privacy might increase the likelihood that, because the vote is secret, an individual can attest to voting one way but actually vote another without any accountability. This would make bribery a risk.

11. B: Choice *B* is correct. The writer notes specifically that they are tools to create a way of life we can enjoy. As such, while dictators do limit freedoms, but no in a way that populations typically enjoy, so Choice *A* is not correct. The passage does note that laws, but freedom ensures we can make our own, but not abuse or misuse so Choice *C* is incorrect. Finally, Choice *D* is incorrect because there is no mention of how we limit who uses the tool.

12. D: Choice *D* is correct. Roosevelt notes that without the processes and discussions that democracy requires, a dictatorship can achieve the same result much more quickly. While it is true that dictatorships may be benevolent, this is not the argument Roosevelt offers, so Choice *A* is incorrect. It is true that multiple factors enable dictators to rise to power, but this is not the reason Roosevelt offers, so Choice *B* is incorrect. Finally, Choice *C* suggests that dictators have been successful and popular, and though that might be true in some instances, it is also not what the passage discusses.

13. C: Choice *C* is correct. The passage states that antitrust laws maintain economic competition and prevent monopolies from limiting people's freedoms. Choice *A* is incorrect as antitrust laws are intended to protect consumers, and while they contribute to a relationship between governments and populations, that's not their primary goal. Choice *B* is incorrect as there are still ways in which businesses can manipulate markets, and so fairness isn't the ultimate outcome. Finally, businesses do compete with the government in certain industries, and that is not the purpose of antitrust laws, so Choice *D* is incorrect.

14. C: Choice *C* is correct. "Promulgated" means to promoted or spread. Therefore, Choices *A*, *B*, and *D* are incorrect as they are opposites and do not suggest spreading or championing an idea.

15. A: Choice *A* is correct. Multiple supporting points throughout the passage support Choice *A*, and paragraph 3 clarifies this main idea clearly. While Choice *B*, Choice *C*, and Choice *D* are all mentioned in the paragraph, they are mentioned as supporting points rather than the main idea.

16. B: Choice *B* is correct. While Choice *A* is true, that's not the reason to include it. The goal of mentioning the two is to compare the current situation to two major movements for democracy and their successful campaigns thereby highlighting the importance of such fights. While his audience might include both American and French citizens, he is speaking to a much larger audience, and that is not the primary reason, so Choice *C* is not the best answer. Finally, Choice *D* is incorrect as the date of the speech does not commemorate both events.

17. A: Choice *A* is correct. The speech highlights the ideals of human freedom and democracy, and altogether it implies that Roosevelt feels very strongly about these ideals. A satirical speech, Choice *B*, is one that scorns or ridicules, and that is incorrect. Choice *C* suggests someone is being attacked, and

240

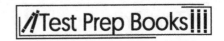

that's not accurate either. Finally, Choice *D* suggest she is appeasing someone, and that isn't correct either.

18. D: Choice *D* is correct. Because freedom and democracy are the main focus of each of the points Roosevelt brings up, it's clear that she values them above other ideals. While Choice *A*, Choice *B*, and Choice *C* might be true, they are not reflected as clearly in the passage as Choice *D* is. Those values are brought up in the passage, but only in support of freedom and democracy.

19. C: Choice *C* is correct. Roosevelt clearly states that her concern is that there is no guarantee a dictator will remain benevolent and no guarantee that power would be returned to the populace. While Choice *A* is true, it is not Roosevelt's concern. Choice *B* is also correct, but not discussed in the passage. Choice *D* is too extreme; Roosevelt does not say it's impossible for a dictator to be benevolent, though she does have concerns about them staying that way.

20. D: Choice *D* is correct. Johnson is passionately speaking about civil rights and racial equality and is aiming to impart this mindset to all Americans.

21. B: Choice *B* is correct. Johnson notes that Selma is an opportunity to right wrongs and seek justice as it relates to the denial of equal rights. Though a bridge played prominent in the Selma protest march, it was not the cause, so Choice *A* is incorrect. A man was killed, but that happened during the protest so could not be the cause. Therefore, Choice *C* is not correct. Finally, though Johnson discusses wealth in this passage, he does not say it is the cause of the events in Selma, so Choice *D* is incorrect.

22. C: Choice *C* is correct. Johnson says the cries created conversation and garnered the attention of the government to redress the issues raised. There is no mention of police response, so Choice *A* is incorrect. Similarly, there is no mention of the turnout at the protest, so Choice *B* is also incorrect. Finally, while Johnson does mention that one life was lost at the protest, he does not present this as cause for hope nor does he say it was "only" one life. Therefore, Choice *D* is also incorrect.

23. D: Choice *D* is correct. Johnson says that this challenge speaks "to the values, and the purposes, and the meaning of our beloved nation." There is no mention of other protests, Choice *A*, and there is no mention or whether those issues are easier, Choice *B*, or harder, Choice *C*, to solve, so those are not correct.

24. A: Choice *A* is correct. Johnson writes that a person's dignity "rests on his right to be treated as a man equal in opportunity to all others." Though Johnson discusses the protests, Choice *B*, American might and abundance, Choices *C* and *D*, they are not the defined as the source of a person's dignity.

25. A: Choice *A* is correct. What is righteous is morally just, and that characterizes Johnson's tone, so Choice *A* is the best answer. Choice *B*, "quixotic," means excessively or foolishly idealistic. To call Johnson's speech quixotic would mean that its goals of dignity and equality were foolish ones. Both scathing, Choice *C*, and vindictive, Choice *D*, suggest anger, harsh language, and bitterness. Johnson speaks of hope and progress, and he does not use language that suggests he is trying to chastise his audience, so these answers are incorrect.

26. D: Choice *D* is correct. Johnson says even if we "defeat every enemy", Choice *C*, "double our wealth" (Choice *B*), or conquer the stars, Choice *A*, the greater failure is for a person to lose "his own soul." In this speech, "soul" refers to a person's moral or spiritual core, and to lose one's soul in this context means to lose moral or spiritual integrity.

241

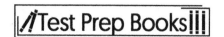

27. C: Choice *C* is correct. Convocation means a gathering or a formal assembly. In this case, the people are summoning the leaders of government to an assembly. Based on context and conventional definitions of the words, Choices *A*, *B*, and *D* are incorrect.

28. C: Choice *C* is correct. The three quotations Johnson offers in this paragraph refer to the three ideals listed in Choice *C*. While there is mention of the military in this paragraph, it is not the purpose of the country, so Choice *A* is incorrect. While America is a world leader, it became a world leader some time after it was founded, so Choice *B* is incorrect. Finally, while America has prided itself on much, the goal was not to create envy, so Choice *D* is incorrect.

29. B: Choice *B* is correct. Johnson says these guardians "fought and died," and he says that they stand as guardians "around the world," referring to American troops. While some American citizens live in other parts of the world, they are not guarding liberty, so that answer is incorrect. "American government", Choice *C*, is singular and "guardians" is plural, so that answer doesn't fit. The protestors are located in Selma and not "around the world," so Choice *D* is also incorrect.

30. A: Choice *A* is correct. According to the research, residents saw the risk of mosquito-borne illnesses as higher during the Zika outbreak despite the risk being higher post hurricane. It does not suggest that they saw no risk from either, so Choice *B* and Choice *C* are incorrect. Choice *D* is also incorrect as they did not see the risks as the same.

31. D: Choice *D* is correct. According to the research, one can infer that concerns about basic necessities like shelter, post-hurricane, may impact rates of mosquito-borne illnesses. There is no connection mentioned between Zika and hurricanes, though the research does compare the two in terms of mosquito problems, so Choice *A* is incorrect. Similarly, Choice *B* is incorrect as though the passage discusses resident concerns of risk and Zika, it does so in connection with mosquito-borne illnesses, not in regard to the spread of Zika specifically. Choice *C* is also incorrect because, again, though discussed together, there's no real correlation discussed in the passage.

32. B: Choice *B* is correct. Based on the information provided, backpack spraying best addresses the need to spray targeted areas with greatest risk. Human exposure to mosquito bites is mentioned, but not to the chemicals used in spraying, so Choice *A* is incorrect. Though the passage mentions community support for spraying, it doesn't specify the type of support, so Choice *C* is incorrect. Finally, while the passage mentions household-level prevention, it doesn't specify how household participation affects spraying, so Choice *D* is also incorrect.

33. A: Choice *A* is correct. According to the passage, CASPERs may help assess community campaigns and reveal community knowledge, attitudes, and practices. Lack of shelter and spraying support are noted directly in reference to post-hurricane concerns, which is an emergency situation, so Choice *B* and Choice *C* are incorrect. While some of the efforts of CASPERs may reveal community risks, particularly as it relates to actual versus perceived risks, it is not listed among the non-emergency applications in the final paragraph and so Choice *D* is incorrect.

34. B: Choice *B* is correct. While backpack spraying is noted as the acceptable option, we cannot determine how communities will move forward with its inclusion in their response without more information, so Choice *A* is incorrect. Similarly, this passaged argues for the inclusion of CASPERs as a tool in emergency and non-emergency situations, but we cannot draw a conclusion regarding future use, so Choice *C* is incorrect. Given the nature of increased storm activity across the world, we cannot be certain that these disease vector problems will remain isolated to island nations, so Choice *D* is

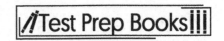

incorrect. However, given the increase in severe storms, we can conclude that risks with mosquito-borne illnesses will also increase, meaning Choice *B* is correct.

35. D: Choice *D* is correct. The primary focus of this paragraph is to discuss how CASPER can be used to assist communities and governments in addressing both emergency and non-emergency issues. While Choices *A*, *B*, and *C* are true, they are supporting details in the paragraph and not the focus of the passage itself.

36. A: Choice *A* is correct. The passage notes, in paragraph 1, that environmental conditions for mosquito breeding and exposure are more favorable after a hurricane. While it might be true that mosquitoes bite less during storms, Choice *B*, or that fewer preventative medications are available, Choice *C*, these are not discussed in the passage. Finally, it is noted that residents seem to be aware of an elevated risk post-hurricane, but awareness does not cause disease, so Choice *D* is incorrect.

37. C: Choice *C* is correct. The passage notes that CASPERs would be incredibly useful in non-emergency situations as well, so Choice *A* is incorrect. Aerial spraying is not mentioned specifically, especially in relation to Zika, so Choice *B* is incorrect. Finally, researchers agree that controlling mosquito-borne diseases involves bite prevention, but also requires control, community knowledge and other factors, so while Choice *D* is part of the solution, it may not be the best option.

38. D: Choice *D* is correct. Both Choice *A* and Choice *B* suggest that researchers and residents are unaware of the lead problem in much of America's water. However, the existence of the research itself contradicts both these answers. Similarly, Choice *C* directly contradicts the research presented in both passages, which not only identify but also track the lead sources.

39. B: Choice *B* is correct. The passage states that public systems can measure water quality and use corrosion inhibitors to improve water quality. While a city may inform residents of high lead levels, that's not noted in this passage regarding the public system's role. Therefore, Choice *A* is incorrect. Similarly, public water systems are not responsible for replacing home piping, Choice *C*. Further, while systems clearly allow and likely encourage research, their objective is to mitigate lead exposure, so Choice *D* is not the best answer.

40. D: Choice *D* is correct. The research suggests that if the lead pipes have been removed from the home, the city's service lines could be a source for lead. Choice *A* and Choice *C* are not discussed in the passage and are, therefore, incorrect. While Choice *B* is possible, it is not presented as the cause nor discussed in the passage.

41. A: Choice *A* is correct. While Choice *B*, Choice *C*, and Choice *D* are all reasonable possibilities, they are not discussed in the article. Though we know researchers do not have all the data, Choice *B*, there is no reference to this being related to source points. We do not get any information about how researchers are adapting the models to new information, Choice *C*, so that is incorrect as well. Finally, there is no data presented regarding how changes in the service lines impact the models being used.

42. C: Choice *C* is correct. There is no data to support Choice *A*; in fact, some of the research suggests that even changes the lines has little initial impact on lead levels. Choice *B* is mentioned as a mitigation and control factor, but it is not suggested that it's the most effective. Choice *D* is not discussed at all. In fact, lead levels are a concern regardless of the water source.

43. A: Choice *A* is correct. There was no mention in passage 1 of lead levels in the water sources themselves, so Choice *B* is incorrect. Similarly, passage 1 discusses corrosion inhibitors, but not as related to their introduction and its impact on the research, so Choice *C* is incorrect. There is no mention of false positives, so Choice *D* is incorrect.

44. D: Choice *D* is correct. Based on the sentence it is used in, one can infer the meaning from the context. Later in the sentence, the writer uses the word "dissolve" in place of "solubility." Choice *B* and Choice *C* are both the opposite of the correct meaning and, therefore, incorrect. Choice *A* is the result of the dissolution and also incorrect.

45. B: Choice *B* is correct. Both passages focus on the need to replace lead service lines in older homes as the first step to addressing lead levels in tap water. High-end water filtration systems are not discussed at all, so Choice *A* is incorrect. Lead levels were found in both types of water sources, so Choice *C* is not the correct answer. While Choice *D* is one of the methods discussed, it is secondary to the replacement of service lines and, therefore, incorrect.

46. B: Choice *B* is correct. In both passages, the researchers focus on the accumulation of minerals and scaling in pipes, problems that must be handled through service line replacement and corrosion inhibitors. While replacing lines in older homes, Choice *A*, is one solution, neither group believes it will resolve the issue. Choice *C* may be true, and though it is discussed in the second passage, it is not discussed in the first passage; nor does either passage discuss its role in future research. Finally, source point pollution is not discussed in either passage though water sources are discussed, so Choice *D* is incorrect.

47. D: Choice *D* is correct. Because of the scope of work, and because of the existence of lead in water up to four years after lead lines have been replaced in the home, one can infer that Choice *D* is the statement researchers would most disagree with. Because they do not discuss tap filtration, we cannot gauge where researchers would stand on how this method would work, so Choice *A* is incorrect. Well water is not without its own issues, particularly in relation to scaling and additional minerals. Researchers would likely agree that the issue is different rather than determining whether it's easier, so Choice *B* is incorrect. Finally, corrosion control, Choice *C*, is a valuable weapon, but researchers would not agree that it's the best option, based on both passages. Instead, they'd likely argue that corrosion control is part of a multi-step process.

Writing and Language Test

1. B: Choice *B* is correct. Here, a colon is used to introduce an explanation. Colons either introduce explanations or lists. Additionally, the quote ends with the punctuation inside the quotes, unlike Choice *C*.

2. A: The verb tense in this passage is predominantly in the present tense, so Choice *A* is the correct answer. Choice *B* is incorrect because the subject and verb do not agree. It should be "Education provides," not "Education provide." Choice *C* is incorrect because the passage is in present tense, and "Education will provide" is future tense. Choice *D* doesn't make sense when placed in the sentence.

3. D: The possessive form of the word "it" is "its." The contraction "it's" denotes "it is." Thus, Choice *A* is wrong. The word "raises" in Choice *B* makes the sentence grammatically incorrect. Choice *C* adds an apostrophe at the end of "its." While adding an apostrophe to most words would indicate possession, adding 's to the word "it" indicates a contraction.

4. C: The word *civilised* should be spelled *civilized*. The words *distinguishes* and *creatures* are both spelled correctly.

5. B: Choice *B* is correct because it provides clarity by describing what "myopic" means in context right after the word itself. Choice *A* is incorrect because the explanation of "myopic" comes before the word; thus, the meaning is skewed. It's possible that Choice *C* makes sense within context. However, it's not the *best* way to say this. Choice *D* is confusingly worded. Using "myopic focus" is not detrimental to society; however, the way *D* is worded makes it seem that way.

6. C: Again, we see where the second paragraph can be divided into two parts due to separate topics. The paragraph's first main focus is education addressing the mind, body, and soul. This first section, then, could end with the concluding sentence, "The human heart and psyche ..." The next sentence to start a new paragraph would be "Education is a basic human right." The rest of this paragraph talks about what education is and some of its characteristics.

7. A: Choice *A* is correct because the phrase "others' ideas" is both plural and indicates possession. Choice *B* is incorrect because "other's" indicates only one "other" that's in possession of "ideas," which is incorrect. Choice *C* is incorrect because no possession is indicated. Choice *D* is incorrect because the word "other" does not end in *s*. Others's is not a correct form of the plural possessive word.

8. D: This sentence must have a comma before *although* because the word *although* is connecting two independent clauses. Thus, Choices *B* and *C* are incorrect. Choice *A* is incorrect because the second sentence in the underlined section is a fragment.

9. C: Choice *C* is the correct choice because the word *their* indicates possession, and the text is talking about "their students," or the students of someone. Choice *A*, *there*, means at a certain place and is incorrect. Choice *B*, *they're*, is a contraction and means *they are*. Choice *D* is not a word.

10. B: Choice *B* uses all punctuation correctly in this sentence. In American English, single quotes should only be used if they are quotes within a quote, making Choices *A* and *C* incorrect. Additionally, punctuation should go inside quotation marks with a few exceptions, making Choice *D* incorrect.

11. B: Choice *B* is correct because the conjunction *and* is used to connect phrases that are to be used jointly, such as teachers working hard to help students "identify salient information" and to "think critically." The conjunctions *so*, *but*, and *nor* are incorrect in the context of this sentence.

12. A: Choice *A* has consistent parallel structure with the verbs *read*, *identify*, and *determine*. Choices *B* and *C* have faulty parallel structure with the words *determining* and *identifying*. Choice *D* has incorrect subject/verb agreement. The sentence should read, "Students have to read ... identify ... and determine."

13. D: The correct choice for this sentence is that "they are ... shaped by the influences." The prepositions "for," "to," and "with" do not make sense in this context. People are *shaped by*, not *shaped for, shaped to,* or *shaped with*.

14. A: To see which answer is correct, it might help to place the subject near the verb. Choice *A* is correct: "Teachers ... must strive" makes grammatical sense here. Choice B is incorrect because "Teachers ... to strive" does not make grammatical sense. Choice C is incorrect because "Teachers must not only respect ... but striving" eschews parallel structure. Choice *D* is incorrect because it is in past tense, and this passage is in present tense.

15. C: Choice *C* is correct because it uses an em-dash. Em-dashes are versatile. They can separate phrases that would otherwise be in parenthesis, or they can stand in for a semicolon. In this case, a semicolon would be another decent choice for this punctuation mark because the second sentence expands upon the first sentence. Choice *A* is incorrect because the statement is not a question. Choice *B* is incorrect because adding a comma here would create a comma splice. Choice *D* is incorrect because this creates a run-on sentence since the two sentences are independent clauses.

16. B: Choice *B* is correct because it removes the apostrophe from *icon's*, since the noun *icon* is not possessing anything. This conveys the author's intent of setting *Frankenstein* apart from other icons of the romantic and science fiction genres. Choices *A* and *C* are therefore incorrect. Choice *D* is a good revision but alters the meaning of the sentence—*Frankenstein* is one of the icons, not the sole icon.

17. C: Choice *C* correctly adds a comma after *style*, successfully joining the dependent and the independent clauses as a single sentence. Choice *A* is incorrect because the dependent and independent clauses remain unsuccessfully combined without the comma. Choices *B* and *D* do nothing to fix this.

18. A: Choice *A* is correct, as the sentence doesn't require changes. Choice *B* incorrectly changes the noun *enlightenment* into the verb *enlighten*. Choices *C* and *D* alter the original meaning of the sentence.

19. B: Choice *B* is correct, fixing the incorrect split of *highlight*. This is a polyseme, a word combined from two unrelated words to make a new word. On their own, *high* and *light* make no sense for the sentence, making Choice *A* incorrect. Choice *C* incorrectly decapitalizes *Ancient*. Since it modifies *Greece* and works with the noun to describe a civilization, *Ancient Greece* functions as a proper noun, which should be capitalized. Choice *D* uses *highlighting*, a gerund, but the present tense of *highlight* is what works with the rest of the sentence; to make this change, a comma would be needed after *Rome*.

20. A: Choice *A* is correct, as *not only* and *but also* are correlative pairs. In this sentence, *but* successfully transitions the first part into the second half, making punctuation unnecessary. Additionally, the use of *to* indicates that an idea or challenge is being presented to the reader. Choice *B*'s *with*, *C*'s *for*, and *D*'s *there before* are not as active, meaning these revisions weaken the sentence.

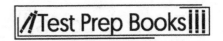

21. D: Choice *D* is correct, adding finer details to help the reader understand exactly what Prometheus did and his impact: fire came with knowledge and power. Choice *A* lacks a comma after *fire*. Choice *B* inserts unnecessary commas since *people* is not part of the list *knowledge and power*. Choice *C* is a strong revision but could be confusing, hinting that the fire was knowledge and power itself, as opposed to being symbolized by the fire.

22. C: Choice *C* reverses the order of the section, making the sentence more direct. Choice *A* lacks a comma after *gods*, and although Choice *B* adds this, the structure is too different from the first half of the sentence to flow correctly. Choice *D* is overly complicated and repetitious in its structure even though it doesn't need any punctuation.

23. B: Choice *B* fixes the two problems of the sentence, changing *faltered* to present tense in agreement with the rest of the passage, and correctly linking the two dependent clauses. Choice *A* is therefore incorrect. Choice *C* does not correct the past tense of *faltered*. Choice *D* correctly adds the conjunction *by*, but it lacks a comma after the conjunction *Yet*.

24. C: Choice *C* successfully applies a comma after *power*, distinguishing the causes of Frankenstein's suffering and maintaining parallel structure. Choice *A* is thus incorrect. Choice *B* lacks the necessary punctuation and unnecessarily changes *lack* to a gerund. Choice *D* adds unnecessary wording, making the sentence more cumbersome.

25. D: Choice *D* correctly inserts an apostrophe into the contraction *doesn't*. Choice *A* is incorrect because of this omission. Choices *B* and *C* are better than the original but do not fit well with the informal tone of the passage.

26. B: Choice *B* is correct, successfully combining the two independent clauses of this compound sentence by adding a comma before "and" to create the effective pause and transition between clauses. Choice *A* does not join the independent clauses correctly. Choices *C* and *D* offer alternate ways of joining these clauses, but since "and" is already part of the sentence, adding the comma is the most logical choice. This also keeps the informal tone set by the rest of the passage.

27. C: Choice *C* correctly fixes the homophone issue of *their* and *they're*. *Their* implies ownership, which is not needed here. The author intends *they're*, a contraction of *they are*. Thus, Choice *A* is incorrect, as is Choice *B*, using the homophone *there*. Choice *D* eliminates the homophone issue altogether, but the sentence becomes more clunky because of that.

28. B: Choice *B* correctly joins the two independent clauses with a comma before *but*. Choice *A* is incorrect because, without the comma, it is a run-on sentence. Choice *C* also lacks punctuation and uses *however*, which should be reserved for starting a new sentence or perhaps after a semicolon. Choice *D* is incorrect because the semicolon throws off the sentence structure and is incorrectly used; the correct revision would have also removed *but*.

29. A: Choice *A* is correct because the sentence does not require modification. Choice *B* is incorrect because it uses the faulty subject/verb agreement, "Physical proof are." Choice *C* is incorrect because a comma would need to follow *exists*. Choice *D* is incorrect because the comma after *science* is unnecessary.

30. D: Choice *D* correctly changes *this* to *the* and retains *validity*, making it the right choice. Choices *A* and *B* keep *this*, which is not as specific as "the" and does not fit the sentence. Choice *C* incorrectly pluralizes *validity*.

31. A: Choice *A* is correct because the sentence is fine without revisions. Choice *B* is incorrect, since removing *there is* is unnecessary and confusing. Choice *C* is incorrect since it inserts an unnecessary comma. Choice *D* introduces a homophone issue: *weather* refers to climatic states and atmospheric events, while *whether* expresses doubt, which is the author's intent.

32. C: Choice *C* correctly changes *continuing* to the present tense. Choice *A* is incorrect because of this out-of-place gerund use. Choice *B* not only does not fix this issue but also incorrectly changes *describe* into a gerund. While Choice *D* correctly uses *continue*, *describe* is incorrectly put in the past tense.

33. D: Choice *D* is correct because it moves the modifying clause "including Native Americans" so that it comes after what it describes: "Ancient civilizations." This adds clarity to the sentence and makes it more direct. Choice *A* uses redundant phrases *as well* and *including*. It also lacks punctuation. Choice *B* is poorly constructed, taking out the clearer *including*. Choice *C* also makes little sense.

34. B: For this question, place the underlined sentence in each prospective choice's position. Leaving the sentence in place is incorrect because the father "going crazy" doesn't logically follow the fact that he was a "city slicker." Choice *C* is incorrect because the sentence in question is not a concluding sentence and does not transition smoothly into the second paragraph. Choice *D* is incorrect because the sentence doesn't necessarily need to be omitted since it logically follows the very first sentence in the passage.

35. D: Choice *D* is correct because "As it turns out" indicates a contrast from the previous sentiment, that the RV was a great purchase. Choice *A* is incorrect because the sentence needs an effective transition from the paragraph before. Choice *B* is incorrect because the text indicates it *is* surprising that the RV was a great purchase because the author was skeptical beforehand. Choice *C* is incorrect because the transition "furthermore" does not indicate a contrast.

36. B: This sentence calls for parallel structure. Choice *B* is correct because the verbs "wake," "eat," and "break" are consistent in tense and parts of speech. Choice *A* is incorrect because the words "wake" and "eat" are present tense while the word "broke" is in past tense. Choice *C* is incorrect because this turns the sentence into a question, which doesn't make sense within the context. Choice *D* is incorrect because it breaks tense with the rest of the passage. "Waking," "eating," and "breaking" are all present participles, and the context around the sentence is in past tense.

37. C: Choice *C* is correct because it is clear and fits within the context of the passage. Choice *A* is incorrect because "We rejoiced as 'hackers'" does not explain what was meant by "hackers" or why it was a cause for rejoicing. Choice *B* is incorrect because it does not mention a solution being found and is therefore not specific enough. Choice *D* is incorrect because the sentence does not give enough detail as to what the problem entails.

38. A: The original sentence is correct because the verb tense and the meaning both align with the rest of the passage. Choice *B* is incorrect because the order of the words makes the sentence more confusing than it otherwise would be. Choice *C* is incorrect because "We are even making" is in present tense. Choice *D* is incorrect because "We will make" is future tense. The surrounding text of the sentence is in past tense.

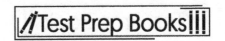

39. B: Choice *B* is correct because there is no punctuation needed if a dependent clause ("while traveling across America") is located behind the independent clause ("it allowed us to share adventures"). Choice *A* is incorrect because there are two dependent clauses connected and no independent clause, and a complete sentence requires at least one independent clause. Choice *C* is incorrect because of the same reason as Choice *A*. Semicolons connect closely related independent clauses on either side of the semicolon. Choice *D* is incorrect because the dash simply interrupts the complete sentence.

40. C: The rule for "me" and "I" is that one should use "I" when it is the subject pronoun of a sentence, and "me" when it is the object pronoun of the sentence. Break the sentence up to see if "I" or "me" should be used. To say "Those are memories that I have now shared" is correct, rather than "Those are memories that me have now shared." Choice D is incorrect because "my siblings" should come before "I."

41. B: Choice *B* is correct because it adds an apostrophe to *ones*, which indicates *one's* possession of *survival*. Choice *A* doesn't do this, so it is incorrect. This is the same for Choice *C*, but that option also takes out the crucial comma after *Jiu-Jitsu*. Choice *D* is incorrect because it changes *play* to *plays*. This disagrees with the plural *Martial arts*, exemplified by having an example of its many forms, *Jiu-Jitsu*. Therefore, *play* is required.

42. C: Choice *C* is the best answer because it most clearly defines the point that the author is trying to make. The original sentence would need a comma after *however* in order to continue the sentence fluidly—but this option isn't available. Choice *B* is close, but this option changes the meaning of the sentence. Therefore, the best alternative is to begin the sentence with *However* and have a comma follow right after it in order to introduce a new idea. The original context is still maintained, but the flow of the language is more streamlined. Thus, Choice *A* is incorrect. Choice *D* would need a comma before and after *however*, so it is also incorrect.

43. A: Choice *A* is the best answer for several reasons. To begin, the section is grammatically correct in using a semicolon to connect the two independent clauses. This allows the two ideas to be connected without separating them. In this context, the semicolon makes more sense for the overall sentence structure and passage as a whole. Choice *B* is incorrect because it forms a run-on. Choice *C* applies a comma in incorrect positions. Choice *D* separates the sentence in a place that does not make sense for the context.

44. D: Choice *D* is the correct answer because it fixes two key issues. First, *their* is incorrectly used. *Their* is a possessive indefinite pronoun and also an antecedent—neither of these fit the context of the sentence, so Choices *A* and *B* are incorrect. What should be used instead is *they're*, which is the contraction of *they are*, emphasizing action or the result of action in this case. Choice *D* also corrects another contraction-related issue with *its*. Again, *its* indicates possession, while *it's* is the contraction of *it is*. The latter is what's needed for the sentence to make sense and be grammatically correct. Thus, Choice *C* is also incorrect.

Math Test

Calculator Questions

1. B: 300 miles in 4 hours is $\frac{300}{4} = 75$ miles per hour. In 1.5 hours, the car will go 1.5×75 miles, or 112.5 miles.

2. The best way to solve this problem is by using a system of equations. We know that Jan bought $90 worth of apples ($a$) and oranges ($o$) at $1 and $2 respectively. That means our first equation is:

$$1(a) + 2(o) = 90$$

We also know that she bought an equal number of apples and oranges, which gives us our second equation $a = o$. We can then replace a with o in the first equation to give:

$$1(o) + 2(o) = 90 \text{ or } 3(o) = 90$$

Which yields:

$$o = 30$$

Thus, Jan bought 30 oranges (and 30 apples).

3. C: Plug in the values for x and y to discover that the solution works, which is:

$$(-3)^2 + (-4)^2 = 25$$

Choices *A* and *B* are not the correct answers since the solution works. Choice *D* is not the correct answer because there is enough information to tell where the given point lies on the circle.

4. First, the train's journey in the real world is:

$$3 \text{ h} \times 50 \frac{\text{mi}}{\text{h}} = 150 \text{ mi}$$

On the map, 1 inch corresponds to 10 miles, so that is equivalent to:

$$150 \text{ mi} \times \frac{1 \text{ in}}{10 \text{ mi}} = 15 \text{ in}$$

Therefore, the start and end points are 15 inches apart on the map.

5. B: The total trip time is $1 + 3.5 + 0.5 = 5$ hours. The total time driving is $1 + 0.5 = 1.5$ hours. So, the fraction of time spent driving is $\frac{1.5}{5}$ or $\frac{3}{10}$. To get the percentage, convert this to a fraction out of 100. The numerator and denominator are multiplied by 10, with a result of $\frac{30}{100}$. The percentage is the numerator in a fraction out of 100, so the answer is 30%.

6. B: The formula for the volume of a cylinder is $\pi r^2 h$, where r is the radius and h is the height. The diameter is twice the radius, so these barrels have a radius of 1 foot. That means each barrel has a volume of:

$$\pi \times 1^2 \times 3 = 3\pi \text{ ft}^3$$

Since there are three of them, the total is:

$$3 \times 3\pi = 9\pi \text{ ft}^3$$

7. A: The tip is not taxed, so he pays 5% tax only on the $10.

The tax is 5% of $10, or $0.05 \times 10 = \$0.50$. Add up $10 + \$2 + \$0.50$ to get $12.50.

8. A: In order to determine the savings needed per day, divide up $150 into four equal parts:

$$\frac{\$150}{4 \text{ d}} = \frac{\$37.5}{\text{d}}$$

251

So, she needs to save an average of $37.50 per day.

9. The number of days can be found by taking the total amount Bernard needs to make and dividing it by the amount he earns per day:

$$\frac{300}{80} = \frac{30}{8} = \frac{15}{4} = 3.75$$

But Bernard is only working full days, so he will need to work 4 days since 3 days is not a sufficient amount of time.

10. A: The value went up by:

$$\$165,000 - \$150,000 = \$15,000$$

Out of $150,000, this is $\frac{15,000}{150,000} = \frac{1}{10}$ or 0.1. To get the percentage, multiply 0.1 by 100 to get 10%.

11. D: The total faculty is:

$$15 + 20 = 35$$

So, the ratio is 35 : 200. Then, divide both of these numbers by 5, since 5 is a common factor to both, with a result of 7 : 40.

12. The journey will be $5 \times 3 = 15$ miles. A car traveling at 60 miles per hour is traveling at 1 mile per minute. The resulting equation would be:

$$\frac{15 \text{ mi}}{1 \frac{\text{mi}}{\text{min}}} = 15 \text{ min}$$

Therefore, it will take 15 minutes to take the journey.

13. A: Taylor's total income is $\$20,000 + \$10,000 = \$30,000$. Fifteen percent of this is $\frac{15}{100} = \frac{3}{20}$. So:

$$\frac{3}{20} \times \$30,000 = \frac{\$90,000}{20}$$

$$\frac{\$9000}{2} = \$4500$$

14. D: Exponential functions can be written in the form: $y = a \times b^x$. The equation for an exponential function can be written given the y-intercept (a) and the growth rate (b). The y-intercept is the output (y) when the input (x) equals zero. It can be thought of as an "original value," or starting point. The value of b is the rate at which the original value increases ($b > 1$) or decreases ($b < 1$). In this scenario, the y-intercept, a, would be $\$1200$, and the growth rate, b, would be 1.01 (100% of the original value combined with 1% interest, or $100\% + 1\% = 101\% = 1.01$).

15. C: The domain consists of all possible inputs, or x-values. The scenario states that the function approximates the population between the years 1900 and 2000. It also states that $x = 0$ represents the year 1900 with x representing the year (where 1900 is $x = 0$) and y representing the population (in thousands). Therefore, the year 2000 would be represented by $x = 100$. Only inputs between 0 and 100 are relevant in this case.

16. D: This problem can be solved by setting up a proportion involving the given information and the unknown value. The proportion is:

$$\frac{21 \text{ pages}}{4 \text{ nights}} = \frac{140 \text{ pages}}{x \text{ nights}}$$

We can cross-multiply to get $21x = 4 \times 140$. Solving this, we find $x \approx 26.67$. Since this is not an integer, we round up to 27 nights. 26 nights would not give Sarah enough time.

17. D: This problem can be solved by using unit conversion. The initial units are miles per minute. The final units need to be feet per second. Converting miles to feet uses the equivalence statement 1 mi = 5,280 ft. Converting minutes to seconds uses the equivalence statement 1 min = 60 s. Setting up the ratios to convert the units is shown in the following equation:

$$\frac{72 \text{ mi}}{90 \text{ min}} \times \frac{1 \text{ min}}{60 \text{ s}} \times \frac{5,280 \text{ ft}}{1 \text{ mi}} = 70.4 \frac{\text{ft}}{\text{s}}$$

The initial units cancel out, and the new units are left.

18. C: The total percentage of a pie chart equals 100%. We can see that CD sales make up less than half of the chart (50%) and more than a quarter (25%), and the only answer choice that meets these criteria is Choice *C*, 40%.

19. B: Since $850 is the price after a 20% discount, $850 represents 80% of the original price. To determine the original price, set up a proportion with the ratio of the sale price (850) to original price (unknown) equal to the ratio of sale percentage (where x represents the unknown original price):

$$\frac{850}{x} = \frac{80}{100}$$

To solve a proportion, cross multiply and set the products equal to each other:

$$(850)(100) = (80)(x)$$

Multiplying each side results in the equation:

$$85,000 = 80x$$

To solve for x, divide both sides by 80:

$$\frac{85,000}{80} = \frac{80x}{80}$$

$$x = 1,062.5$$

Remember that x represents the original price. Subtracting the sale price from the original price ($1,062.50 − $850) indicates that Frank saved $212.50.

20. C: $40N$ would be 4,000% of N. $\frac{40}{100}$.

21. C: An x–intercept is the point where the graph crosses the x–axis. At this point, the value of y is 0. To determine if an equation has an x-intercept of −2, substitute -2 for x, and calculate the value of y. If the value of −2 for x corresponds with a y–value of 0, then the equation has an x-intercept of −2. The only answer choice that produces this result is Choice *C*.

$$0 = (-2)^2 + 5(-2) + 6$$

22. C: There are 34 girls who are potty-trained out of a total of 52 girls:

$$34 \div 52 = 0.65 = 65\%$$

23. A: A sample statistic indicates information about the data that was collected (in this case, the heights of those surveyed). A population parameter describes an aspect of the entire population (in this case, all twelve-year-old boys in the United States). A confidence interval would consist of a range of heights likely to include the actual population parameter. Measurement error relates to the validity of the data that was collected.

24. C: To ensure valid results, samples should be taken across the entire scope of the study. Since all states are not equally populated, representing each state proportionately would result in a more accurate statistic.

25. D: Subtract the center from the x- and y-values of the equation and square the radius on the right side of the equation. Choice *A* is not the correct answer because you need to square the radius of the equation. Choice *B* is not the correct answer because you do not square the centers of the equation. Choice *C* is not the correct answer because you need to subtract (not add) the centers of the equation.

26. D: The slope is given by the change in y divided by the change in x. Specifically, it's:

$$slope = \frac{y_2 - y_1}{x_2 - x_1}$$

The first point is $(-5, -3)$, and the second point is $(0, -1)$. Work from left to right when identifying coordinates. Thus the point on the left is point 1 $(-5, -3)$ and the point on the right is point 2 $(0, -1)$.

Now we need to just plug those numbers into the equation:

$$slope = \frac{-1 - (-3)}{0 - (-5)}$$

It can be simplified to:

$$slope = \frac{-1 + 3}{0 + 5}$$

$$slope = \frac{2}{5}$$

27. B: The figure is composed of three sides of a square and a semicircle. The sides of the square are simply added:

$$8 \text{ in} + 8 \text{ in} + 8 \text{ in} = 24 \text{ in}$$

The circumference of a circle is found by the equation $C = 2\pi r$. The radius is 4 in, so the circumference of the circle is 25.13 in. Only half of the circle makes up the outer border of the figure (part of the perimeter) so half of 25.13 in is 12.565 in. Therefore, the total perimeter is:

$$24 \text{ in} + 12.565 \text{ in} = 36.565 \text{ in}$$

255

The other answer choices use the incorrect formula or fail to include all of the necessary sides.

28. A: The first step is to determine the unknown, which is in terms of the length, l.

The second step is to translate the problem into the equation using the perimeter of a rectangle:

$$P = 2l + 2w$$

The width is the length minus 2 centimeters. The resulting equation is:

$$2l + 2(l - 2) = 44$$

The equation can be solved as follows:

$2l + 2l - 4 = 44$	Apply the distributive property on the left side of the equation
$4l - 4 = 44$	Combine like terms on the left side of the equation
$4l = 48$	Add 4 to both sides of the equation
$l = 12$	Divide both sides of the equation by 4

The length of the rectangle is 12 centimeters. The width is the length minus 2 centimeters, which is 10 centimeters. Checking the answers for length and width forms the following equation:

$$44 = 2(12) + 2(10)$$

The equation can be solved using the order of operations to form a true statement: $44 = 44$.

29. B: $3x^2 - 3x + 11$. By distributing the implied one in front of the first set of parentheses and the -1 in front of the second set of parentheses, the parentheses can be eliminated:

$$1(5x^2 - 3x + 4) - 1(2x^2 - 7) = 5x^2 - 3x + 4 - 2x^2 + 7$$

Next, like terms (same variables with same exponents) are combined by adding the coefficients and keeping the variables and their powers the same:

$$5x^2 - 3x + 4 - 2x^2 + 7 = 3x^2 - 3x + 11$$

No Calculator Questions

30. Kristen bought four DVDs, which would cost a total of $4 \times 15 = \$60$. She spent a total of $100, so she spent $\$100 - \$60 = \$40$ on CDs. Since they cost $10 each, she must have purchased $40 \div 10 = 4$ CDs.

31. 85% of a number means multiplying that number by 0.85. So, $0.85 \times 20 = \frac{85}{100} \times \frac{20}{1}$, which can be simplified to:

$$\frac{17}{20} \times \frac{20}{1} = 17$$

Therefore, the student got 17 questions correct.

32. A: To find the fraction of the bill that the first three people pay, the fractions need to be added, which means finding the common denominator. The common denominator will be 60.

$$\frac{1}{5} + \frac{1}{4} + \frac{1}{3} = \frac{12}{60} + \frac{15}{60} + \frac{20}{60} = \frac{47}{60}$$

The remainder of the bill is:

$$1 - \frac{47}{60} = \frac{60}{60} - \frac{47}{60} = \frac{13}{60}$$

33. The average is calculated by adding all six numbers, then dividing by 6. The first five numbers have a sum of 25. This means $\frac{(25+n)}{6} = 6$, where n is the unknown number. Multiplying both sides by 6, we get $25 + n = 36$, which means $n = 11$.

		1	**1**
	⊘	⊘	
·	·	·	·
⓪	⓪	⓪	⓪
①	①	●	●
②	②	②	②
③	③	③	③
④	④	④	④
⑤	⑤	⑤	⑤
⑥	⑥	⑥	⑥
⑦	⑦	⑦	⑦
⑧	⑧	⑧	⑧
⑨	⑨	⑨	⑨

34. C: Kimberley worked 4.5 hours at the rate of $10 / h and 1 hour at the rate of $12 / h. The problem states that her time is rounded to the nearest hour, so the 4.5 hours would round up to 5 hours at the rate of $10 / h.

$$(5h) \times \left(\frac{\$10}{h}\right) + (1h) \times \left(\frac{\$12}{h}\right) = \$50 + \$12 = \$62$$

35. C: In order to find the percentage by which the value of the car has been reduced, the current cash value should be subtracted from the initial value and then the difference divided by the initial value. The result should be multiplied by 100 to find the percentage decrease.

$$\frac{20,000 - 8,000}{20,000} = 0.6$$

$$(0.60) \times 100 = 60\%$$

36. A: This problem can be solved by simple multiplication and addition. Since the sale date is over six years apart, 6 can be multiplied by 12 for the number of months in a year, and then the remaining 4 months can be added.

$$(6 \times 12) + 4 = ?$$

$$72 + 4 = 76$$

37. D: This problem can be solved using basic arithmetic. Xavier starts with 20 apples, then gives his sister half, so 20 divided by 2.

$$\frac{20}{2} = 10$$

He then gives his neighbor 6, so 6 is subtracted from 10.

$$10 - 6 = 4$$

Lastly, he uses $\frac{3}{4}$ of his apples to make an apple pie, so to find remaining apples, the first step is to subtract $\frac{3}{4}$ from one and then multiply the difference by 4.

$$\left(1 - \frac{3}{4}\right) \times 4 = ?$$

$$\left(\frac{4}{4} - \frac{3}{4}\right) \times 4 = ?$$

$$\left(\frac{1}{4}\right) \times 4 = 1$$

38. B: To find the value of n, multiply $\frac{5}{2}$ by the reciprocal of $\frac{1}{3}$ and simplify:

$$\frac{5}{2} \div \frac{1}{3} = \frac{5}{2} \times \frac{3}{1} = \frac{15}{2} = 7.5$$

39. A: The total fraction taken up by green and red shirts will be:

$$\frac{1}{3} + \frac{2}{5} = \frac{5}{15} + \frac{6}{15} = \frac{11}{15}$$

The remaining fraction is:

$$1 - \frac{11}{15} = \frac{15}{15} - \frac{11}{15} = \frac{4}{15}$$

40. C: If she has used $\frac{1}{3}$ of the paint, she has $\frac{2}{3}$ remaining. The mixed fraction can be converted because $2\frac{1}{2}$ gallons is the same as $\frac{5}{2}$ gallons. The calculation is:

$$\frac{2}{3} \times \frac{5}{2} = \frac{5}{3} = 1\frac{2}{3} \text{ gal}$$

259

41. C: The volume of a cylinder is $\pi r2h$, and $\pi \times 6^2 \times 2$ is $72\,\pi$ cm³. Choice A is not the correct answer because that is only $6^2 \times \pi$. Choice B is not the correct answer because that is $2^2 \times 6 \times \pi$. Choice D is not the correct answer because that is $2^3 \times 6 \times \pi$.

42. B: The first step is to calculate the difference between the larger value and the smaller value.

$$378 - 252 = 126$$

To calculate this difference as a percentage of the original value, and thus calculate the percentage *increase*, 126 is divided by 252, then this result is multiplied by 100 to find the percentage: 50%, or Choice B.

43. A: Setting up a proportion is the easiest way to represent this situation. The proportion is $\frac{20}{x} = \frac{40}{100}$, and cross-multiplication can be used to solve for x. Here, $40x = 2,000$, so $x = 50$.**44.**

To solve the problem, a proportion is written consisting of ratios comparing distance and time. One way to set up the proportion is $\frac{3}{48} = \frac{5}{x}$ or $\left(\frac{distance}{time} = \frac{distance}{time}\right)$, where x represents the unknown value of time. To solve a proportion, the ratios are cross-multiplied:

$$(3)(x) = (5)(48)$$

$$3x = 240$$

The equation is solved by isolating the variable, or dividing by 3 on both sides, to produce $x = 80$.

45. The perimeter is found by calculating the sum of all sides of the polygon:

$$9 + 9 + 9 + 8 + 8 + s = 56$$

where s is the missing side length. Therefore, $43 + s = 56$. The missing side length is 13 cm.

46. When x and y are complementary angles, the sine of x is equal to the cosine of y. The complementary angle of 30 is $90 - 30 = 60$ degrees. Therefore, the answer is 60 degrees.

47. Start with the original equation: $x - 2xy + 2y$, then replace each instance of x with a 2, and each instance of y with a 3 to get:

$$2^2 - 2 \times 2 \times 3 + 2 \times 3^2$$

$$4 - 12 + 18 = 10$$

48. If Ray will be 25 in three years, then he is currently 22. The problem states that Lisa is 13 years younger than Ray, so she must be 9. Sam's age is twice that, which means that the correct answer is 18.

		1	8
	/	/	
.	.	.	.
0	0	0	0
1	1	**1**	1
2	2	2	2
3	3	3	3
4	4	4	4
5	5	5	5
6	6	6	6
7	7	7	7
8	8	8	**8**
9	9	9	9

PSAT Practice Tests #3, #4, #5, and #6

To keep the size of this book manageable, save paper, and provide a digital test-taking experience, practice tests 4-6 can be found online. Scan the QR code or go to this link to access it:

testprepbooks.com/bonus/psat

The first time you access the tests, you will need to register as a "new user" and verify your email address.

If you have any issues, please email support@testprepbooks.com

Dear PSAT Test Taker,

We would like to start by thanking you for purchasing this study guide for your PSAT exam. We hope that we exceeded your expectations.

Our goal in creating this study guide was to cover all of the topics that you will see on the test. We also strove to make our practice questions as similar as possible to what you will encounter on test day. With that being said, if you found something that you feel was not up to your standards, please send us an email and let us know.

We would also like to let you know about other books in our catalog that may interest you.

SAT

This can be found on Amazon: amazon.com/dp/1637759878

ACT

amazon.com/dp/163775583X

ACCUPLACER

amazon.com/dp/1637750250

CLEP College Composition

amazon.com/dp/163775129X

We have study guides in a wide variety of fields. If the one you are looking for isn't listed above, then try searching for it on Amazon or send us an email.

Thanks Again and Happy Testing!
Product Development Team
info@studyguideteam.com

FREE Test Taking Tips Video/DVD Offer

To better serve you, we created videos covering test taking tips that we want to give you for FREE. **These videos cover world-class tips that will help you succeed on your test.**

We just ask that you send us feedback about this product. Please let us know what you thought about it—whether good, bad, or indifferent.

To get your **FREE videos**, you can use the QR code below or email freevideos@studyguideteam.com with "Free Videos" in the subject line and the following information in the body of the email:

   a. The title of your product

   b. Your product rating on a scale of 1-5, with 5 being the highest

   c. Your feedback about the product

If you have any questions or concerns, please don't hesitate to contact us at info@studyguideteam.com.

Thank you!

Made in the USA
Las Vegas, NV
30 July 2023

75433330R00151